THE MUTE STONES SPEAK

THE
MUTE
STONES
SPEAK

THE STORY
OF
ARCHAEOLOGY
IN
ITALY

PAUL MacKENDRICK

W · W · NORTON & COMPANY

New York · London

First published in the Norton Library 1976
by arrangement with St. Martin's Press, Inc.

Books That Live
The Norton imprint on a book means that in the publisher's
estimation it is a book not for a single season but for the years.
W. W. Norton & Company, Inc.

Library of Congress Cataloging in Publication Data

MacKendrick, Paul Lachlan, 1914–
    The mute stones speak.

    (The Norton Library)
    Bibliography: p.
    Includes index.
    1. Italy—Antiquities. I. Title.
DG431.M3   1976   937   75-35677
ISBN 0-393-00805-3

Printed in the United States of America

5   6   7   8   9   0

TO MY WIFE

ACKNOWLEDGMENTS

This book owes much to many: to the Trustees of the American Academy in Rome, the John Simon Guggenheim Memorial Foundation, and the Research Committee of the University of Wisconsin Graduate School, for giving me the opportunity to spend three years in Italy; to Laurance and Isabel Roberts, for hospitality and moral support; to Axel Boëthius, for friendship and instruction; to Ernest Nash, for photographs and advice; to Mrs. Inez Longobardi, the best and most helpful of librarians and friends; to Ferdinando Castagnoli, for sharing with me his incomparable knowledge of the topography of Rome and Latium; to R. I. W. Westgate and Alston Chase, who taught me Latin at Harvard and have been my friends for thirty years; to the staff of the St. Martin's Press: Diane Wheeler-Nicholson, and Fred J. Royar, for giving the book so handsome a dress; especially to my colleague J. P. Heironimus, for meticulous proofreading which saved me from much error; and to Frank E. Brown, who introduced me to archaeology and is hereby absolved from responsibility for all untoward results of the introduction. My overarching debt is acknowledged in the dedication.

CONTENTS

ILLUSTRATIONS

1

Prehistoric Italy

In May of 1945 two young British Army officers, John Bradford and Peter Williams-Hunt, based with the R.A.F. at
Foggia in the province of Puglia, near the heel of Italy,
found that the World War II armistice left them with time
on their hands. Both trained archaeologists, they readily prevailed upon the R.A.F. to combine routine training flights
with pushing back the frontiers of science. The result of
their air reconnaissance was to change profoundly the
archaeological map of Italy.

The value of air-photography for archaeology had long
been known; as early as 1909 pictures taken from a balloon
had revealed the plan of Ostia, the port of ancient Rome.
But the English, especially such pioneers as Major G. W. G.
Allen and O. G. S. Crawford, early took the lead in interpreting, on photographs taken usually for military purposes,
vegetation-marks showing the presence and plan of ancient
sites buried beneath the soil, and invisible to the ground-
ling's eye. Where the subsoil has been disturbed in antiquity
by the digging of a ditch, the increased depth of soil will
produce more luxuriant crops or weeds; where soil-depth
is decreased by the presence of ancient foundations, walls,
floors, or roads, the crop will be thin, stunted, lighter in

color. Air-photographs taken in raking light, just after sunrise or just before sunset in a dry season, especially over grassland, will highlight these buried landscapes. The Tavoliere, the great prairie where Foggia lies, thirty by fifty-five miles in extent, suits these conditions admirably; its mean annual rainfall is only 18.6 inches (0.6 in July) or half that of Rome, and Rome is a dry place, at least in summer. So Bradford and Williams-Hunt had high hopes for their project.

In a Fairchild high-wing monoplane, in which the position of struts and nacelles does not interfere with the operation of a hand-held camera, they took oblique shots at 1,000 feet with an air camera of 8-inch focal length. For vertical shots they used, at 10,000 feet, air cameras of 20-inch focal length, mounted tandem to produce overlap for stereoscopic examination, which makes pictures three-dimensional. The thousands of resulting photographs were at a scale of about 1:6000, or ten inches to the mile, over four times as large as the best available ground maps (the 1:25,000 series of the Italian Istituto Geografico Militare.)

Bradford, realizing the archaeological value of the millions of air-photographs taken during the war by the British and American Strategic Air Commands, prevailed upon the authorities to deposit prints, giving complete coverage for Italy, in Rome (with the British and Swedish Schools) and the American Academy. The initiative of Prof. Kirk H. Stone procured a similar set for the University of Wisconsin. The stereoscopic study of these collections will mean great strides in Italian archaeology. The accuracy of the data obtained is amazing: ditches estimated from the photographs with a good micrometer scale to be four feet wide proved when measured on the ground to be precisely that.

What the photographs revealed, scattered over the 1650 square miles of the Tavoliere, were over 2000 settlements, some up to 800 yards across, surrounded by one to eight ditches. Within the ditched area, and approached by in-turned, tunnel-shaped entrances, were smaller, circular patches, which looked like hut-enclosures, or "compounds." Three examples of the sites photographed will illustrate typical settlements. At a site identified on the map (Fig. 1.1) as San Fuoco d'Angelone, eight miles northeast of Foggia, the photographs showed a ditch-enclosed oval measuring 500 x 400 feet, and an inner circle 260 feet across, with what proved to be the characteristic funnel-shaped opening. At Masseria Fongo, four miles south of Foggia, the oval was estimated at 480 yards long, with a 12-foot entrance and 12-foot ditches. At Passo di Corvo (Fig. 1.2), eight miles northeast of Foggia, the enclosure measured 800 x 500 yards, and the details were revealed by masses of flowers, yellow wild cabbage, mauve wild mint, white cow-parsley.

So much for results from the study of photographs. The next step for Bradford was to spend a fruitful season in the study. Archaeology is a comparative science: to know one site is to know nothing; to know a thousand is to see some factors unifying all. Thus the settlement-shapes of the Tavoliere are reminiscent of the fortified stronghold of Dimini in Thessaly (Fig. 1.3), dated by its excavation in the late neolithic age, which in Greece means about 2650 B.C. They also look like the fortified site of Altheim near Munich (Fig. 1.4), also late neolithic, which in Germany means about 1900 B.C. Culture in Europe moved from east to west; in general the farther west the site, the later it reached its successive levels of culture. The Tavoliere sites, lying geographically between Dimini and Altheim, might well be intermediate in date also; by their shape, at any rate, they are almost certainly to be dated sometime in the neolithic period. So much can be guessed before the indispensable next step is taken. The next step is excavation.

Modern archaeological excavation is neither haphazard

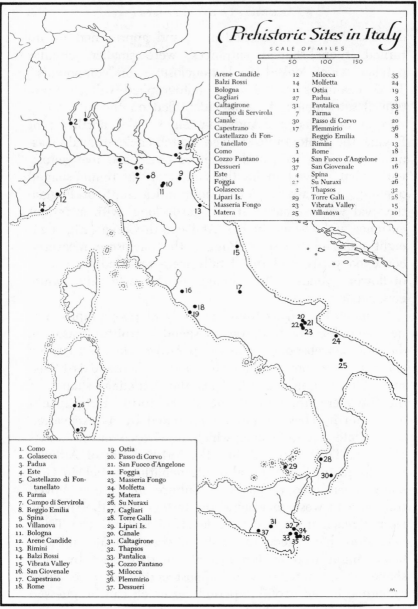

Prehistoric Sites in Italy

SCALE OF MILES

0   50   100   150

Arene Candide	12	Milocca	35
Balzi Rossi	14	Molfetta	24
Bologna	11	Ostia	19
Cagliari	27	Padua	3
Caltagirone	31	Pantalica	33
Campo di Servirola	7	Parma	6
Canale	30	Passo di Corvo	20
Capestrano	17	Plemmirio	36
Castellazzo di Fon-		Reggio Emilia	8
tanellato	5	Rimini	13
Como	1	Rome	18
Cozzo Pantano	34	San Fuoco d'Angelone	21
Dessueri	37	San Giovenale	16
Este	4	Spina	9
Foggia	22	Su Nuraxi	26
Golasecca	2	Thapsos	32
Lipari Is.	29	Torre Galli	28
Masseria Fongo	23	Vibrata Valley	15
Matera	25	Villanova	10

M.

FIG. 1.1   Prehistoric sites in Italy.

FIG. 1.4   Altheim, a late Neolithic site near Munich. →
(H. Bengtson, *Grosser historischer Weltatlas*, 44f)

FIG. 1.2 Passo di Corvo, low-oblique air photo (May 1945, by John Bradford) across the Neolithic settlement, 7 miles N.E. of Foggia. Crop-marks revealed the parallel lines of surrounding ditches (in foreground and background), with many enclosures inside.

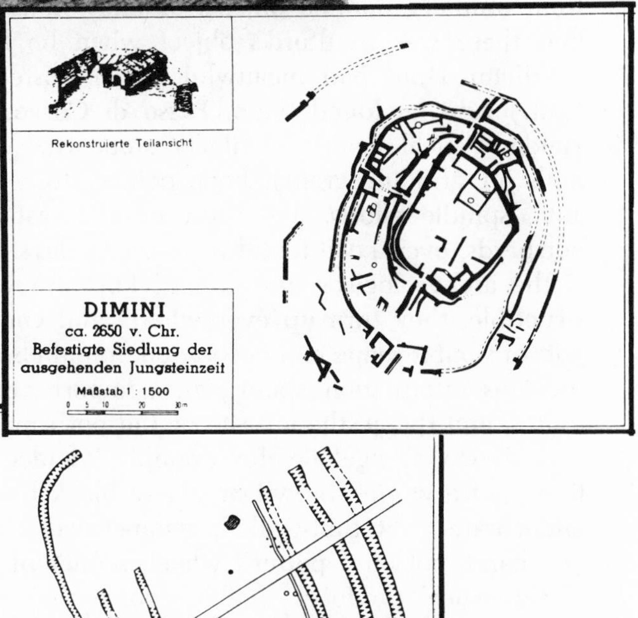

FIG. 1.3 Dimini, a late Neolithic site in Thessaly. (H. Bengtson, *Grosser historischer Weltatlas*, 44a)

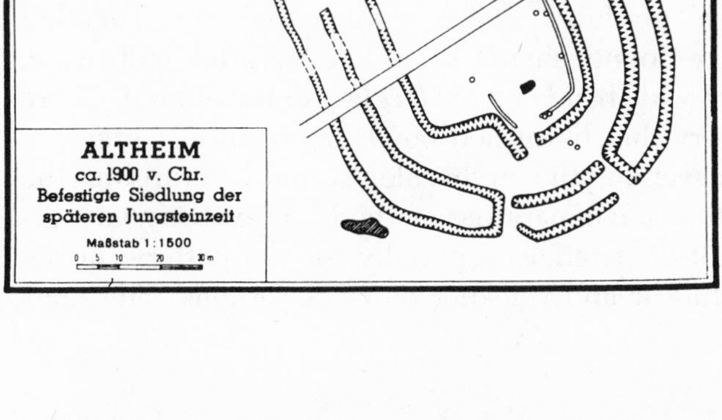

Rekonstruierte Teilansicht

DIMINI
ca. 2650 v. Chr.
Befestigte Siedlung der
ausgehenden Jungsteinzeit

Maßstab 1 : 1500

0 5 10   20   30 m

festgestellter
Grabenverlauf
angenommener
Grabenverlauf
Pfahlgräbchen
o o Pfostenlöcher
Wohngruben

ALTHEIM
ca. 1900 v. Chr.
Befestigte Siedlung der
späteren Jungsteinzeit

Maßstab 1 : 1500

0 5 10   20   30 m

nor a treasure hunt. It is a scientific business, preceded by careful survey, conducted with minute attention to levels and strata (the level in which an object is found determines its relative date; comparison with similar objects found elsewhere that can be dated determines its absolute date), and followed by scrupulous recording and publication of the evidence. A dig is not a treasure hunt. Naturally an archaeologist is pleased if he turns up gold or precious stones, but he knows in advance that an old stone age site will produce neither, but rather something infinitely more valuable, an intimate knowledge of man's past, gained from ordinary humble objects of daily household use. To find these was Bradford's object when he began to dig. (Williams-Hunt had meanwhile been posted to the Far East.) And he found them. Passo di Corvo, for example, yielded typical neolithic artifacts: stone axes, querns (hand-mills for grinding grain), bone points, stone sickles, pendants, spindle-whorls, and, best of all, vast quantities of potsherds, over 4,000 found in fourteen days. The potsherd is the archaeologist's best friend. Pots are virtually indestructible, they turn up everywhere, and comparison with pots of similar shape and decoration, found elsewhere, yields precious information about dates, imports, exports, trade-routes, and the aesthetic taste of the pot's maker and user.

S. Fuoco d'Angelone, for example, yielded typical neolithic pottery: rich brown or glossy black burnished ware, undecorated but thin-walled, symmetrical, and well-made (by hand, not on a potter's wheel; sooner or later the use of the wheel produces shoddy commercialism). Together with it were found sherds of a fine-textured buff ware, painted with wide bands (*fasce larghe*) of tomato red. There were also very thin burnished bowls in cream and gray.

After excavation, the archaeologist must return to the study and to the comparative method; an exacting and exciting pursuit of parallels, especially for the pottery, in the hope of dating it and tracking down its origins. The facts are recorded in technical excavation reports, often buried in obscure or local journals. Oftener, the results of excavation are unpublished (it is always more fun to dig than to write.) In that case, the facts are treasured up in the notes or the memories of the excavator, often a local archaeologist. He belongs to a splendid breed, burning with enthusiasm, brimful of knowledge, and eager to share what he knows, in conversation if not in print.

So Bradford read and talked, and found his parallels. The wares he had excavated were familiar; they had been found elsewhere in the heel of Italy, especially opposite or in Matera, in Lucania, and Molfetta, in Puglia, between Barletta and Bari, in contexts dated 2600-2500 B.C. And this pottery proves to have affinities, too, with that of Thessalian Sesklo, a neolithic site not far from Dimini. This same type of pottery can be traced across the Balkans into Illyricum, and thence across the Adriatic to Bradford's sites, giving in the process a glimpse of neolithic man as a more daring seafarer than had previously been thought.

And so, by patient, detailed work like Bradford's, the newly-discovered sites are fitted into and enrich the pattern of the neolithic world. The total mapping fills a huge gap in the picture of the findspots of Neolithic sites in Italy. Before 1945, some 170 were known; now the Tavoliere alone makes up more than that number. And Passo di Corvo becomes the largest known neolithic site in Europe.

The things the archaeologists did not find are instructive, too. No weapons were found: the inference is that the Tavoliere folk were unwarlike. There is no evidence that the sites survived into the Bronze Age: it looks as though, like unwarlike peoples all too often elsewhere, they were wiped out in an invasion.

It is clear from the artifacts and the site-plans that neolithic man on the Tavoliere lived like neolithic man elsewhere in Italy, that the culture was on the whole uniform. He lived in a wattle-and-daub hut with a sunken floor, a central hearth, and a smokehole—the remote and primitive predecessor of the atrium-and-impluvium house of historic Roman times, whose central apartment had a hole in the roof with a pool below to catch rain water. Fortunately for us, his wife was a slovenly housekeeper: from her rubbish we can reconstruct her way of life. In his enclosures he penned the animals he had domesticated: other Italian sites have yielded the bones of the sheep, goat, horse, ox, ass, and pig. The dog has not yet become man's best friend in the neolithic Tavoliere. Primitive man in Italy had a rudimentary religion: the Ligurian cave of Arene Candide has yielded statuettes of big-breasted, pregnant women, which probably had something to do with a fertility cult. In another Ligurian cave, Balzi Rossi, over 200,000 stone implements have been found. Not far up the Adriatic coast from Foggia, in the Vibrata valley, lie the foundations of 336 neolithic huts. We know something, too, of neolithic man's burial customs, and macabre enough they seem: skulls have been found smeared with red ochre; apparently the flesh was stripped from the corpse—a practice called in Italian *scarnitura*—and the stain applied to the bared bone. All this suggests a level of culture far below that which the Near East was enjoying at the same time: Passo di Corvo's mud huts are contemporary with the Great Pyramid of Egypt, with palaces and temples in Mesopotamia (see Fig. 1.5). But there is no evidence that neolithic man in Italy was priest-ridden or tyrannized over, as the Egyptians and Akkadians were; he is rather to be thought of as the ancestor of the sturdy peasant stock which was to form the backbone of Roman Italy.

Bradford's methods are scientific, but archaeology has not always been the exact science it is today. Americans may be proud that the first recorded scientific excavation took place in Indian mounds in Virginia. The date was 1784, and the excavator was Thomas Jefferson. But thereafter archaeo-

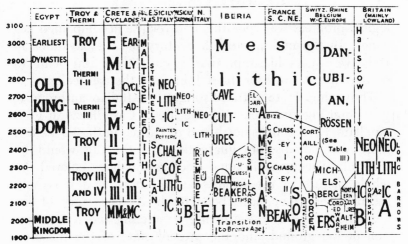

FIG. 1.5 Comparative table of early cultures.
(C. F. C. Hawkes, *The Prehistoric Foundations of Europe*, Table IV)

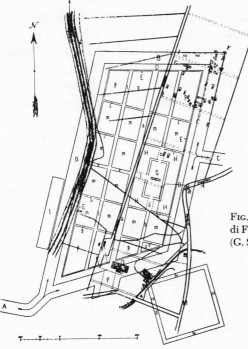

FIG. 1.6 *Terramara* at Castellazzo di Fontanellato, Pigorini's plan.
(G. Säflund, *Le terremare*, Pl. 93)

logical progress was sporadic, and relapse accompanied advance. In the mid-nineteenth century most excavations in
Italy were more like rape than science, their aim being to
dredge up treasures for the nobility and the art-dealers.

Thus when in 1889 the distinguished Italian anthropolo-
gist Luigi Pigorini excavated the site of Castellazzo di Fontanellato, twelve miles northwest of Parma, in the Po Valley,
there was no absolute guarantee that the dig would be
scientific. Yet Pigorini's announced results have colored the
whole picture of the Bronze Age in Italy, and it is only
recently that they have been doubted. The story of his
announced results, the growing scepticism, the reexamina-
tion of the ground, and the present state of the question
is an illuminating if sobering one.

What Pigorini was after was the evidence for the prehistoric settlements which have come to be called *terremare*.
They owe their discovery, their name, and their destruction
to the fertilizing quality of the earth of which they are
composed. *Terra marna* is the name in the dialect of Emilia
for the compost heaps formed by the decay of organic matter in certain mounds of ancient date, mostly south of the
Po. Farmers repeatedly found potsherds and other artifacts,
often of bronze, in these mounds, and Pigorini determined
to examine them before all the evidence should be dispersed. Castellazzo di Fontanellato is the most famous of
his efforts.

He found clear, though meager, evidence in pottery and
metal artifacts (axes, daggers, pins, razors) of a Bronze
Age culture, but no report of the levels in which he found
these objects survives, and indeed in this as in most *terremare* the farmer's shovel has completely upset the levels.
Roman terracotta, medieval pottery, and prehistoric bronze
axe-heads jostle one another in confusion. Besides, the prehistoric site has been continuously inhabited, and, in con-
sequence, the soil continuously turned over, ever since
Roman times.

Pigorini apparently dug isolated, random trenches rather than the continuous ones which would have enabled him to trace a ground-plan securely. It is hard to see, without more evidence than he supplies, how the grandiose grid of his ultimate plan (Fig. 1.6) could be deduced from the disconnected series of trenches figured on his earliest one. Though he had to contend with the most vexatious swampy conditions, working in the midst of constant seepage and ubiquitous mud, in which a rectangular grid could hardly have survived, he was nevertheless able to persuade himself, at Castellazzo, of the existence of a ditch and a rampart, reinforced by wooden piling. (Post-holes and piles he certainly found, and photographed.)

By 1892 he had convinced himself that his site had a trapezoidal plan, surrounded by a ramparted ditch thirty yards wide and ten feet deep. (Some of his dimensions suggest a prehistoric unit of measure in multiples of five; others a foreshadowing of the Roman foot of twenty-nine centimeters.) Running water derived from a tributary of the Po supplied the hypothetical ditch, which was crossed on the south by a wooden drawbridge thirty yards wide and sixty yards long. South of the site Pigorini claimed to have found a cemetery (M) perfectly square in plan, for cremation urn-burials, and westward another, rectangular one.

In 1893 he announced the discovery, within the rampart, halfway along its east side, of a mound in a reserved area or *templum* (G), surrounded by its own ditch; in 1894 this *templum* became the *arx*, or citadel of the settlement, having in its midst a sacrificial trench (*mundus*) containing in its floor, for the deposit of the sacrificial fruits, five sink-holes each equipped with a wooden cover.

In 1895 and 1896 he published claims to have found within the rampart a grid of streets (*cardines* and *decumani*), which he held to be the ancestor of the grid in Roman camps and Roman colonies. The total plan was alleged to resemble that of primitive Rome (Roma Quad-

Fig. 1.7 Su Nuraxi, a Sardinian *nuraghe*. (*Illustrated London News*)

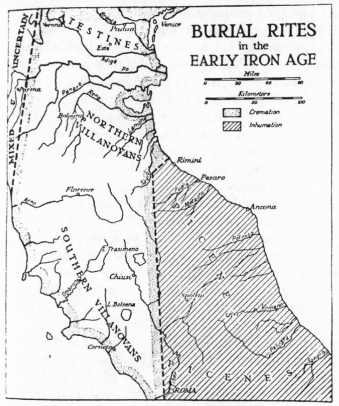

Fig. 1.8 Cremating and inhumating peoples of prehistoric Italy.
(D. Randall-MacIver, *Italy before the Romans*, p. 45)

rata), and the wooden bridge was compared to Rome's early wooden one across the Tiber, the Pons Sublicius. At another site one of Pigorini's pupils claimed to have found traces of a ritual furrow like that with which hundreds of years later the Romans were to mark the line of the future walls of a colony. For Pigorini and his school regarded the *terremare* folk as the ancestors of an Iron Age people called Villanovans, and ultimately of the Romans of historical times.

Since Pigorini's death in 1920 other archaeologists have been moved to go over the ground again, revising his findings and his inferences. Having excogitated his grid plan for Castellazzo di Fontanellato, Pigorini seems to have generalized from it rather more widely than the evidence warranted. While rectangular or square plans are not denied for some *terremare* (modern investigators enumerate ten), many sites are oval, not unlike Bradford's Tavoliere hut-settlements. In fact the *terremare* plan varies more than Pigorini was willing to admit. Furthermore, parallel in date to the *terremare* are unmoated hut villages and true lake dwellings. (The *terremare* are lake dwellings without the lake, presumably a reminiscence in the minds of immigrants from beyond the Alps of their primordial homes.)

But while we must grant to his critics that Pigorini had, to say the least, a strong imagination, we need not go so far as one of his detractors who argued that the *terremare* are Bronze Age pigsties. One site has an area of thirty-five acres, which is a bit large for a pigsty.

The *terremare* are important: they preserve the memory of an immigrant population, distinct in culture from the aborigines. The distinguishing marks of this new culture are knowledge of metal-working, a pottery identifiable by its exaggerated half-moon handles, and the practice of cremation rather than inhumation. On the evidence, we must suppose that this new culture emerged about 1500 B.C. as a fusion of indigenous hut-dwellers and immigrant lake-dwellers. Bronze bits found in their settlements show that they had domesticated the horse, and there is some evidence, outside the *terremare,* for dogs as well, described by Randall-MacIver as "doubtless good woolly animals of a fair size."

In fact the Bronze Age in Italy of which the *terremare* are a part represents a considerable cultural development beyond the level of the Neolithic Tavoliere folk. Cave dwellings from Liguria show a people using wagons and ox-drawn plows. Chemical analysis of their copper shows that some of it comes from central Germany, though a copper ingot from Sardinia betrays by its impressed double-ax trade-mark some connection with Minoan Crete. (The *terremare* are contemporary with Mycenae.) Bronze Age women wore jewelry: jadeite arm rings, necklaces of pierced red coral, bored stones, or clamshells. Curious stamps called *pintaderas* were used to impress a pattern in color on the body. A horned mannikin, with penis erect, from Campo di Servirola, now in the museum of Reggio Emilia, may be evidence for fertility cult, like the neolithic female idols from the Ligurian caves.

The Po valley in the Bronze Age was a melting pot in which a variety of cultures, indigenous and immigrant, mingled. What is to be read from the excavations is almost a recapitulation in this early period, in terms of creative imitation of imported and native forms and ideas, of the whole cultural history of Rome. To our knowledge of this culture, and to our appreciation of the importance of scrupulous archaeological recording, the curious story of Pigorini's *terremare* contributed not a little.

The island of Sardinia to the archaeologist is a fascinating curiosity, isolated, until recently, by its unhealthy climate and its odd dialect. In prehistoric times, however, while Sardinia's development does not parallel that of the mainland, its level of culture appears from archaeological finds and monuments to have been higher, not lower, than that of Italy proper. This superior level seems to have been due to Sardinia's richness in metals. To protect the wealth, the prehistoric islanders built enormous watchtowers, called *nuraghi*, which developed into veritable feudal castles with villages nestling at their feet.

Recent excavations (1951-56) by Professor Giovanni Lilliu of the University of Cagliari have cast clearer light on Sardinia's culture. He excavated the huge *nuraghe* of Su Nuraxi, at Barumini, some thirty miles north of Cagliari. When he began, Su Nuraxi was a small hill covered with ruins, earth, and scrub. Now six campaigns have revealed a truncated conical tower (Fig. 1.7), built, without mortar, of huge many-sided blocks of basalt. Clustered about the tower he found a small village; the whole complex—tower plus the village—is surrounded by other *nuraghi* on neighboring hills. To the original single tower four others, with upper courses of dressed stone, were added in a cloverleaf pattern, linked by a curtain-wall enclosing a court sixty feet deep, with a reservoir fifteen feet deep for drinking water. The central tower is three stories high, with a corbelled or false-vaulted roof built of gradually converging horizontal courses. The upper stories were reached by a spiral stair in the thickness of the wall. Lilliu meticulously observed stratigraphy; for dating, he submitted samples of carbonized matter from the towers to laboratories in Milan, and was told that the Carbon 14 process dates his remains as 1270 B.C. ± 200 years.

The C^{14} method of dating, an American device discovered and perfected by Professor W. F. Libby and his associates at the University of Chicago Institute of Nuclear Studies, is sufficiently new to deserve a word of explanation here. All living matter has a uniform radioactivity associated with its carbon content. The supply of the radioactive isotope C^{14} ceases when living matter, wood, foliage, etc., dies. Scientists can calculate the time elapsed since death by counting the residual radioactivity of C^{14} in the organic specimen, since the rate of decay can be described by specifying how long it takes for half the number of atoms in a given sample to disintegrate. For C^{14} this period, called its "half-life," is 5700 years. If the present assay of a specimen of organic matter, for instance, is 12.5 C^{14} explosions per minute per gram of carbon, an ancient organic sample assaying at 6.25 would be 5700 years old (the half-life of C^{14}). Checking with samples of known date has proved the method accurate within 200 years either way. For most classical objects found in association with organic matter this is valueless, since a trained archaeologist can date a pot, an inscription, or an architectural block by eye within fifty years or less. But the method is invaluable for making more precise the great sweeps of time in prehistory. Thus the lowest C^{14} date for Su Nuraxi, 1070 B.C., would take it almost into the Iron Age in Italy; at this date culture on the mainland was much more primitive.

Lilliu calls the period of the four added towers Lower Nuragic I, and dates it 800-750 B.C. These smaller towers contain each a single cell with two rows of loopholes. They are guard-posts, and are equipped with speaking-tubes for the guard's use when challenging.

In the next period, Upper Nuragic I, dated by Lilliu 750-500 B.C., the earth having subsided, the four towers and the walls were reinforced. The ground-level entrance was blocked, and replaced by a new entrance twenty-one feet higher, accessible only by ladder. Battlements now replaced the loopholes. Stone balls found in the excavations were apparently the projectiles hurled from these battlements. From a watchtower added to the central *nuraghe* come conch shells, perhaps intended to be sounded like trumpets.

The surrounding village, of 200 or 300 huts, separated by narrow labyrinthine passages, housed the troops; the chief lived in the tower. The village, hard-hit when the Carthaginians sacked it late in the sixth century B.C., survived in decadence till the late first century B.C. The typical oval or rectangular plan of an early Su Nuraxi village hut resembles that of the Bronze Age in Sicily or Cyprus. One contained a pit for votive offerings. Sixty round huts, with lower courses in stone, have been dated in Upper Nuragic I. They would have been roofed, like shepherd huts in Sardinia to this day, with logs and branches weighted by stones. One larger circle has seats around its inner perimeter. It was equipped with shelves, a niche, a stone basin, and a sacred stone (a model of a *nuraghe*). Lilliu thinks this must have been the warriors' council chamber.

Su Nuraxi yielded artifacts in stone, terracotta, bronze, iron, lead, and amber, the latter showing connections with trade routes to the Baltic. Lilliu found axes, millstones, pestles, and bronze votive statuettes. Pottery and *fibulae* (humble safety-pins, whose shapes, varying from age to age, are a help in dating) suggest connections with Phoenicia—via Carthage—and Etruria, whose rich and, in certain respects, mysterious culture is discussed in the next chapter.

In a later phase, after the Carthaginian invasion, the huts have fan-shaped rooms, each devoted to a specialized occupation, baking, oil-pressing, stone-tool making. A pair of stone boot-trees, or shoe-lasts, presumably from a cobbler's shop, was one of the more curious finds. Gewgaws in glass paste, poor, decadent, commercialized, but traditional in design, testify to the material and aesthetic poverty of this period. Only the last phase yielded tombs, but a huge stele with a curved top may have marked the entrance to what the peasants call a Giant's Grave, a Stone Age slab-edged tomb, forming a corridor sometimes as much as twenty yards along, from which two wings branch off to form a semicircular approach.

This scientific dig provides a fixed foundation for future research into earlier ages on Sardinia. Lilliu is understandably excited about the "dynamic spirit" revealed by the creators of this amazingly early massiveness, but like all massiveness, whether of pyramid, ziggurat, or Roman Imperial palace, it undoubtedly justifies the unhappy inference that with all this grandeur went autocracy.

Perhaps the mainland political system in the early Iron Age was less rigid; at any rate it can boast no architectural remains as sophisticated as the Sardinian *nuraghi*. But the artifacts, especially from graves, are more numerous than for the Bronze or Neolithic Ages, and the graves show that roughly speaking the peninsula was divided in the early Iron Age between two cultures (Fig. 1.8): the folk west of a line drawn from Rome to Rimini cremated their dead; those east of that line inhumed them. In and near Rome the two burial rites are mingled: the significant inference from this fact will be explained later. Because the finds are so much more numerous on the mainland, the resulting inferences involve a much more complex subdivision into cultures and periods. We may single out three sets of inferences, based primarily on three major archaeological efforts. The first is Pericle Ducati's work at Bologna, which distinguished four cultural phases, named from Villanova, the village where a major cemetery was found, and from the Benacci and Arnoaldi estates, whence key finds come. The second centers at Este, near Padua, famous for its bronze *situle* or buckets finely decorated by punching from the back, in the technique called *repoussé*. The third is Paolo Orsi's exemplary work in Sicily and South Italy. The complex chronology is best set out in a tabular view (see facing page).

The cremation cemetery excavated as early as 1853 at Villanova, near Bologna, produced artifacts (ossuary urns, *fibulae,* razors, hairpins, distaffs, bracelets, fish hooks, tweezers, *repoussé* bronze belts [see Fig. 1.9]) which match objects found later at other sites farther south, in Latium

THE IRON AGE

DATES	ITALY			SICILY	GREECE & AEGAEAN
	North	*Central*	*South*		
900	Proto-Villanovan		Torre Galli, Canale	Siculan III	Troy VIII Geometric pottery
850	Benacci I				
800		Early Etruscans			
750	Benacci II	Alban & Forum graves	Pantalica South		
700				Gk. col., Syracuse	Oriental-izing pottery
650	Arnoaldi	Etruscan tombs			
600				Rise of Carth. Empire	
550					
500	Marzabotto	Roman republic. Cape-strano warrior			Black-figure ware Troy IX
450					Red-figure ware
400	La Tène Culture				

and Etruria; e.g., the village in the process of excavation since 1955 at San Giovenale, near Bieda, by H. M. King Gustav VI of Sweden. Thus the inference is warranted that this whole area was inhabited in the early Iron Age by a people unified in culture. Since the Villanovans, unlike the aborigines, cremated their dead, we infer that they were foreigners, probably invaders; that they descended from the *terremare* folk is not proven. That they lived in wattle-and-daub huts roofed with carved beams is inferred from the hut-urns (Fig. 1.10) in which the Southern Villanovans (in Rome and Latium) placed the ashes of their dead. Though these huts show no great advance over those of the Tavoliere or *terremare* folk, the people who lived in them were skilled artisans, producing fine bronze work. The finest example, from the late Arnoaldi period in Bologna (*ca.* 525 B.C.), is the Certosa *situla* (Fig. 1.11), where the scenes portrayed are so vivid that even a funeral comes to life. In one band is a vignette of rustic festival, where a slave drags a pig by the hind leg, a piper plays, and the lord of the manor ladles his wine while he waits for a dinner of venison. The deer is being brought on a pole by two slaves, while a curly-tailed dog marches beneath.

Three other areas of Iron Age digs are worthy of mention. One is Este, whose culture in general resembles Bologna's, with fine bronze buckets, belts, and pendants. A second is Golasecca, near Lago Maggiore, where, as at Como, the finds reveal a people making a living as transport agents, forwarding artifacts back and forth between the Transalpine country, Etruria and the Balkans. The graves yield safety-pins, bronze buckets, small jewelry of bronze, iron, amber and glass, horse-bits, chariot-parts, helmets, spears, and swords. A third is the territory of Picenum, on the central Adriatic coast; here the tombs are filled (Fig. 1.12) with maces, greaves, breastplates, even chariots, as might be expected from the ancestors of those thorns in Rome's flesh,

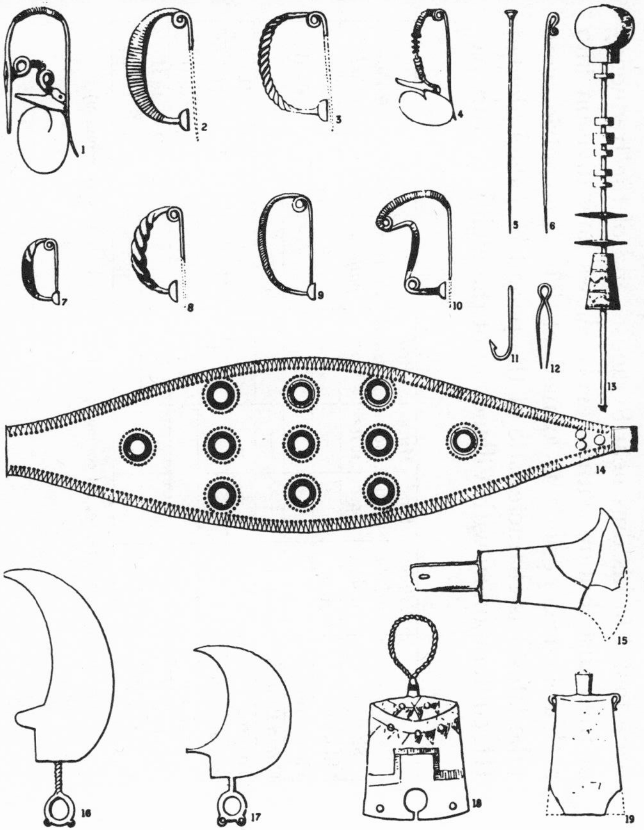

Fig. 1.10   A hut-urn.
(D. Randall-MacIver, *Italy before the Romans*, fac. p. 66)

Fig. 1.9   Villanovan artifacts.
(D. Randall-MacIver, *Villanovans and Early Etruscans*, Pl. 2)

the warlike Samnites. The unique Warrior of Capestrano (Fig. 1.13), found in Picenum, shows how remote Picene culture was, about 500 B.C., from the influences affecting the rest of the peninsula.

Finally, a brief word about Sicily in prehistory. Recent excavations of over 400 graves in the Lipari Islands, and of a Siculan village near Leontini, whose huts have front porches, and otherwise resemble those of Latium, has established closer connections with the mainland than used to be thought possible. But our main knowledge of Siculan culture results from the earlier excavations of Paolo Orsi, near Syracuse, and on either side of the toe of Italy, at Torre Galli and Canale. These provided a model of archaeological method. The following table, resulting from Orsi's careful observation of the strata in which pots of various fabrics were found in his digs near Syracuse, and of the frequency of their distribution within levels, shows how division into archaeological periods is arrived at. The Geometric ware (the latest) is characteristic of the period he called Siculan III, contemporary with Villanovan of the eighth century B.C.

Site	Yellow surface ware	Fine grey ware	Myce-naean ware	Red polished ware	Feather-pattern	Geo-metric	Siculan Period
Milocca	+ +		−				Early II
Plemmirio		+					Early II
Cozzo Pantano	+	+	−		=		II
Thapsos	−	+ +	+ +				II
Pantalica, N.		=		+ +		−	II
Caltagirone		=		+	=	+	Late II
Dessueri		=		−	−		Late II
Pantalica, S.				+	+ +	+	Early III

(= signifies very rare; −, not common; +, not unusual; + +, very common)

FIG. 1.12 Picene tomb-furniture from Fabriano.
(F. von Duhn and F. Messerschmidt,
Italische Gräberkunde, 2, Pl. 31)

FIG. 1.11 The Certosa *situla*.
(D. Randall-MacIver, *The Iron Age in Italy*,
frontispiece)

FIG. 1.13 Chieti, Museum. The Warrior
of Capestrano. (Italian Ministry of Public
Instruction)

Orsi's sites at Torre Galli and Canale are urn fields, dated by the Geometric pottery (meander and swastika patterns, the latter perhaps to insure good luck) in the eighth century. They show a trade with Greece 150 years before the first Greek colony was founded in South Italy.

If the prehistoric folk who lived on the Tavoliere, in the *terremare,* and around the *nuraghi,* if the later Villanovans and Siculans have any reality for us, we owe our insights into their culture to the patience, critical spirit, and intelligence of Bradford, Pigorini's critics, Lilliu, Ducati, Orsi, and other archaeologists. Their work has pushed back the frontiers of Italian history nearly two millennia, and revealed to us how the energy and capacity for creative borrowing of provincial Italians contributed to the ultimate strength and coherence of the Roman state, or how the Italians fought the Romans when they proved high-handed. To Roman culture of historical times another great contribution was made by the Etruscans.

2

The Etruscans

Between Tiber and Arno there flourished, while Rome was still a collection of mud huts above the Tiber ford, a rich, energetic, and mysterious people, the Etruscans, whose civilization was to influence Rome profoundly. Their riches have been known to the modern world ever since the systematic looting of the fabulous wealth of their underground tombs began, as early as 1489. Visitors to the Vatican and Villa Giulia Museums in Rome, and, better still, the Archaeological Museum in Florence, can marvel at the splendid weapons, rich gold-work, and handsome vases with which more or less scientific grave-robbers have enriched the collections in the last hundred years. Travellers to Tarquinia, on the Tuscan seaboard, can wonder at the strange, vivid paintings and seemingly indecipherable inscriptions on the walls of mysterious and intricate underground chambers. Etruscan bronze-work inspired the sculptors of the Renaissance, Etruscan tombs were drawn by the pen of the great engraver Piranesi, Etruscan cities and cemeteries were described by perhaps the most interesting author, certainly the best stylist, who ever wrote on archaeology, the Englishman George Dennis.

Dennis' *Cities and Cemeteries of Etruria,* though its last

edition appeared in 1883, is still the best general introduction to Etruscology. His achievement is the more remarkable in the light of the conditions under which he worked: execrable roads, worse lodging, and malaria stalking the whole countryside. In his day Etruscan tombs were exploited exclusively in the interest of the art dealers, with methods utterly unscientific. Artifacts without commercial value were ruthlessly destroyed: it is heart-rending to read Dennis' account of the rape of Vulci:

> "Our astonishment was only equalled by our indignation when we saw the labourers dash [coarse pottery of unfigured and . . . unvarnished ware, and a variety of small articles in black clay] to the ground as they drew them forth, and crush them beneath their feet as things 'cheaper than seaweed.' In vain I pleaded to save some from destruction; for though of no remarkable worth, they were often of curious and elegant forms, and valuable as relics of the olden time, not to be replaced; but no, it was all *roba di schiocchezza*—'foolish stuff'—the [foreman] was inexorable; his orders were to destroy immediately whatever was of no pecuniary value, and he could not allow me to carry away one of these relics which he so despised."

Unfortunately, looting of this kind produced much of the material in our museums, whose precise findspots (from the German *Fundort,* the precise place where an archaeologically significant object was found) are consequently often not known. On the other hand scientific excavation, when it came, in the mid-nineteenth century found still some tombs unplundered.

Our knowledge of Etruscan civilization is almost entirely a triumph of this modern scientific archaeology, since written Etruscan, with no known affinities, is still largely undeciphered, though scientific methods have made large strides possible. In the last three generations archaeologists have attacked and in great measure solved the problem of the origin of the Etruscans, the nature of their cities, their political organization, their religious beliefs and practices, the degree of originality in their creative arts, their life and customs. The result is a composite picture of the greatest people to dominate the Italian peninsula before the Romans.

As to origins, the Etruscans might have been indigenous, or come down over the Alps, or, as most of the ancients believed, have come by sea from Asia Minor. The difference of their burial customs and, probably, their language from those of their neighbors makes it unlikely that their ruling class was native like, for example, the Villanovans; the archaeological evidence for their links with the North is very late, and the Northern theory has tended to fall along with the discrediting of Pigorini's notions (based, as we saw, on unwarranted reconstruction of the *terremare*) about a single line of descent for Etruscan and Italic peoples. There remains the theory of Near Eastern origin, first stated in the fifth century B.C. by the Greek historian Herodotus, and recently (in the 1930's) given some slight support by Italian excavators' discovery of an inscription dated about 600 B.C. on the island of Lemnos, off the coast of Asia Minor opposite Troy. Though the Lemnian dialect is non-Indo-European, and therefore, like Etruscan, cannot be read, its archaic letters can be transliterated. Beginning with the bottom center line (Fig. 2.1), continuing with the line on the far left, and reading *boustrophedon* (alternately from right to left and from left to right, like an ox plowing), it reads *evistho zeronaith zivai/ sialchveiz aviz/ maraz mav/ vanalasial zeronai morinail/ aker tavarzio/ holaiez naphoth ziazi*. The resemblance to the alphabet and the art-forms of the Aules Feluskes stele from Etruscan Vetulonia (Fig. 2.2) is obvious. The particular letter-form transcribed as *th* occurs elsewhere only in Phrygia in Asia Minor. The

Fig. 2.1
Lemnos. Inscription in local dialect,
   similar to Etruscan.
(M. Pallottino, *Etruscologia*, Pl. 4)

Fig. 2.2
Vetulonia. Aules Feluskes stele.
   (M. Pallottino, *Etruscologia*,
   Pl. 21)

very words and word-endings of the Lemnian stele can be found on Etruscan inscriptions. Thus the inscription shows at the very least that on an island "geographically intermediate between Asia Minor and Italy a language very similar to Etruscan was employed by some persons." The ancient tradition localizing the original home of the Etruscans somewhere in or near northwest Asia Minor receives here some archaeological support.

But the important thing is not where they came from, but how their culture was formed. The archaeological evidence justifies the hypothesis that they were a small but vigorous military aristocracy from the eastern Mediterranean, established in central Italy, where they built, by borrowing and merging, upon a structure created by the Villanovans. A new approach, the analysis of bones from Etruscan tombs to ascertain the blood types of their ancient occupants, may, by comparison with the persistent blood types of modern Tuscans, enable the archaeologist to determine what proportion of the ancient population was native and what intrusive.

Archaeology tells us, too, that Etruscan civilization is a culture of cities. Ancient literary sources speak of a league of twelve Etruscan places (Fig. 2.3), most of which have yielded important archaeological material: from Veii, the great terracotta Apollo; at Cerveteri, Vetulonia, Orvieto, and Perugia, the remarkable rock-cut tombs; at Tarquinia, Vulci, and Chiusi, strikingly vivid tomb-paintings; at Bolsena, Roselle, and Volterra, mighty fortification walls; at Populonia, the slag-heaps from the iron works which made Etruria prosperous. But the most interesting, and some of the latest, evidence for Etruscan city-planning and fortifications comes from three sites, two in the northern Etruscan sphere of influence: Marzabotto on the River Reno, fifteen miles south of Bologna; Spina, near one of the seven mouths

FIG. 2.3 Early Italy, to illustrate Etruscan and other sites. Inset: early Rome.
(V. Scramuzza and P. MacKendrick, *The Ancient World*, Fig. 32a)

of the Po; and one in northern Etruria itself, Bolsena, ancient Volsinii.

The first recorded excavations at Marzabotto date from the 1860's, but the ruins had been known since 1550. The striking discovery at Marzabotto was that the site (dated by pottery in its necropolis to the late sixth or early fifth centuries B.C.) had a regular, oriented, rectangular grid of streets (Fig. 2.4), enclosing house-blocks (*insulae*) averaging 165 x 35 yards. The main north-south street, or *cardo*, and the main east-west street, or *decumanus*, were each over forty-eight feet wide, the minor streets one third as broad. The streets were paved, as they were not in Rome until 350 years later. Drains ran beneath all the streets except the reserved area (the Romans were to call it the *pomerium*) just inside the circuit-wall. The house-plans resemble closely the fourth-century ones discovered in the

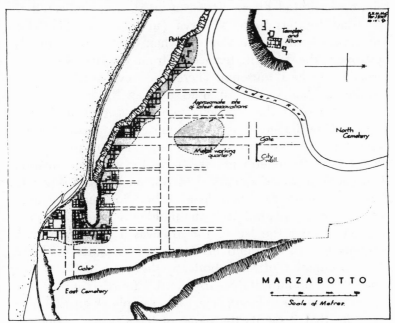

FIG. 2.4   Marzabotto: grid plan.
(J. B. Ward Perkins, "Early Roman Towns in Italy," Fig. 5)

1930's at Olynthus, on the Chalcidice Peninsula in Greece, by an American expedition. The house-doors had locks and keys. A number of the buildings were recognizable as shops, with back rooms for living quarters.

Bearing in mind the sobering experience of Pigorini's unwarranted claims about a grid plan for the *terremare*, we might be tempted to scepticism about Marzabotto, except for two facts: Brizio, the excavator, himself expressed doubts, as early as 1891, about Pigorini's reconstruction; furthermore, a re-examination of the site in 1953 confirmed the authenticity of Brizio's findings.

The city is dominated, on the high ground to the northwest, by an *arx*, bearing the footings, some of considerable size with impressive moldings, of five structures, temples or altars. One of them, facing south, and divided at the back into three *cellae*, is the prototype of the Roman Capitolium, decorated by an Etruscan artist, and dedicated to the triad Jupiter, Juno, Minerva (in Etruscan, Tin, Uni, Menerva). Until World War II, when they were wantonly destroyed, the finds in terracotta from the arx were preserved in the local museum. There were revetments, plaques forming a thin veneer of fired clay, with nail-holes for affixing them to the wooden frame of a typical Tuscan temple. They included archaic antefixes: ornamental terracotta caps to mask the unsightly ends of half-round roof tiles. Terracotta revetments like these, for wooden construction, continue to be canonical in Roman temples down to the first century B.C.: marble as a building material does not come into use until after the middle of the second century B.C. Under the lee of the arx was a necropolis with contents like those found in Gallic graves, mute evidence of the occupation of Marzabotto by the wave of Gauls that brought terror into Italy early in the fourth century B.C. In sum, Marzabotto is so perfect an example of an Etruscan town-site that it merits the name of the Etruscan Pompeii.

Marzabotto remained for many years the only known

Etruscan site with a grid plan. Lying as it does outside Etruria proper, it was clearly the product of Etruscan expansion northward. Since 1922 reclamation by drainage canals has revealed the necropolis of another northern outpost, Spina, near one of the mouths of the Po. Working under the greatest difficulties from mud and seepage, archaeologists had unearthed the contents of no less than 1213 tombs, often finding golden earrings and diadems gleaming in the mud against the skulls in the burials. These precious ornaments, together with necklaces of northern amber, perfume-bottles in glass paste and alabaster from Egypt, and Greek black- and red-figured vases, are now the pride of the Ferrara Museum. Though the vases are Greek, both Etruscans and Greeks lived in the site together, as is proved by *graffiti* in both languages scratched on the pottery. The spot, commanding the Adriatic, would be the ideal port of entry for foreign luxury goods imported to satisfy the taste for display of wealthy Etruscans. Wealthy as they were, they were all equal in the sight of Charun: the skeletons were regularly found with small change, to pay the infernal ferryman, clutched in the bony fingers of their right hands. Pathetic graves of children contained jointed dolls and game counters.

This rich and crowded cemetery was all that was known of Etruscan Spina until further drainage operations in 1953, in the Pega Valley, south of the original site (Fig. 2.5), brought to light not only 1195 new tombs, but also further surprises. In October, 1956, an air-photograph in color revealed beneath the modern irrigation canals the grid plan (Fig. 2.6), resembling Marzabotto's, of the port area of the ancient Etruscan city. This time the *decumanus* is a canal, sixty-six feet wide, and the marshy site is revealed as a sort of Etruscan Venice. Later air-photographs showed evidence of habitation over an area of 741 acres, large enough for a population of half a million. Since the artifacts of this vast city are a little later in style than those

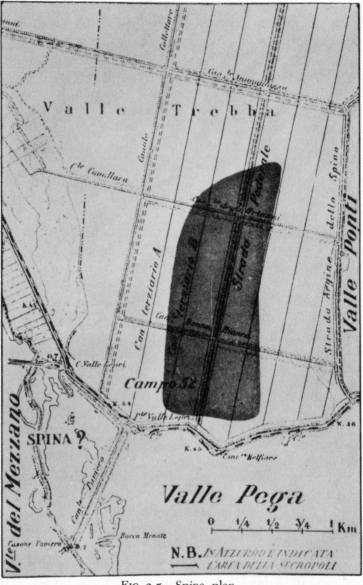

FIG. 2.5   Spina, plan.
(S. Aurigemma, *Il R. Museo di Spina in Ferrara*, Pl. 4)

of Marzabotto, we assume that Spina flourished a little later. Almost no weapons were found in the graves: Spina apparently felt secure on her landlocked lagoon, but she reckoned without attacks from the landward side. Few vases datable later than the late fifth century are found in the graves: the inference is that Spina fell, about 390 B.C., before the same Gallic invasion that despoiled Marzabotto. The two sites together reinforce each other in giving evidence for the use by Etruscan city-planners of the kind of square or rectangular grid of streets later made famous by Roman colonies and Roman camps; unfortunately the question is still open whether the Etruscans invented the grid used in Italy or whether it was a Greek import.

Archaeology tells us something about Etruscan fortifications, too, not least important being some recent negative evidence: many polygonal walls in Etruria and Latium, formerly believed Etruscan, are now proved to be of Roman date. But excavations conducted since 1947 at Bolsena by the French school in Rome have unearthed walls that are genuinely Etruscan, surrounding an Etruscan site, and with Etruscan letters hacked on the blocks. The marks, concentrated on strategic sections of the wall, were probably apotropaic, intended to work as magic charms against the enemy. One section of the wall was only one block thick. It could not have been self-standing; it must have been intended as the spine of an *agger* or earthwork. Just such a spine was a part of Rome's earliest walls, and a similar technique is to be seen in early earthworks at Anzio and Ardea. The discovery of these walls has clinched the identification of Bolsena with Etruscan Volsinii, one of the twelve cities, and the scene of regular meetings of the Etruscan League. On the same site were found some temple foundations, but the district is rich farmland, and it proved impossible to dig over a wide enough area to discover whether Volsinii, like Marzabotto and Spina, had a grid plan.

Grid plans suggest a sophisticated, if rigid, political organization for Etruscan cities. Evidence for the political life of a civilization normally comes from literature and inscriptions, very little from artifacts. Yet the Aules Feluskes stele from Vetulonia, already mentioned, shows a figure carrying a double-headed ax. Later, axes were carried by the consul's twelve bodyguards whom the Romans called lictors. There seems to be a connection between the number twelve and the twelve cities of the Etruscan confederacy. Vetulonia has yielded another object of great interest to those who would understand Etruscan political organization and Rome's debt to it. In the Tomb of the Lictor was found, besides a chariot and a metal coffer containing gold objects wrapped in gold leaf, a double-headed iron ax (Fig. 2.7) hafted onto a single iron rod surrounded by eight others. This is obviously the prototype of the Roman *fasces,* and indeed Silius Italicus, a Roman epic poet of the Silver Age, assigns the origin of the fasces to Vetulonia. Such artifacts suggest that the ruler of an Etruscan city, whether king or aristocrat, was surrounded by considerable pomp.

Etruscan political organization, according to Latin literary sources, at one stage embraced Rome, and an Etruscan inscription on a shiny black dish of the ware called *bucchero,* in Rome, goes a little way to confirm this. More impressive confirmation comes from a frescoed Etruscan tomb in Vulci, discovered by A. François in 1857. The fresco has a historical subject, a battle scene, portraying two camps, populated with figures labelled in Etruscan letters. The figures in one camp are labelled Aule and Caele Vipina (in Latin, Vibenna), and Macstrna (in Latin, *magister*); in the other, a figure labelled Cneve Tarchunies Rumach (in Latin, Cn. Tarquinius Romanus), a member of the dynasty of Roman kings which in the historical tradition is alleged to have come from Etruria. Aule Vipina's name recurs in a votive inscription, from a context dated

FIG. 2.6   Spina: grid plan, air-photograph. (ENIT, *Italy's Life*, p. 91)

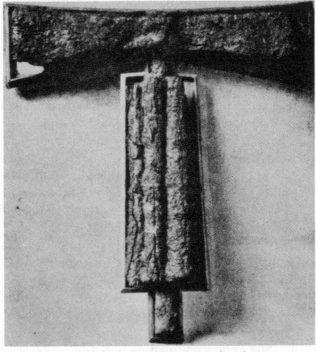

FIG. 2.7   Vetulonia: fasces from the Tomb of the Lictor.
(M. Pallottino, *Etruscologia*, Pl. 22)

in the sixth century B.C., found at Veii on a *bucchero* sherd. The conclusion is inescapable that A. and C. Vibenna were actual historical figures, Etruscan leaders involved in a political struggle for the domination of Rome. Macstrna is identified in Roman tradition with Servius Tullius, a good king whose rule falls, according to the literary tradition, between the tyrannical reigns of the two Tarquins. The fresco may represent an episode in Servius Tullius' life unknown to the Roman tradition, before he became king in Rome; he is represented rescuing C. Vibenna from the Romans, and killing Tarquin. Thus archaeology here not only confirms the literary tradition of Rome's Etruscan kings; it suggests something about the internal policy of sixth-century Etruscan cities, the existence in them, perhaps by a constitutional transformation from an archaic kingship, of a strong military authority, like that of the *magister populi* or dictator of the later Roman Republic. Etruscan tomb inscriptions, with their many personal names, show that official Etruscan nomenclature included—as did the later Roman—the name of the clan. Clan organization is in origin aristocratic. As later in Rome aristocrats with a clan organization overthrew the original monarchy, so too, we may suppose, the clans operated in Etruria.

In the example just cited, light is thrown on Etruscan political organization by the inscriptions on the fresco, and it is in fact to inscriptions in the Etruscan alphabet (Fig. 2.8) that we owe most of what we know about Etruscan politics. For, paradoxically, though Etruscan, as a non-Indo-European language, is technically indecipherable (in the sense that the longest inscriptions in it cannot be entirely translated), valid inferences can be made about some of the short ones. For example, one of the inscriptions on the wall of the Tomb of Orcus at Tarquinia, discovered in 1868 (Fig. 2.9), reads in part *zilath : amce : mechl : rasnal*, at first sight a most unlikely combination of letters. Another Tarquinian inscription, this time from a sarcophagus in the

Typical Letterings	Archaic Letterings (vii–v cent.)	Late Letterings (iv–i cent.)	Modern Equivalents	Typical Letterings	Archaic Letterings (vii–v cent.)	Late Letterings (iv–i cent.)	Modern Equivalents
A	A	A	a	⊞			(s)
B			(b)	O			(o)
⊃	⊃	⊃	c(k)	↑	↑	↑	p
⊂			(d)	M	M	M	ś
⊒	⊒	⊒	c	Q	Q		q
⊐	⊐	⊐	v	⊂	⊂	⊂	r
I	I	‡	z	₹	₹	₹	s
⊟	⊟	⊟	h	T	T	✝	t
⊗	⊗	⊙	δ (th)	Y	Y	V	u
I	I	I	i	X	X,+		ś
K	K		k	φ		φ	φ (ph)
↓	↓	↓	l	↓		↓	X (ch)
M	M	m	m		8	8	f
↑	↑	↑	n				

FIG. 2.8
Etruscan alphabet.
(M. Pallottino,
The Etruscans, p. 259)

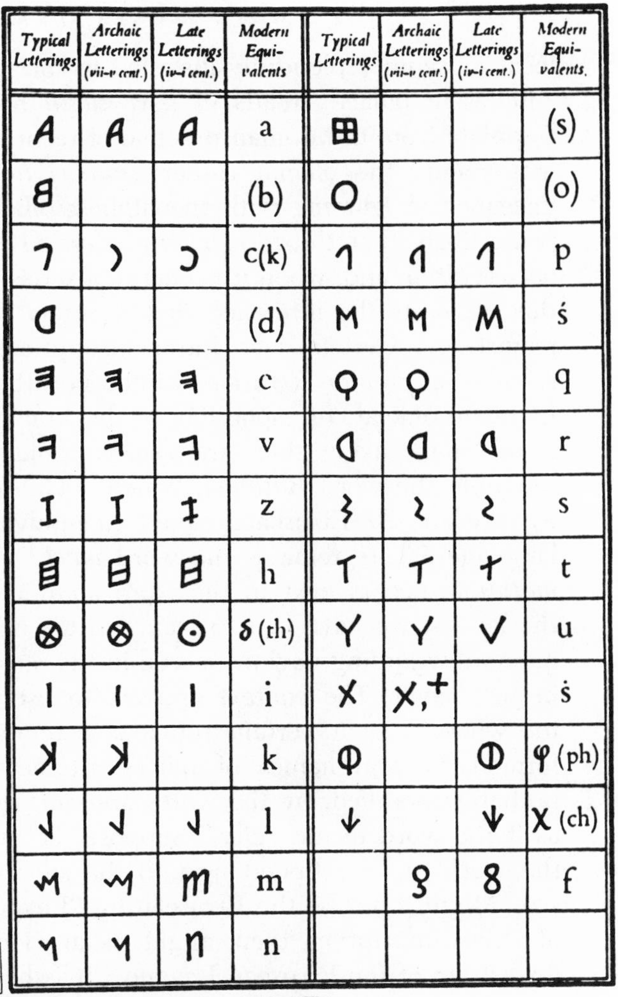

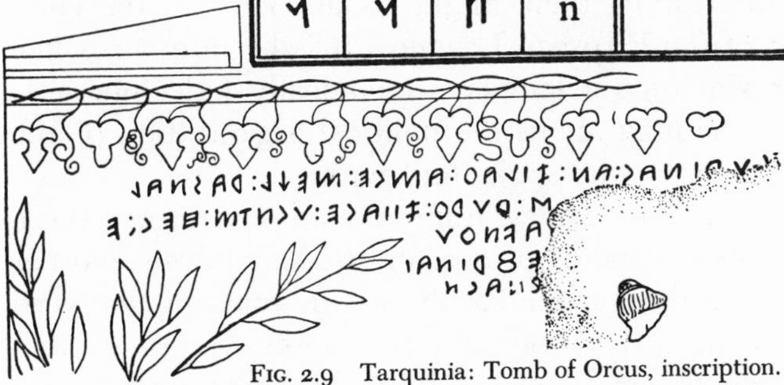

FIG. 2.9 Tarquinia: Tomb of Orcus, inscription.
(*Corpus Inscriptionum Etruscarum*, no. 5360)

local museum (splendidly installed in the fifteenth century Vitelleschi palace) reads in part *zilath rasnas*. If we extrapolate from the Roman practice of recording on funerary monuments the official career (*cursus honorum*) of the deceased (beginning with the highest offices held), it appears likely that the term *zilath* refers to a magistracy. It occurs often, and, when it occurs in a series, it occurs early; this warrants the inference that it refers to an important magistracy. Certain late Latin inscriptions from Etruria refer to a *praetor Etruriae*. Might not the *zilath* be the Etruscan official corresponding to the Roman praetor? This is the more likely since the words *rasnal, rasnas* closely resemble the word *Rasenna,* which a Greek historian tells us is what the Etruscans called themselves in their own language. There remains the word *mechl.* A similar word, *methlum,* occurs next to the word *spur* in a curious text, the longest we have in Etruscan, written on the cloth of a mummy wrapping now preserved in the museum of Zagreb, in Jugoslavia. The context appears to list the institutions for whose benefit certain religious ceremonies were performed. Several names of offices are accompanied, and probably modified, by the words *spureni, spurana.* It looks as if the word means "city." Suppose the other institution, the *methlum,* mentioned next to the *spur,* were of larger size. Might it not be the Etruscan for "League"? The Tomb of Orcus inscription, then, might mean, "He was the chief magistrate of the Etruscan League." It is by inferences like these that we force a language technically indecipherable to tell us something about the political organization of the mysterious people who spoke and wrote it.

Another example comes from a long inscription on a scroll held in the hands of a sculptured figure on another sarcophagus in the Tarquinia museum. It contains the word *lucairce.* In the text of the Zagreb mummy-wrapping mention is made of ceremonies celebrated *lauchumneti,* presumably a noun with an ending showing a place relation, and obviously related in root to *lucairce*. And both seem connected with the word *lucumo*, used in Latin to refer to Etruscan chiefs or kings. *Lucairce* contains the ending -*ce* which we interpreted on the Tomb of Orcus inscription as verbal; it might mean "was king (or chief)." In that case *lauchumneti*, with its locative ending, might mean "in the (priest)-king's house" (Latin *Regia*). Thus by reasoning from the known to the unknown we can find evidence from the Etruscans themselves that at some stage they were ruled by kings. Since the Tarquinia sarcophagus with the scroll is on the evidence of artistic techniques dated late (second century B.C., a date at which the Roman Republic fully controlled Etruria), we must suppose that by that date the *lucumo* had been reduced to a mere priestly function, much as in Rome itself the priest who in Republican times discharged the sacred duties once performed by Rome's kings (*reges*) was still called the *rex sacrorum*.

A final example. On Etruscan inscriptions occurs a root *purth-*, with by-forms *purthne, purtsvana, eprthne, eprthni, eprthnevc*. This looks like the root which occurs in the name of the king of Clusium, transliterated by the Romans Lars Porsenna, he who in the *Lays of Ancient Rome* swore by the Nine Gods. The same root probably occurs in the Greek *prytanis*, which means something like "senator." Clearly another official of importance is referred to here.

In sum, archaeologists looking for evidence of Etruscan political organization have found such outward signs of pomp as fasces, plus evidence for magistrates resembling the later Roman dictator, praetor, priest-king, senator, and for cities probably combined into a league.

If inscriptions can be made to yield this kind of evidence, what can we say about the state of our knowledge about the Etruscan language in general? The same kind of combinatory method applied to other inscriptions yields with patience results justifying the statement that progress, though agonizingly slow, is being made. Many short inscriptions can be read entire: they are usually funerary, and give the names, filiation, and age of the deceased. Here is an example, from yet another sarcophagus in the Tarquinia museum:

> *partunus vel velthurus   satlnal-c   ramthas clan*
> "Partuni Vel of Velthur and of Satlnei Ramtha the son,
> *avils   XXIIX lupu*
> of years 28,   dead."

Here for translation one assumes that Etruscan, while not Indo-European in its roots, is an inflected language, where an *-s* or *-l* ending shows possession, and the enclitic *-c*, like the Latin *-que*, means "and." Another example shows similar case-endings, uses vocabulary we have seen before, and adds a place-name:

> *Alethnas Arnth   Larisal   zilath Tarchnalthi amce*
> "Alethna Arnth (son) of Laris praetor at Tarquinia was."

Altogether some 10,000 Etruscan inscriptions are known. Of these only three are of any length: the Zagreb mummy-wrapping, a tile from Capua, and the previously mentioned scroll from Tarquinia. The next seven taken together total less than 100 words. Given this material, there is some bitter truth in the statement that if we could unlock the secret of Etruscan, we would have the key to an empty room. But whole cities in Etruria remain to be dug; there is no knowing what new inscriptions excavations now in progress at Vulci, Roselle, or Santa Severa may turn up, including perhaps a bilingual, where identical texts in Etruscan and a known language like Latin may solve the puzzle, as the Greek of the Rosetta Stone made possible the deciphering of Egyptian hieroglyphics. Etruscan loan-words in Latin tell us something: *antemna,* "yard-arm"; *histrio,* "actor"; *atrium,* "patio"; *groma,* "plane-table" suggest Etruscan predominance on the sea and the stage, in domestic architecture and surveying. But we know more than loan-words: the known vocabulary in Etruscan amounts now to 122 words, in seven categories, including time-words (*e.g.*, the names of several months), the limited political vocabulary already discussed, names for family relationships, some three dozen verbs and nouns, and the same number of words from the field of religion.

It is about Etruscan religion, and especially funerary rites, that we are best informed. The Etruscans had the reputation of being the most addicted to religious ceremonial of any people of antiquity, and we learn much about Etruscans living from Etruscans dead. We know what sort of documentation to expect on religious matters from an Etruscan tomb, by extrapolating back from rites which the Romans believed they had inherited from Etruria, especially in the area of foretelling the future by examining the livers of animals (hepatoscopy) or observing the flights of birds (augury). One of the most curious surviving documents of Etruscan superstition is the bronze model of a sheep's liver (Fig. 2.10) found in 1877 near Piacenza, on the upper Po, and now in the Civic Museum there. The liver is split in two lengthwise. From the plane surface thus provided three lobes project. The plane surface itself is subdivided into sixteen compartments (Fig. 2.11); over each compartment a god presides. The same sixteen subdivisions were used in the imaginary partition of the sky for augury, and the same principle governed the layout and orientation of cities like Marzabotto and probably Spina. The same superstition found in Babylonia directs our attention once more to the probable Near Eastern origin of the Etruscan ruling class. The priest would take his position at the cross-point of the intended *cardo* and *decumanus* of the city, facing south (we recall that the three-celled temple on the *arx* at Marzabotto faces south).

Fig. 2.10 Piacenza, Civic Museum. Bronze model of sheep's liver, used in foretelling the future. (ENIT, *Italy's Life*, p. 37)

The half of the city behind him was called in Latin the *pars postica* (posterior part), the part in front of him the *pars antica* (anterior part); on his left was the *pars familiaris* (the lucky side; hence thunder on the left was a good omen) on his right the *pars hostilis* (unlucky). To the subdivision of the earth below corresponded a similar subdivision of the sky above; either was called in Latin (using

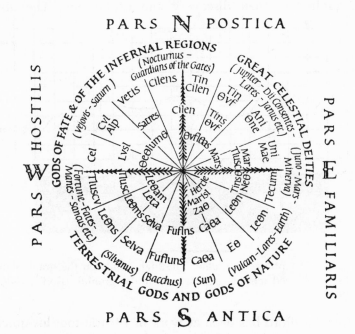

FIG. 2.11 Piacenza liver, schematic representation.
(M. Pallottino, *The Etruscans*, p. 165)

a concept clearly derived from Etruscan practice) a *templum*, "part cut off," a sacred precinct, terrestrial or celestial. From the Piacenza liver and the orientation of Marzabotto we can deduce both the orderliness of the Etruscan mind and the ease with which it degenerated into rigidity and superstition. For this deadly heritage the Etruscans apparently found in the Romans willing recipients; often, but

not always, for old Cato said, "I cannot see how one liver-
diviner can meet another without laughing in his face."

The vast number of Etruscan tombs and the richness of
their decoration and furnishings tell us much about another
aspect of the Etruscans' religion: their view of the after-
life. About this the fabulous painted tombs of Tarquinia
tell us most, and bid fair to tell us more as new methods
are applied to their discovery and exploration. The ubi-

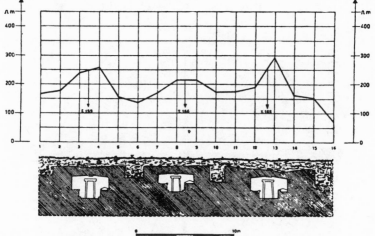

Fig. 2.12   Potentiometer profile. The high points on the graph show
where hollowed tomb-chambers exist under ground. (ENIT, *Italy's
Life*, p. 106)

quitous Bradford has been at work in Etruria too; his quick
eye has detected on air-photographs over 800 new tomb-
mounds at Tarquinia alone, and new methods of ground
exploration, worked out by the dedicated Italian engineer
C. M. Lerici, have enormously speeded the work of exploration. Electrical-resistivity surveying with a potentiometer,
sensitive to the difference between solid earth and empty
subterranean space, makes possible the rapid tracing of a
profile showing where the hollows of Etruscan tombs exist
underground (Fig. 2.12). A hole is then drilled large enough
to admit a periscope; if the periscope shows painted walls,

or pottery, a camera can be attached to make a 360-degree photograph. By this method Lerici reports exploring 450 tombs in 120 days. This work, rapid as it is, is being done none too soon; land redistribution schemes, good for the farmer, bad for the archaeologist, are changing the face of south Etruria day by day; deep plowing and the planting of vines and fruit trees are destroying or obscuring the archaeological picture.

Dennis would hardly lament the passing of the conditions he so graphically describes: "Among the half-destroyed tumuli of the Montarozzi [at Tarquinia] is a pit, six or eight feet deep, overgrown by lentiscus; and at the bottom is a hole, barely large enough for a man to squeeze himself through, and which no one would care to enter unless aware of something within to repay him for the trouble, and the filth unavoidably contracted. Having wormed myself through this aperture, I found myself in a dark, damp chamber, half-choked with the *debris* of the walls and ceiling. Yet the walls have not wholly fallen in, for when my eyes were somewhat accustomed to the gloom, I perceived them to be painted, and the taper's light disclosed on the inner wall a banquet in the open air." Modern gadgetry like Lerici's has destroyed some of the romance; there is something graphic about descriptions like Mengarelli's of opening a tomb at Cerveteri in 1910, in the presence of the local and neighboring landlords, the Prince and Princess Ruspoli and the Marchese Guglielmi. As the blocks of the entrance were removed one by one, and sunlight was reflected into the tomb by mirrors, there were to be seen against the black earth objects of gleaming gold, and priceless proto-Corinthian vases resting on shreds of decomposed wood, which were all that was left of the funeral bed, while other vases were to be seen fixed to the wall with nails.

The Tomb of Hunting and Fishing at Tarquinia, discovered in 1873, gives us our most attractive picture (Fig. 2.13) of how Etruscans in their palmiest days viewed the next world. The tomb is dated by the black-figured Attic vases it contained in the decade 520-510 B.C., when the Etruscan ruling class was still prosperous. A more charming invitation to the brainless life could hardly be imagined. The most vivid scene is on the walls of the tomb's inner room, which are conceived as opening out into a breezy seascape, with a lively population of bright birds in blue, red, and yellow, frisky dolphins, and boys, friskier still, at play. Up a steep rock striped in clay-red and grass-green clambers a sun-burnt boy in a blue tunic, who appears to have just pushed another boy who is diving, with beautiful form, into the hazy, wine-dark sea. On a nearby rock stands another boy firing at the birds with a slingshot. Below him is a boat with an eye painted on the prow (to ward off the evil eye; fishing boats are still so painted in Portugal). Of the boat's four passengers, one is fishing over the side with a flimsy handline, while beside the boat a fat dolphin turns a mocking somersault. All is life, action, humor, vitality, color; such is the notion of blessed immortality entertained by a people for whom God's in his heaven, all's right with the world.

A quarter of a century or so after the Tomb of Hunting and Fishing was painted, the Etruscans suffered a major naval defeat at the hands of Greeks off Cumae. Rome, expanding, eventually took over the iron mines of Elba and the iron-works of Populonia, and Etruscan prosperity declined agonizingly to its end. Let us look at a Tarquinian tomb of the period of the decadence; e.g., the Tomb of Orcus again. There, beside one of the loveliest faces ever painted by an ancient artist (Fig. 2.14), is portrayed one of the most hair-raising demons a depressed imagination could conceive (Fig. 2.15). Its flesh is a weird bluish-green, as though it were putrefying. Its nose is the hooked beak of a bird of prey. The fiend has asses' ears; its hair is a tangled mass of snakes. Beside its monstrous wings rises

FIG. 2.13   Tarquinia: Tomb of Hunting and Fishing, fresco.
(M. Pallottino, *Etruscan Painting*, p. 51)

FIG. 2.14   Tarquinia: Tomb of Orcus, portrait of the lady Velcha. (MPI)

FIG. 2.15   Tarquinia: Tomb of Orcus, the demon Charun. (MPI)

a huge crested serpent, horribly mottled. In its left hand the demon holds a hammer handle. An inscription identifies him as Charun, the ferryman of the dead; it is to pay this monster that the skeletons of Spina clutch their bronze small change in their right hands. The contrast between the gaiety of the scenes in the Tomb of Hunting and the gloomy prospect of the lovely lady—her name is Velcha—in the clutches of this grisly demon has been held to epitomize the contrast between the views of an after life entertained by a prosperous and by an economically depressed people.

Other finds cast further light. The Capua tile prescribes funerary offerings to the gods of the underworld. An inscribed lead plaque from near Populonia is a curse tablet, in which a woman urges Charun or another infernal deity, Tuchulcha, to bring his gruesome horrors to bear on members of her family whose death she ardently desires. Bronze statuettes give details of priestly dress (conical cap tied under the chin, fringed cloak) or show Hermes, Escorter of Souls, going arm-in-arm with the deceased to the world below. The total picture is one of a deeply religious, even superstitious people, attaching particular importance to the formalities of their ritual relations with their gods, and obsessed with the after life, of which they take a progressively gloomier view as their material prosperity declines.

What can archaeology tell us about Etruscan cultural life? Of art for art's sake there seems to have been very little, of literature none, except for liturgical texts. The Etruscans excelled in fine large-scale bronze work, like the famous Chimaera of Arezzo or the Capitoline Wolf, but their minor masterpieces in bronze deserve mention also, especially the engraved mirrors, the cylindrical cosmetic boxes called *ciste*, and the statuettes whose attenuated bodies appeal strongly to modern taste. Their painting at its best shows in its economy of line how intelligently they borrowed from the Greeks, in its realism how sturdily they maintained their own individuality. In architecture, Etruscan temples, having been made of wood, do not survive above their foundation courses, but recent discoveries of terracotta temple-models at Vulci tell us something about their appearance, and masses of their terracotta revetment survive, brightly-painted geometric, vegetable, or mythological motifs, designs to cover beams, mask the ends of half-round roof tiles, or (in pierced patterns called *à jour* crestings) to follow the slope of a gable roof. Made from molds, the motifs could be infinitely repeated at small expense, an aspect of Etruscan practicality which was to appeal strongly to the Romans.

But the Etruscans' artistic genius shows at the best in their architectural sculpture in painted terracotta, freestanding or in high relief. Their best-known masterpiece in this genre is the Apollo of Veii (Fig. 2.16), designed for the ridgepole of an archaic temple. Discovered in 1916, it is now in the Villa Giulia museum in Rome. The stylized treatment of the ringlets, the almond eyes, the fixed smile are all characteristic of archaic Greek art, and the fine edges of the profile, lips, and eyebrows suggest an original in bronze. But this is no mere copy. It is the work of a great original artist, probably the same Vulca of Veii who was commissioned in the late sixth century B.C. to do the terracottas for the Capitoline temple in Rome. The sculptor is telling the story of the struggle between Apollo and Hercules for the Hind of Ceryneia: the god is shown as he tenses himself to spring upon his opponent; the anatomical knowledge, the expression of mass in motion, and the craftsmanship required to cast a life-size terracotta (a feat which even now presents the greatest technical difficulties) are all alike remarkable.

A set of antefixes (used, as we have seen, to cover the ends of half-round roof-tiles), from the archaic temple at Satricum in Latium, in the same museum, are noteworthy

FIG. 2.16 Rome, Villa Giulia Museum.
Apollo of Veii, terracotta. (MPI)

FIG. 2.17 Rome, Villa Giulia Museum. Terracotta antefix
of satyr and nymph, from Satricum. (MPI)

for their humor. They represent a series of nymphs pursued by satyrs. The satyrs are clearly not quite sober, and the nymphs are far from reluctant. In a particularly fine piece (Fig. 2.17) the satyr frightens the nymph with a snake which he holds in his left hand, while he slips his right hand over her shoulder to caress her breast. Her gestures are almost certainly not those of a maiden who would repel a man's advances.

A third Etruscan masterpiece in terracotta, of later date, but still showing the same striking vitality as the two pieces just described, is the pair of winged horses in high relief (Fig. 2.18), first published in 1948, which come probably from the pediment of the temple called the Ara della Regina, on the site of the Etruscan city (as opposed to the necropolis) of Tarquinia, and now in the Tarquinia museum. The proud arching of the horses' necks, their slim legs, their rippling muscles are rendered to make them the quintessence of the thoroughbred, so that we forget that the delicate wings would scarcely lift their sturdy bodies off the ground. In these three masterpieces art is none the less vibrant for being put at the service of religion. Here is created a new Italic expressionistic style, so admirable that many would hold that Italian art did not reach this level again until the Renaissance.

Just as archaeology's finds can convince us of the vitality of Etruscan art, so they can bring to life ancient Etruscan life and customs. Most illuminating in this area are two tombs from Cerveteri, ancient Caere, one of the great cities of the Etruscan dodecapolis, twenty-five miles up the coast-road from Rome, and close, too, in cultural relations. Here again Bradford has been at work, spotting over 600 new tombs, but the one that tells us most about Etruscan every-day life has been known since 1850. It is the fourth-century Tomb of the Reliefs (Fig. 2.19), with places for over forty

FIG. 2.18   Tarquinia, Museum. Winged horses, terracotta relief,
from Ara della Regina. (MPI)

FIG. 2.19   Cerveteri: Tomb of the Reliefs, interior. (MPI)

bodies. The front and back walls of this tomb, and two pillars in the middle, are covered with representations in low relief of Etruscan weapons and objects in daily use; here, as elsewhere in Etruscan tombs, but in far more detail, the tomb-chamber reproduces the look of a room in an Etruscan house. Such chambers served again as shelters in modern times—against bombs in World War II. In the central recess in the farthest wall is a bed for a noble couple. It is flanked by pilasters bearing medallions of husband (on the left) and wife (on the right). On the husband's side appears the end of a locked strongbox, covered with raised studs or bosses, with a garment lying folded on top. On the wife's side is a sturdy knotted walking-staff, a garland, necklaces, and a feather fan. The couch has lathe-turned legs; it is decorated with a relief of Charun and the three-headed dog Cerberus, with a serpent's tail. The couch rests on a step on which a pair of wooden clogs awaits their master's need. Above the couch, and continuing all the way around the room, is a frieze of military millinery: helmets with visors, helmets with cheek-pieces, the felt cap worn under the helmet to keep the metal from chafing, swords, shields, greaves or shin guards, and a pile of round objects variously interpreted as missiles, decorations for valor, or balls of horse-dung. The central pilasters, with typical Etruscan economy, are decorated only on the sides visible from the door. What is represented is the whole contents of an Etruscan kitchen. Identifiable objects include a sieve, a set of spits for roasting, a knife-rack, an inkpot, a dinner gong, a game board (not unlike those provided in English pubs for shove-ha'penny) with a bag for the counters, and folding handles; a ladle, mixing spoons, an egg-beater, pincers, a duck, a tortoise, a cat with a ribbon around its neck, playing with a lizard; a belt, a pitcher, a long thin rolling pin for making macaroni, a pickaxe, a machete, a coil of rope, a pet weasel teasing a black mouse, a *lituus* (the augur's curved staff), a wine-flask of the familiar Chianti shape, a knapsack, and a canteen. Over and flanking the door are *bucrania* (ox-skulls), wide, shallow sacrificial basins, and a curved war-trumpet or hunting-horn. Surely never a household embarked better equipped for the next world. This tomb is as good as a documentary film; nothing ever found by archaeology brings Etruscan daily life more vividly before our eyes.

While the Tomb of the Reliefs is full of homely details of Etruscan life, the Regolini-Galassi tomb, also at Cerveteri, was crammed with objects of conspicuous consumption and conspicuous waste. The tomb is named for its discoverers, General Alessandro Regolini and Fr. Vincenzo Galassi, arch-priest of Cerveteri in 1836. Its contents are datable in the eighth or seventh century B.C. It consists of a long narrow entrance-way or *dromos,* two oval side-chambers, and a long narrow main tomb-chamber roofed with a false vault, "now," says Dennis, "containing nothing but slime and serpents." When it was entered through a hole in the roof on April 21, 1836, an incredible treasure of gold, silver, bronze, and ceramics, over 650 objects in all, burst upon the workmen's gaze. All was cleared with feverish haste in less than twenty-four hours, and no detailed inventory was compiled until seventy years later. The riches are fabulous; to quote Dennis again, "here the youth, the fop, the warrior, the senator, the priest, the belle, might all suit their taste for decoration—in truth a modern fair one need not disdain to heighten her charms with these relics of a long past world." In those days, Etruscan objects were not allowed to languish in a museum. A report of 1839 states, "a few winters ago the Princess of Canino [wife of Lucien Bonaparte] appeared at some of the [British] ambassador's fêtes with a *parure* of Etruscan jewellery which was the envy of the society, and excelled the *chefs-d'oeuvre* of Paris or Vienna." Though the contents of the tomb have been now for many years the pride of the Gregorian Museum in the Vatican, the definitive publication did not appear until 1947.

The tomb contained three burials, including one of a woman of princess' rank. With one of the males was buried his chariot (which was first dismantled and its wooden parts ceremoniously burned); his funeral car, plated with bronze in a sword-like leaf design; and his bronze bier, with a raised place for the head and a latticework of twenty-nine thin bronze bars. With the woman was buried a priceless treasure of gold, of baroque barbarity: a magnificent golden *fibula;* a great gold pectoral (Fig. 2.20) decorated in *repoussé* with twelve bands of animal figures (this, one would like to think, was what the Princess of Canino wore to the ambassador's party); gold and amber necklaces; massive gold bracelets and earrings to match the pectoral; silver bracelets, rings, pins, a spindle, and buckets, the latter decorated with fantastic animals; ivory dice; a bronze wine-bowl, with a beautiful green patina, decorated with six heads of lions and griffins, turned inwards; and (reconstructed) a great bronze-plated chair of state with footstool, the whole ornamented with vegetable and animal motifs; the arms end in horse's heads, the back legs in cow's hoofs. To the second male burial belonged a set of splendid bronze parade-shields; a bronze incense-burner on wheels, with a rim of lotus-flowers in bronze; a bronze vase-stand, with a conical base surmounted by two superimposed oblate spheroids, supporting a bronze container for the vase, the whole ornamented in *repoussé* with bulls and winged and wingless lions; bowls in silver and silver-gilt, decorated with horsemen, footsoldiers, archers, lancers, chariots, lions, dogs, bulls, vultures, and palm trees, in a style that might be Egyptian, Cypriote, or Syrian. Such of the treasure as is imported from the Near East bespeaks the wealth of Etruscan overlords; such as is of local manufacture bespeaks the skill of Etruscan craftsmen.

From other places, other clues to Etruscan life and cus-

FIG. 2.20 Vatican City, Vatican Museum: gold pectoral from the
Regolini-Galassi tomb, Cerveteri. (Musei Vaticani)

toms. We may end with two observations, both taken from tombs in Tarquinia: Etruscan women were treated on a par with men; Etruscan sports were sometimes of barbaric cruelty. The Tomb of the Leopards in Tarquinia (fifth century B.C.) shows women (with dyed hair) reclining on the same dining-couch with men; later (Tomb of the Shields, third century B.C.) women sat at meals, while men reclined, but the sexes dined together; there was no Oriental seclusion. The Tomb of the Chariots, also in Tarquinia, shows women along with men in the stands watching athletic events: horse-racing, the pole-vault, boxing, wrestling, discus-throwing, and running. A tomb discovered by Lerici just in time to be restored for the 1960 Olympic Games in Rome is called the Tomb of the Olympic Victors, and shows similar events.

But Etruscan spectator sports were not always so innocent. On the right wall of the Tomb of the Augurs in Tarquinia, a masked figure, in a false beard, a blood-red tunic, and a conical cap, is portrayed inciting a fierce hound to attack a hairy-chested figure, nude but for a loin-cloth and carrying a club; his eyes are blinded by a sack tied over his head, and his movements are impeded by a cord held by a bystander. The victim is already bleeding from several savage bites. Unless, handicapped as he is, he can club the dog to death, he will surely be torn to bits. Perhaps this sanguinary and savage scene represents human sacrifice (and, if so, it is none the less forbidding), but it is a tempting hypothesis that what we have pictured here is a predecessor of the kind of spectacle the Romans later enjoyed in their amphitheaters, when gladiators fought to the death. Gladiatorial contests were in fact traditionally of Etruscan origin, first imported from Etruria for certain funeral games in 264 B.C.

We end, then, where we began, with archaeological evidence for Etruscan influence, for good or for ill, upon Rome. As with the story of prehistoric man in Italy, the Etruscan story is one of influences in part originating in the Near East, in part indigenous, creating a civilization with durable elements that could be and were transmitted, playing a predominant rôle in forming the culture of ancient Italy. The Etruscans are important in themselves, of course, but it is a mistake to assume, because their language, unique on the Italian peninsula, is non-Indo-European, that their culture is isolated, too. As a culture of cities, Etruria must have had its effect, not without cross-fertilization from Greek practice, upon Roman town-planning. Etruscan political forms and practice recur in Roman usage. The language claims our attention for the light it throws, however dimly, on Etruscan politics, religion, and family life, and for the challenge it has presented to modern scientific scholarship to penetrate its mystery. Etruscan religion, as illuminated by archaeological finds, has its own fascination, foreshadows Roman formalism, and is noteworthy for changing, under the stress of political and economic decline, from an optimistic to a pessimistic view of the after-life. Etruscan art, especially terracotta sculpture, shows a striking vitality, humor, and independence; Etruscan architecture makes its impact upon Roman. Finally, the evidence of artifacts as to Etruscan daily life shows a standard of material comfort, and even of luxury, not to be achieved again on the peninsula for two hundred years. Etruscan equality of sexes foreshadows the independence of Roman women; the brutality of Etruscan games is to strike an answering chord in sadistic Roman breasts. Etruria has its own intrinsic fascination, yet for the Western world its major interest must lie in its legacy to Rome. When Etruscan culture was at its brilliant, golden height, Rome was a primitive village of wattle-and-daub huts. Archaeology has been able to trace the metamorphosis of those huts into palaces, with all the concomitant story of grandeur and barbarity; to that metamorphosis the rest of this book will be devoted.

3

Early Rome

Everyone remembers that Augustus left Rome a city of marble, but too few people recall that he found it a city of brick. The picture of Rome in most people's minds is of a marble metropolis, proud mistress of a Mediterranean Empire. This to be sure she eventually became, but the archaeological evidence is that until the end of the third century B.C. Rome looked tawdry, with patched temples and winding, unpaved streets. To trace the development is fascinating, and archaeology is our chief guide.

The story that we read from the earth begins not in Rome itself but in the Alban Hills, extinct volcanoes in the Roman Campagna, sixteen miles southeast of Rome, close to Castel Gandolfo, the lovely lakeside spot where nowadays the Pope has his summer palace. Here, in a pastureland called the Pascolare di Castello, some peasants in 1817 were cutting trenches for planting vineyards. Under the topsoil of the Alban Hills is a thick bed of solid lava, called tufa, which seals in a layer of ashes. In digging their trench the peasants cut through the lava seal and revealed large *dolia*, jars of rough clay, each of which contained, in an urn shaped like a miniature oval hut, the ashes of a cremation burial, together with *fibulae*, objects in amber

and bronze, and numerous vases. It was not until fifty years
later that a committee of experts, including the same Pigorini who afterwards overstepped his evidence about the
terremare, first connected the burials with the city of Alba
Longa, traditionally founded in the mists of prehistory by
the son of Aeneas. In 1902, in cremation graves from a
necropolis to which we shall return, on the edge of the
Roman Forum itself, hut-urns and artifacts were found so
similar to those from the Pascolare that the inference of
cultural connection was inescapable. Whether Alba Longa
was the metropolis and Rome the colony, as stated by the
literary sources, or the other way about, was not evident
from the artifacts.

A necropolis or graveyard implies an inhabited site. The
inhabited site of Alba Longa was destroyed by the Romans
about 600 B.C. Where was the inhabited site that used the
Forum in Rome as a necropolis? It could hardly have been
the Forum itself, which was a swamp not drained and fit
for habitation until about 575 B.C., a date which, as we
shall see, marks the end of the necropolis. Could it have
been the Palatine Hill which rises from the south side of
the Forum? At first sight it seemed unlikely that any evidence for prehistoric habitation could be found on the
Palatine, since the hill was covered with the substructures
of Imperial palaces. But beneath these as early as 1724
were found the remains of the mansions of Republican
nabobs (recorded in literature, too, as having lived here),
and beneath these in turn why should there not lie the
traces of even earlier dwellings? Vergil had pictured Aeneas
humbly entertained on the Palatine by Evander, and lodged
in a hut with swallows under the eaves. Excavations published in 1906 by the great Italian archaeologist G. Boni
(who lived in a villa on the Palatine, and whose memorial bust appropriately adorns the Farnese Gardens there)
found under the Flavian Palace traces of huts containing
artifacts matching those found in the Forum necropolis.

These artifacts fell into two phases. The first included the rough handmade pottery called *impasto,* which we have already seen to be characteristic of Villanovan sites; serpentine *fibulae* (which match those found in the First Benacci period at Bologna); ware incised with a clamshell in dogtooth, meander, and swastika patterns, or with a rope-like clay *appliqué;* pierced beads, spools, and a curious kind of Dutch oven with a perforated top, examples of which were known from the Forum necropolis and the Alban Hills, but not elsewhere. Artifacts of a different and more developed type, belonging, therefore, to a second phase, included pots with thinner walls, sharper profiles (as seen in elevation drawings), and more complicated handles; they are decorated with spirals and semicircles, apparently compass-drawn. There was even a miniature clay sheepdog, his curly coat represented by circles impressed with a metal tube or a hollow reed. Such artifacts match those found in the evolved Villanovan culture, dated in the first half of the sixth century B.C. This culture is contemporary with a rich, sophisticated one in Etruria, but the techniques in Rome and its vicinity are much more primitive than in Etruria. We conclude that the Palatine village was infinitely less prosperous than, say, the contemporary Etruscan cities of Caere or Tarquinia. But equally primitive artifacts are found in the Alban Hills burials, certain tombs on the Quirinal and Esquiline Hills in Rome (discovered when the city expanded after Italy's unification in the 1870's), and in burials in hollowed-out tree-trunks from the Forum necropolis, the latter now on display in the Forum Antiquarium.

In 1907 D. Vaglieri began excavations in the southwest corner of the Palatine which revealed cuttings in the rock. These were actually, though Vaglieri did not recognize them as such, cuttings for early Iron Age huts, the date being an inference from the artifacts, whose stratification Vaglieri did not record. After a sharp controversy with

Pigorini (whose prestige, because of public interest in the *terremare*, was then at its height), the dig was suspended, leaving one hut half-excavated. Here, in this intact area, excavations were resumed in 1948 by a younger specialist in the prehistoric archaeology of Italy, S. M. Puglisi. This time, the methods were rigorously scientific, and the cultural strata were observed and recorded with meticulous care. Puglisi recognized that a scientific dig requires the constant presence on the site during working hours of a competent archaeologist; no precise results can ever be obtained by an excavation director who visits his site only a couple of times a week, since unsupervised workmen can hardly be expected to respect levels of stratification, preserve the right artifacts, or keep accurate excavation notebooks, without which, of course, no scientifically valid conclusions can be drawn.

In the area left undug by Vaglieri, Puglisi was able to distinguish five levels, which have been schematically reproduced on the walls of the Palatine Antiquarium. The top level consisted of nine feet of ancient dump. But the four levels beneath the dump amounted to six-and-a-half feet of compact, undisturbed strata, of which the bottom eight inches represented what had collected on the hut floor while it was still in use. Here the sherds were very tiny, for they had been walked on, it being the regular practice of Iron Age man—and woman—to live comfortably in the midst of their own debris. The hearth (one of the Dutch ovens was discovered in fragments *in situ*) was near the center of the hut, very close to a cutting for a central supporting post—the first evidence ever found for such construction. But there was no danger of setting the central post on fire, since the cooking flame was entirely enclosed within the clay of the oven. Bits of fallen wattle-and-daub revealed the wall-construction. There were animal bones and impasto sherds bearing the marks of fire, but none of the shiny black pottery called *bucchero* (the best examples

of which are rarely found in Rome in contexts earlier than
700 B.C.) and no painted ware. This level, then, belonged
to the first phase of the Iron Age, dated, by parallels with
the finds from beneath the Flavian Palace, about 800-700
B.C. (The traditional date of Rome's founding is 753.) The
lowest level being so shallow, and the sherds showing the
marks of fire, the inference is that the hut had not been
occupied very long before it was burned down.

The contents of the next superimposed level, two feet
deep, show that the site was next used as a kitchen-midden
or refuse-heap. Here the deposits resemble those from a
well (dug long ago but never described in a detailed scientific article), in the sanctuary of Vesta in the Forum, which
is dated in the second phase of the Iron Age (700-550 B.C.),
corresponding in the tradition to the reigns of the five
Roman Kings from Numa to Servius Tullius.° These finds
include polished *impasto,* with high or twisted handles and
out-turned rims; slat-smoothed ware covered with a thin
coating or engobe of reddish clay, ornamented with double
spirals and palmettes, and of a size to fit on the Dutch
ovens; sherds of fine *bucchero* (the first evidence of imports from Etruria), and of a coarser grey local imitation;
painted ware, of the style known as sub-Geometric, imported from south Italy, and also some local imitations identified by their cruder technique.

The next higher level shows fat-bodied "bloodsucker"
fibulae, and flanged tiles, some with horses molded in low
relief, betraying a completely different and more sophisticated building technique, like that used in Etruscan temples. The artifacts matched those found in the level under

° It will be convenient to record here for future reference the traditional
dates (B.C.) of Rome's seven kings:

Romulus: 753-716   Etruscan Dynasty:
Numa Pompilius: 716-672   Tarquinius Priscus: 616-578
Tullus Hostilius: 672-640   Servius Tullius: 578-534
Ancus Marcius: 640-616   Tarquinius Superbus: 534-509

the late Republican House of the Griffins and under the "House of Livia" on the Palatine, and in the upper strata of the shrine of Vesta well; they are associated with the huts built in the Forum after it was drained; that is, with a transitional period after about 575 B.C. The lower date suggested by the archaeological finds for this second phase corresponds to the dates assigned by the literary tradition to Rome's Etruscan kings, Tarquin I, Servius Tullius, and Tarquin the Proud.

The hut itself (Fig. 3.1) was a large one (12 x 16 feet), sunk about a yard into the tufa of the hill, with six cuttings for the perimetral posts, two for a front porch, and one for the central support. The cuttings, averaging fifteen inches in diameter, are wider than is necessary for posts to support so flimsy a structure; the logs were probably held upright by wooden or stone wedges. The hut, reconstructed, represents a historical fact very much like what Vergil had in mind when he described the sleeping quarters assigned by Evander to Aeneas, and such *capanne* can be found in out-of-the-way places of the countryside near Rome even today. Lucretius, Vergil, and Livy all knew what a Bronze and an Iron Age meant; their generation venerated a replica of the "Hut of Romulus" on the Palatine. It suited Augustus' propaganda purpose to stress Rome's rise from humble origins; so, too, to us, archaeology's picture of Rome's primitive beginnings may well make the story of her later expansion seem more impressive, and her domination of subject peoples less overbearing.

Archaeology's second major contribution to our knowledge of early Rome is provided by Boni's excavation of the Forum necropolis (Fig. 3.2), the results of which are displayed with great clarity in the Forum Antiquarium, installed in the cloister of the church of S. Francesca Romana in the Forum itself. The surviving part of the necropo-

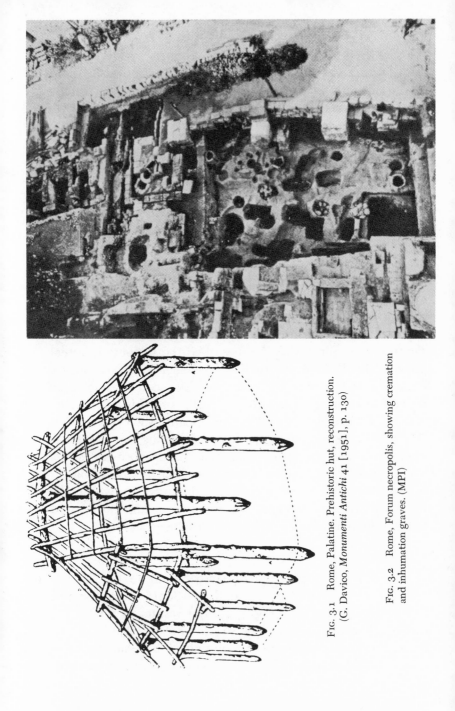

FIG. 3.1 Rome, Palatine. Prehistoric hut, reconstruction. (G. Davico, *Monumenti Antichi* 41 [1951], p. 130)

FIG. 3.2 Rome, Forum necropolis, showing cremation and inhumation graves. (MPI)

lis stretches between the Temple of Antoninus and Faustina, on the north side of the Forum, and a late Republican structure to the east which was pretty certainly (to judge from the built-in beds, the narrow rooms, and the analogy with a building similar in plan at Pompeii, certainly identified by its erotic pictures) a house of ill-fame. The original extent west and southward was probably much greater. The graves have now been filled in, but their sites are marked by plots of grass, round for cremation graves, oblong for inhumation ones. The two types sometimes cut into each other; what inferences are warranted by this fact are better postponed until we have discussed the grave contents.

The Forum nowadays is an austere, even at first sight a forbidding place. It looks much more attractive in a painting by Claude Lorraine or a print by Piranesi, with a double row of olives planted down the middle, romantic broken columns, oxen and peasants scattered about the flowered greensward in picturesque confusion, and the Arch of Septimius Severus buried up to its middle. But picturesqueness is not everything. The Forum is history, stark history; every stone is soaked in blood. To understand that history, mere picturesqueness had to be sacrificed; Boni's graves are not picturesque; they are informative. From them the historical imagination can create a picture of Rome's beginnings which no Piranesi print could rival.

Sixteen feet of picturesqueness had to be cleared before Boni could reach the necropolis level. The cremation tombs are small circular wells, most of them containing, as in the Alban Hills tombs, a *dolium* or large jar, covered by tufa slabs. In the *dolia* were found ash-containers, often in the shape of miniatures of huts like the full-sized ones on the Palatine. The oblong graves contained rough sarcophagi of tufa, or coffins made of hollowed-out oak logs. Both types of tomb contained, intact on discovery, tomb furniture not differing much between the types, and not differing much from the finds in the bottom two levels of Puglisi's Palatine hut; *i.e.,* rough *impasto,* decorated with incised spirals, parallel lines (done with a comb) or zigzags; *bucchero,* some *fibulae* inlaid with amber, glass beads, tiny enamel plaques, remains of funeral offerings of food. It is all very humble, a far cry from the Regolini-Galassi treasure, though some of the tombs are of the same date. The finds show that the necropolis was in use from the ninth to the sixth centuries B.C. The site was, as we saw, on the edge of a swamp; when the swamp was drained, the cemetery went out of use, and huts, of which more later, were built over it.

In the necropolis, sometimes inhumation graves cut into cremation ones, sometimes vice versa. There is thus no ground for assuming that the cremation graves are older, especially as the grave-contents of the two types are so similar. The difference is not one of time but of funeral practice, as today; it suggests two different populations living peacefully together. The cremators were related to the people whose graves were found so long ago in the Alban Hills, and, as we have seen, to the Palatine hut-dwellers. Who were the inhumers? We know that other Roman hills than the Palatine were inhabited from very early times, though the natural features of the Palatine seem to give it priority: plenty of fodder, abundant water within easy reach, a retreat made safe at night by the hill and the river for the people and their livestock.

But habitation of the Esquiline and Quirinal Hills in the sixth century is attested by a number of tombs from a total of 164 found there in the 1870's. The finds from these were never scientifically recorded, and they have never been published, but it is noteworthy that they include weapons, which are absent from the cremation-graves in the Forum. It looks as though the Esquiline folk were invaders, with a more warlike tradition than the Palatine hut-dwellers. The Esquiline folk might earlier have used the Forum necropo-

lis for inhumation. We know that the Sabines buried their
dead. Literary tradition (the Rape of the Sabine Women)
records that the early Romans got their wives from among
the Sabines. Numa Pompilius, the second of the legendary
Roman kings, bears a Sabine name. Might not the two
types of graves in the Forum necropolis represent the peaceful fusion of cremating Latins and inhuming Sabines who
had laid aside their warlike ways?

On top of the Forum necropolis, when the swamp was
drained, huts were built. The archaeological evidence for
this phase of early Rome's history was provided by Boni's
stratigraphic excavation (recently confirmed by the Swede
Einar Gjerstad) to the northwest of the site of the equestrian statue of the Emperor Domitian in the middle of the
Forum. Gjerstad dug a trench sixteen feet long and eleven
feet wide, down to virgin soil, which he found nineteen
feet below the present Forum level. On the earth wall of
the trench the story of the centuries could be read in the
successive levels (Figs. 3.3 and 3.4). Between levels three
and nineteen, six pavements could be counted, but level
nineteen takes us, to judge by the pots found in it, only
back to about 450 B.C. In layers twenty to twenty-two,
Gjerstad found three pebble pavements, which he dates
about 575 B.C. If he is right in assigning to this date the
beginning of monarchic Rome, he has pushed its date down
in our direction over 150 years from the traditional 753 B.C.
But there is more history below this. Strata twenty-three
to twenty-eight are remains of huts, similar to but (pottery
again) later than the ones on the Palatine. Gjerstad dates
them in two phases: 650-625 and 625-575 B.C. Rather than
push the traditional date down so far, it seems plausible to
suppose that these huts represent the period assigned by
the literary tradition to the early kings, and to argue that
the sophisticated period, symbolized by the Forum's earliest

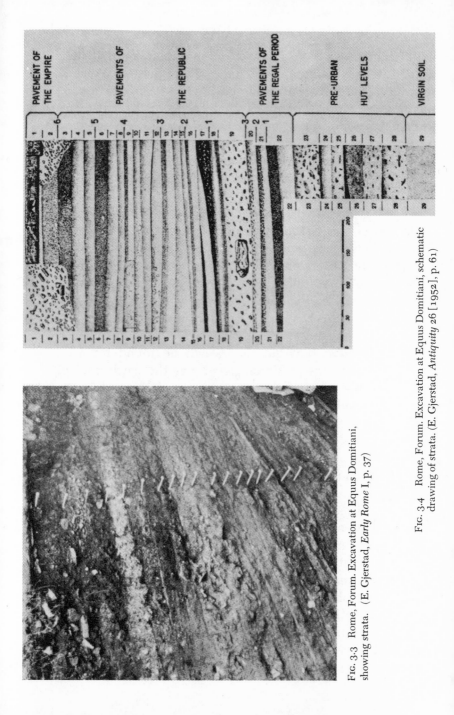

FIG. 3.3 Rome, Forum. Excavation at Equus Domitiani, showing strata. (E. Gjerstad, *Early Rome* I, p. 37)

FIG. 3.4 Rome, Forum. Excavation at Equus Domitiani, schematic drawing of strata. (E. Gjerstad, *Antiquity* 26 [1952], p. 61)

PAVEMENT OF THE EMPIRE

PAVEMENTS OF THE REPUBLIC

PAVEMENTS OF THE REGAL PERIOD

PRE-URBAN

HUT LEVELS

VIRGIN SOIL

pebble pavement, was inaugurated by Rome's earliest Etruscan king, Tarquin I.

These other huts confirm the other archaeological data, which show that what later was unified into urban Rome was originally a group of simple hut-villages clustered on various hills, the Forum huts having spilled down, as it were, from the village on the Palatine. The huts in the level just above the Forum necropolis represent a still earlier stage of this spillover; they antedate the earliest huts in Gjerstad's twenty-nine levels. By the date of Gjerstad's earliest pebble pavements, the huts in the necropolis area have been replaced by a more developed domestic architecture, perhaps with rooms opening on a central court. These houses have rectangular plans, mud-brick, wood-braced walls, and tufa foundations. At the spillover stage, the villagers from the various hills formed some kind of confederation symbolized archaeologically by the two types of graves in the Forum necropolis, and in literature by the tradition of the joint religious festival called the Septimontium.

The period of the first pebble pavement (575 B.C.) is one of major change, from village to urban life, to a city now for the first time boasting a civic center, destined to become the world's most famous public square, the Roman Forum. Of the same date are the earliest remains on the Capitoline Hill, which was to be the *arx* or citadel of historic Rome. Of the same date are the earliest artifacts from the Regia, which later generations revered as the palace of the kings. Of the same date is a sophisticated phase of the round shrine of Vesta, which encircled the sacred flame, symbol of the city's continuity. The literary tradition would date the last two earlier, at least to Numa's reign. However no architectural remains have so far been discovered which associate them with the earlier date.

In his interpretation of the archaeological evidence about the date of the beginning of the Roman Republic, Gjerstad is just as iconoclastic as about the dating of the kings. His argument, more ingenious than convincing, is that an event as important politically as a change from a monarchy to a republic should be reflected in the artifacts, changing from richer to poorer, whereas no such objective evidence of a cultural break is visible in the levels dated by him (perhaps more closely than the facts warrant) at 509 B.C. Such a cultural break does not come until some fifty years later, when Etruscan imports cease. There are grave difficulties in pushing the date of the Roman Republic's beginning down so far, of which the chief is a list (the *Fasti*) of pairs of consuls 509-450 B.C. where many names are too obscure to have been invented. Gjerstad's excavation, in sum, is important as confirming the accuracy of Boni's methods, and as telling us much about the village stage of Rome, but the absolute chronology cannot be said to be as yet firmly fixed, nor the traditional one definitely upset.

Apart from absolute chronology, what unequivocal evidence can archaeology provide that early Rome was ruled by kings? The ideal evidence would be an inscription, and one was discovered in 1899 in the Forum near the Comitium, where, in the open air in front of the Senate House, the popular assembly met. The inscription is called the *lapis niger* stele, because it lies under a later pavement of black marble (*lapis niger*), now preserved under a deplorable corrugated iron roof. But the stone on which it is carved is not marble but tufa, identified as having come from the quarries of Grotta Oscura in the territory of Veii, some nine miles north of Rome.

On the various kinds of tufa or volcanic stone in use in early Rome there hangs a tale. In 1924 an American, Tenney Frank, published an epoch-making study of Roman building materials in which he put the dating of Roman monuments on a firmer basis by distinguishing several different kinds of tufa used by Roman builders at successive dates. Subsequent studies have blurred the dividing lines and shown the possibility of overlap, but Frank's nice eye for discriminating tufas has revolutionized the architectural history of the Roman Republic. The following table illustrates Frank's methods:

Type	Characteristics	Quarries	Where used
Cappellaccio	flaky dark grey ash	Rome	Capitoline temple (509 B.C.)
Grotta Oscura	friable greyish yellow	2½ mi. N. of Prima Porta	Forum stele, "Servian" Wall, Tullianum (prison)
Fidenae	flecked black fragments (scoriae)	Castel Giubileo, 5 mi. N. of Rome	Castrum, Ostia (338 B.C.) Argentina Temple A (ca. 200 B.C.)
peperino	peppered; can be carved	Marino (Alban Hills 11 mi. SE)	Tomb of Scipios (early 3rd cent.) Altar, Argentina C (ca. 186 B.C.)
sperone	coarse-grained brown	Gabii (12 mi. E)	Milvian Bridge (109 B.C.)
Monteverde	reddish, olive streaks	Across Tiber	Sullan pavement nr. Lapis niger
Anio	brown	Cervara (35 mi. ENE)	Tomb of Bibulus (before 50 B.C.)

The *lapis niger* stele, inscribed on tufa of the second type in this series, could be of the very late sixth century

FIG. 3.5 Rome, Forum: *lapis niger* stele. Note the word RECEI, which may be evidence for the historicity of Rome's kings. (P. Goidanich, *Mem. Acc. It.* 7.3 [1943], Pl. 9)

FIG. 3.6 Rome, Forum. Rostra, third phase (fourth-third century B.C.). (E. Gjerstad, *Skrifter* 5 [1944], p. 142)

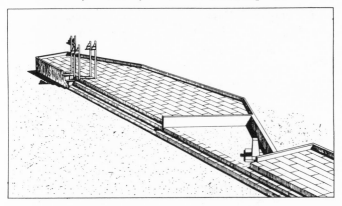

B.C., and this date is borne out by the very archaic letter-styles (Fig. 3.5), which resemble those on the Aules Feluskes stele from Etruscan Vetulonia. Interpreting what the stone says is not made easier by the fact that the top is cut off and the lines are inscribed *boustrophedon* (like the Lemnian stele among other examples), so that in successive lines the beginning and the end are alternately missing. In the left-hand column below is printed the latest text of the letters as they appear on the stele; in the right-hand column, a translation into classical Latin, filling the blanks; below, a translation of this oldest of all Latin inscriptions:

QVOI HOI	QVI · HV[nc locum violaverit,
SAKROS ∶ ESE	manibus] SACER · SIT;
ED SORD	ET SORD[ibus qui haec contam-
OKAFHAS	inet l]OCA, FAS
RECEI ∶ IO	REGI, IV[dicio ei hab-
EVAM	ito, adimere rem pr]EVAM ·
QVOS ∶ RE	QVOS · RE[x per hanc senserit
M ∶ KALATO	vehi via]M, KALATO-
REM HAB	REM, HAB[enis eorum, iubeto
TOD ∶ IOVXMEN	ilic]O · IVMEN-
TA ∶ KAPAI ∶ DOTAV	TA · CAPIAT, VT · A V[ia stati-
M ∶ I ∶ TER PE	M · ITER PE[r aversum locum
M ∶ QVOI HA	pergant puru]M · QVI HA[c]
VELOD ∶ NEQV	VOLET, NEQV[e per purum
IOD ∶ IOVESTOD	perget, iudic]IO, IVSTA
LOIVQVIOD QO ∶	LICITATIONE, CO[ndemnetur].

"Whosoever defiles this spot, let him be forfeit to the shades of the underworld, and whosoever contaminates this spot with refuse, it is right for the king, after due process of law, to confiscate his property. Whatsoever persons the king shall discover passing on this road, let him order the summoner to seize their draft animals by the reins, that they may turn out of the road forthwith and take the proper detour. Whosoever persists in traveling this road, and fails to take the proper detour, by due process of law let him be sold to the highest bidder."

Obviously the inscription thus restored and interpreted, marks a spot which is taboo, its ill-omened nature being further emphasized by the later black marble pavement, which was fenced off by a balustrade of thin white marble slabs set on edge. Beside the stele is a U-shaped shrine or altar,* on a higher level and therefore of a later date than the inscription. Archaeology provides no clue to the purpose of this structure, but learned Romans believed it marked the tomb of Romulus, their first king. This would be a sacred spot indeed, not to be profaned by the feet of men or animals. From one edge of the shrine run the remains of a semicircular platform with steps (Figs. 3.6 and 3.7), also later in date than the inscription. The platform was the Rostra, so called because of its decoration, after 338 B.C., with the bronze *rostra* or ramming-beaks of captured enemy war-galleys. The Rostra was in historical times the speakers' platform; from it in one of its phases resounded the sonorous oratory of Cicero. But it was also the spot from which traditionally funeral orations were delivered, while modern men wearing, according to Roman custom, the death-masks of their ancestors sat behind the orators in curule chairs on the platform. To the logical Roman mind a platform beside the tomb of the first king would seem the appropriate place for funeral speeches.

Since American excavations at Rome's Latin colony of

---

* Professor Ferdinando Castagnoli and Dr. Lucos Cozza reported in 1959 the discovery, at Pratica di Mare, ancient Lavinium, sixteen miles south of Rome, of a series of thirteen such altars, together with an inscription on bronze, with lettering like that of the *lapis niger* stele. They date their finds in the late sixth century B.C.

FIG. 3.7   Rome, Forum. Rostra, fifth phase (Sullan).
(E. Gjerstad, *op. cit.*, p. 143)

Cosa in 1953 identified as a Comitium a circular, step-surrounded space in front of the local Senate House, it appears that the semicircular steps leading to the platform in Rome were Rome's Comitium, and new excavations to prove or disprove this were started in 1957.

Careful equations between the fifteen levels in the Comitium and the twenty-nine levels near the equestrian statue of Domitian prove the Comitium a monument of the Roman Republic: the first phase coincides with the Republic's beginning, and its last with Caesar and Augustus, in the late first century B.C., when the Republic ends. Thereafter freedom of speech, and an arena for it, were but a memory. But the first Rostra rose where it did because the founders of the Roman Republic associated it with the first of Rome's kings.

The *lapis niger* inscription, which refers twice to a king, rests on a base which cannot be older than the sack of Rome by the Gauls in 390 B.C. (for the base is on the same level as the second of the Comitium pavements, laid over traces of a major fire, and the Gauls set Rome on fire). But an inscription of course is a movable monument, and the present location of the stele may not be where it was originally set up. Furthermore, letter styles so archaic are probably older than 390 B.C.: the alternatives, then, are either that the stele, of venerable antiquity, was reset, on a new platform, as a part of rearrangements after the fire, or that it is a deliberately archaizing copy of a much older original. The theory that the king (*rex*) referred to is not the temporal monarch, but the *rex sacrorum,* a Republican priest of later Republican times who inherited the king's religious functions, is virtually ruled out by the letter-styles.

The *lapis niger* stele presents one aspect of primitive Roman religion under the kings: the taboo. Another is the pious tending of the sacred flame on the public hearth, a rite performed in historical times by the Vestal Virgins in Vesta's shrine at the east end of the Forum. The superstructure of the shrine as now restored there yielded no remains earlier than the Gallic fire, but the round plan must reflect the shape of a primitive straw hut of the Palatine type, with central hearth and smoke-hole, and the earliest artifacts, from the previously mentioned well there, are dated in the seventh and sixth centuries B.C. The shrine of Vesta, then, preserves another memory of Rome of the kings.

Kings, like ordinary mortals, need a dwelling place. Traditionally in Rome, this was the Regia (related in root to *rex,* "king"), on the trapezoidal plot between the Forum necropolis and Vesta's shrine (see plan, Fig. 3.8). Romans believed its first occupant was the Sabine Numa, the second

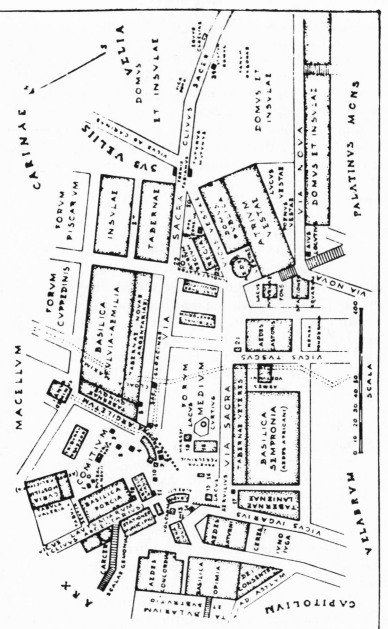

Fig. 3.8 Rome, Republican Forum. (G. Lugli, *Roma Antica*, Pl. 3)

and most pious of the kings, but no archaeological remains confirm so early a date (traditionally 716-672 B.C.). It seems unlikely that the king could have dwelt there before the necropolis was closed, for the king was a priest, and it was unlucky for a priest to look upon a cadaver, or upon death. The earliest datable masonry remains are a foundation in *cappellaccio* of about 390 B.C., another evidence of rebuilding after the Gallic fire. But there might well have been, before the fire, a more primitive structure in wood, revetted in terracotta; indeed, fragments of terracotta revetment, some of a late sixth or early fifth century style and some even earlier, were found there, as well as a grey *bucchero* sherd scratched with the word *rex* in archaic letters. The Regia, as it stands, is the result of at least three rebuildings, the last in 36 B.C. It still has an old-fashioned air: ancient, straggling, intractable, very holy: the shape of its ground-plan never changing from beginning to end. In keeping with the Etruscan tradition—as at Marzabotto—the building is oriented north and south. Its south side was a dwelling, later the office of the Pontifex Maximus; among the great Romans who worked in this building was Julius Caesar. The rest of the Regia was an area partly unroofed. It was a shrine of Mars, hung with shields and a magic lance that quivered at the threat of war. The Pontifex Maximus recorded yearly, day by day, on a whitened board in the Regia, events in which he and his fellow priests had a professional interest: temple-dedications, religious festivals, triumphs, eclipses, famines, rains of blood, births of two-headed calves, and other prodigies. Fragments of this lost archaeological record, piously kept by the pontiffs, turn up in extant Roman history: Livy often refers to them at the end of his account of a year, particularly an unlucky year.

Orientation like the Regia's is an Etruscan practice, and it is with domination by the Etruscans that we should expect Rome's primitive simplicity to evolve into something more like grandeur. The literary tradition ascribed to the Etruscan, Tarquin the Proud, Rome's last king, a great Temple of Jupiter on the Capitoline Hill, built by the forced labor of Roman citizens, and decorated by Etruscan artisans like Vulca of Veii, the sculptor of the Apollo (page 52). It took World War I to confirm this literary tradition archaeologically. The Italians, on the Allied side in that war, ousted the Germans from their Embassy, splendidly situated on the Capitoline Hill in the Palazzo Caffarelli, and remodelled the palace into a museum. In the process was revealed a massive podium, sixteen feet high, built without mortar of blocks of *cappellaccio,* the oldest of Rome's building stones. Fortunately, diagonally opposite corners were found, making it possible to establish how impressive were the podium's dimensions: roughly 120 x 180 feet. Three corners of the podium having been isolated, archaeologists were able to fit into the plan the remains of a substructure which had been found in 1865 under the Palace of the Conservatori. This substructure, now built impressively into a corridor of the Conservatori Museum, proved to be the support for columns. The platform as a whole, then, was the podium of a temple, the largest of its time, over twice the size, for example, of the one at Marzabotto. Traces of the settings for the columns proved them to be placed too wide apart to be connected by architraves in stone; they must instead have been great wooden beams. The wood would have been revetted or faced with terracotta, and in fact enough fragments of terracotta revetments were found on the site to establish this temple as decorated in the typical Etruscan style. If its sculptures were as striking as the Apollo of Veii, they were masterpieces indeed. The temple, repeatedly and ever more grandiosely rebuilt—in one phase it was roofed with gilded bronze, and the cult statue was gold and ivory—was the center and symbol of Rome's religious life. Here the triumphal processions ended. Here the triumphing general, surrounded by his spoils of victory, descended from his chariot drawn by four white horses, and passed through the open doors and the clouds of incense to give thanks to Jupiter the Best and Greatest for his victory. From the cliff behind the temple, the Tarpeian rock, traitors were thrown to their deaths; here, in 133 B.C., Tiberius Gracchus, the friend of the people, was murdered. Religion, dignity, pride, greed, pomp, tragedy: all are the stuff of Roman history; all are here, and archaeology illumines their story. Horace boasted that his poetry would endure "so long as, with the mute Vestal, the Pontifex climbs up to the Capitoline Temple." For him as for us Rome was the Eternal City, and the Capitoline was the symbol of its permanence. Through the assaults of riot, fire, earthquake, poverty, popes, barbarians, limekilns, wind, rain, and earth, the foundations have endured.

The literary tradition tells us how Rome's Etruscan monarchy fell: of Tarquin's despotism and his son's rape of Lucrece, daughter of a Roman aristocrat, whose husband avenged her and allegedly became one of Rome's first pair of consuls. It tells us how the Roman nobles rose, drove out the Tarquins, and founded the Roman Republic. Archaeology cannot confirm the traditional date (indeed the founding of temples, Etruscan style, continues, as we saw, for half a century after 509). But about the middle of the fifth century the contents of the tombs on the Esquiline begin to grow mean and shabby. Contact with Etruria has been cut off, and the Romans make a virtue of necessity, pass sumptuary laws against excessive display, and practice simplicity and frugality. The late fifth century B.C. in Rome, as archaeology reveals it, is a period of isolation, stagnation, and retrenchment.

Hardly had the new Roman Republic rallied to conquer Veii (traditionally in 396 B.C., after a ten-year siege, like Troy's), when the Gauls descended from the north with fire and sword. Rome bought them off, and, resisting the temptation to move to Veii, fell to rebuilding, mindful of how its ancestors had built their city up out of forest and swamp; in love with their protecting hills, their fruitful open spaces, their busy river. The building was done plan-lessly; the main concern was to strengthen defenses.

The primitive Rome of separate villages on the hills had been defended, at most, by separate palisades and ditches. It is with King Servius that literature associated the Rome of impressive buildings and a beetling wall, of squared stone, sturdy enough to repel all invaders. With how much justification Roman historians called the wall "Servian," we are now to learn. The tradition associates Rome's earliest wall with Servius Tullius, who falls between the two Tar-quins, and certain surviving traces of earthwork and ma-sonry, plus the Cloaca Maxima, or Great Drain through the Forum, are assigned by some archaeologists to the sixth century. Indeed until 1932 most scholars accepted the sixth-century date for the whole early circuit. But in that year the Swedish archaeologist Gösta Säflund (who seven years later was to explode Pigorini's myth about the *terremare*) published the results of some painstaking fieldwork which radically changed the picture.

Beginning with the Palatine and working counter-clock-wise, Säflund examined every inch of the surviving circuit ascribed to Servius (see Fig. 2.3), and for stretches which had been torn down during Rome's great expansion (after she became the capital of a united Italy in the 1870's) he had access to unpublished notes and sketches by Boni and another great nineteenth-century Italian archaeologist, Ro-dolfo Lanciani. Everywhere he paid careful attention to materials, techniques, dimensions, mason's marks, the rela-tion of the wall to terrain, neighboring tombs, and ancient artifacts found in its context. It was chiefly from the build-ing material that Säflund drew his conclusions.

The stone was in the main Grotta Oscura tufa, which he

knew from Tenney Frank's studies to have been in use in the year (378 B.C.) in which Livy says the censors contracted to have a wall built of squared stone. Furthermore, some of the Esquiline tombs already mentioned, containing mid-fourth century artifacts, were outside the line of the Grotta Oscura wall, while some of the tombs containing archaic artifacts were inside. The Romans rarely buried their dead within a city wall: the inference is that at the date of the earlier tombs, Rome had no proper ring-wall, while by the date of the later (fourth-century) tombs a circuit wall had been built. The Great Drain through the Forum is also of Grotta Oscura, and is therefore probably to be dated in 378, like the wall, though some feeder lines are in *cappellaccio,* which, as we have seen, was the earliest volcanic stone the Romans used, and we know—because we know the Forum swamp was drained by 575 B.C.—that there must have been some sort of drainage system—possibly open ditches—earlier than 378.

But Säflund found Fidenae tufa also. This he knew, again from Frank's study, to have been in use from about 338 B.C. down into the second century. It had been used to patch the wall in places. What more appropriate time for such repairs than when Hannibal was threatening the city, in 217 B.C.? Thereafter, Roman and Latin colonies, advanced bases, served her in the office of a wall, and her own fortifications were allowed to fall into disrepair.

But there are places in Rome's wall where Monteverde stone has been used for arches, rising from footings set in concrete; in other places the wall has a concrete core faced with Anio tufa. Säflund knew that concrete was little in use in Roman building before 150 B.C., and that it had become a favorite material by Sulla's time (see p. 129). Sulla had marched on Rome in 88 B.C. and taken it; he must have reinforced the wall to keep his enemy Marius from duplicating his own feat. And Sulla included the bridgehead on the far side of the Tiber in his circuit, reinforced the Aventine Hill, and added *ballistae* (great catapults for shooting stones) in arched casemates flanking the main gates.

Thus Säflund distinguished three building periods for the so-called "Servian" Wall, though none as early as King Servius Tullius. One section of earth work or *agger*, on the Quirinal Hill, faced in part with small blocks of *cappellaccio*, looked older than 378 B.C., and Säflund knew from

Fig. 3.9   Rome, "Servian" Wall of 378 B.C., surviving stretch beside Termini railway station. (Photo Paul MacKendrick)

observations at Ardea, Cerveteri (and, as we now know, Anzio) that the use of the earthwork was standard in the sixth century to reinforce weak places on hilly sites. Some early sixth-century sherds, but none later, were found *under* the agger. This helps to confirm that the agger was a part of Rome's sixth-century, genuinely Servian defenses, never a complete ring-wall, but an adjustment and reinforcement of natural defenses, later incorporated into the circuit wall of 378 B.C. A splendid stretch of the facing of this reinforced agger, 100 yards, survives today by the Termini railroad station (Fig. 3.9).

But Säflund's careful observations did more than redate the wall in its several phases. By comparison of the mason's marks, hacked in Greek letters on the heads of the Grotta Oscura blocks only, with similar marks found on the blocks of the fortifications of the Euryalus above Syracuse, in Sicily (built in the late fifth century B.C. by Dionysius I), Säflund was able to demonstrate that Rome's wall was built by Sicilian workmen, Rome not having the manpower or the skill at the time. (Dionysius for his wall had employed 6000 men and 500 yoke of oxen.)

The wall of 378 B.C. is evidence that Rome had emerged from the doldrums into which the Republic had begun to sink. Before 390 B.C. she had depended on men, not walls. The Gallic sack had proved her not invincible, and had also, as war emergencies will, produced a new sense of solidarity. The wall symbolizes it, and so does the bill passed in 367 B.C. (while the wall was still under construction), opening the highest office in the Republic to plebeians. Thus a reinforced oligarchy was formed, which by 338 B.C. could beat its once powerful enemies, the neighboring settlements linked in the Latin League; proudly (even arrogantly) mount the beaks of enemy ships on the new Rostra; and embark upon a career of Manifest Destiny in Italy. The Republic had reached adulthood.

There were other outward and visible signs of the Republic's new maturity and prosperity. The gods deserve their reward for fighting on the side of the biggest battalions, and so the expanding Republic built temples. In another age of arrogant expansion, in 1926, not long before Säflund began his work on the walls, slum clearance in front of the Argentina theater (on the site of the portico of Pompey's theater, where Caesar was murdered) revealed the foundations of four Republican temples (Fig. 3.10), nowadays the haunt of countless tomcats. The gods to

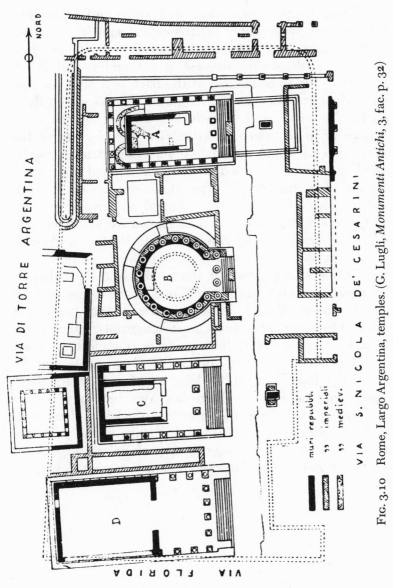

FIG. 3.10   Rome, Largo Argentina, temples. (G. Lugli, *Monumenti Antichi*, 3, fac. p. 32)

whom the temples were dedicated being unknown, they were named, with proper archaeological sobriety, Temples A, B, C, and D. The foundations of Temple C, the third from the north, are the deepest; it is therefore the oldest. It is set in the Italic manner at the back of a high podium, built of Grotta Oscura tufa; its mason's marks match those on the "Servian" wall. Clearly it was built by the same masons or in the same tradition. The podium carries the distinction of being the oldest surviving datable public building in Rome. Terracotta revetments found in excavating are of fourth century type. Besides meanders, the so-called "Greek frets" or "key" design, an angular pattern of lines winding in and out, their decorative motifs include strigil patterns: parallel troughs, made by the workman's thumbs in the wet clay, and then painted in contrasting colors. The strong curve of the profile resembles that of the strigil or scraper used by athletes in the gymnasium to remove caked oil and dirt from their bodies; hence the name. The roof's peak and corner ornaments, called *acroteria,* have spikes set in the clay to discourage birds from perching and committing nuisances. This temple and its three later fellows are still a long way from the grandiose marble and gold of the Augustan Age, but they are an equally long way from the primitive wattle-and-daub huts of the Palatine village. They mark a stage in the painstakingly unravelled archaeological story of Rome's expansion, which we shall follow at various newly-excavated sites in Italy.

4

Roman Colonies in Italy

Rome's wall begun in 378 B.C. took twenty-five years to build. However secure she might feel behind it, immediately beyond the gates lurked enemies. To the north the Gauls, to the east and south, Italic tribes (whom Rome successively feared, rivalled, dominated, and invited to partnership; of these the Samnites were the most fearsome), on the seas the Syracusan and Carthaginian navies—all represented a clear and present danger. Rome's population being inadequate to keep legions in the field, much less a fleet at sea, against all these threats at once, she evolved a system of advanced bases, called Latin colonies (Fig. 4.1), manned partly with trustworthy local non-Romans, though with a hard core of Roman legionaries. This avoided undue drain on the Roman manpower, and placed the responsibility for frontier defense upon frontiersmen who had the greatest interest in their own security.

During the last thirty years the efforts of archaeologists of several nations; for example, Italians at Ostia, Belgians at Alba Fucens, Americans at Cosa have added much to the sum of our knowledge of these frontier outposts: their fortifications, street plan, public buildings, housing arrangements, and the surveyed ("centuriated") quarter-sections of land (allotments) stretching away from the walls into the countryside round about. From these brute facts inferences can be drawn, about what prompted the founding of these outposts (was the motive always military?), about relations with neighbors and with Rome, about communications, about economic, social, and cultural life.

At Ostia, at the Tiber's mouth, historical tradition said that there had been Romans settled since the days of King

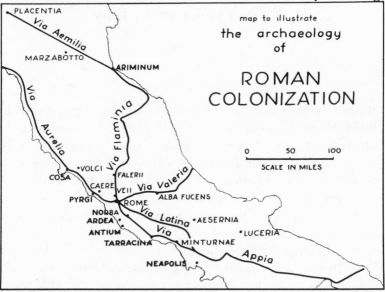

FIG. 4.1   Roman colonization.
(P. MacKendrick, *Archaeology* 9 [1955], p. 127)

Ancus Marcius, and that, even earlier, Aeneas had landed there and built a camp. In 1938 the great Italian archaeologist Guido Calza began soundings to ascertain the date of the oldest surviving stratum. The area he chose was beneath Ostia's Imperial Forum, where the two main streets, the *cardo* and the *decumanus,* crossed. (The Via Ostiensis, from Rome to the river mouth, determined the line of the *decumanus.*) What he found (Fig. 4.2) was a set of walls enclosing a rectangle 627 feet long and 406 feet wide. The

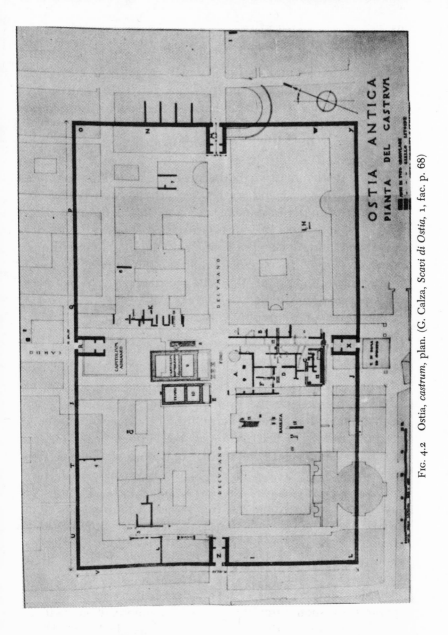

Fig. 4.2 Ostia, *castrum*, plan. (G. Calza, *Scavi di Ostia*, 1, fac. p. 68)

wall was built of roughly squared blocks of tufa in a technique not unlike that of Rome's wall of 378 B.C., but since there was Fidenae stone in it, Calza dated the wall somewhat later than 378. The wall was pierced by four gates of two rooms each, with portcullis. The south gate was demolished in the early Empire to provide space for a temple of Rome and Augustus; the north gate gave way under Hadrian to the massive podium of a Capitolium, but the footings of the east and west gates survive, well below the level of the Imperial pavement. Calza found drains within the walls, and traces of four other streets (unpaved) besides the *cardo* and *decumanus*, but no identifiable buildings. Some terracotta revetments found in the area suggest an unidentified temple of the third century B.C. No traces earlier than the late fourth-century wall have been found in the excavated area of Ostia. Either Ancus Marcius' foundation is a myth, or it was planted in some thus far undiscovered spot, of which all the plowing and digging in the neighborhood has left no trace.

What Calza found at Ostia was a coastguard station, or *castrum*, planted by the Romans at the river's mouth once their control of the sea was established by their victory over Antium's navy (which produced the bronze beaks on the Rostra). The normal complement of such a station was 300 men. A contingent of that size could have manned Ostia's *castrum* wall with one soldier every six feet. Thus the prime motive of the founding was military, and the *castrum* plan is like the familiar and standard plan of a Roman army camp. But the civilian plan antedated the military: Polybius in his description of the Roman camp of about 150 B.C. says that it was planned *like a town* (*i.e.*, with a rectangular grid like Marzabotto). And Ostia's function must from the beginning, or soon after, have been commercial as well as military. Its site at the river mouth was as ideal for collecting the customs as for guarding the coast. Grain from Egypt and Sicily to feed Rome may from the earliest days have

been landed here and stored in warehouses for later ship-
ment upriver by barge. At all events history records the
appointment as early as 267 B.C. of a special finance officer
or *quaestor* for Ostia, and Calza found the footings of warehouses of Republican date. The terracotta revetments mentioned above date from this period. The houses and shops
remained humble for seven generations, but those generations saw the departure of many a fleet, and the arrival of
many a consignment of grain. An inscription dated in 171
B.C. marking the limits of public land in Ostia shows that
by then it had expanded far beyond the *castrum* walls. But
the story of Ostia's development, her new wall under Sulla,
new theater under Augustus, new port under Claudius, new
garden apartment houses under Trajan, and the rest, belong
to later chapters.

In the last half of the fourth century Rome fought two
wars against the Samnites. Alba Fucens (Fig. 4.3) in the
Abruzzi, one of her advanced bases in the Second Samnite
War, has been explored since 1949 by the Belgians. It lies
3315 feet above sea level, on the Via Valeria sixty-eight miles
east-northeast of Rome. (The sixty-eighth milestone of the
Valeria was found *in situ* inside the colony wall.) Alba's
site dominates five valleys. The Latin colony of 6000 families planted here in 303 B.C. assured Rome's communications
on two sides of Samnium, eastward to the Adriatic and
southeastward through the Liris valley.

The pride of Alba is its walls, nearly two miles of them,
surrounding the three hills on which the colony lies. The
material is limestone, which breaks at the quarry into irregular, polygonal blocks. These are set without mortar.
The excavators distinguished four different building techniques in the wall. They assumed that the roughest sectors,
built of enormous blocks, were the oldest, coeval with the
foundation of the colony. These polygonal walls, common
all over central Italy, used to be called Pelasgian or Cyclo-

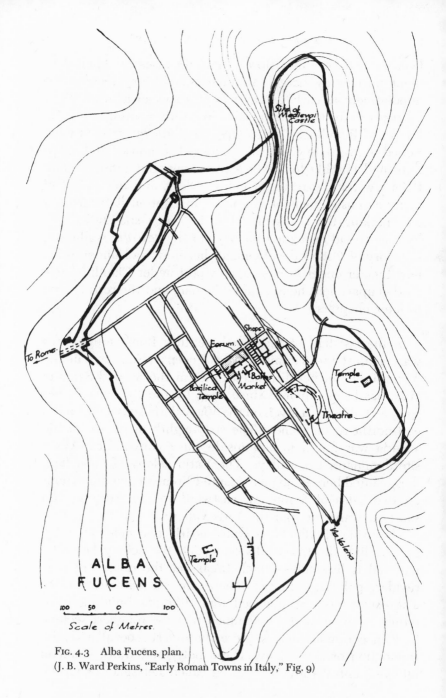

Site of
Medieval
Castle

To Rome

Forum

Shops

Basilica
Temple

Baths
Market

Temple

Theatre

Via Valeria

A L B A
F U C E N S

100 50 0 100

Scale of Metres.

FIG. 4.3 Alba Fucens, plan.
(J. B. Ward Perkins, "Early Roman Towns in Italy," Fig. 9)

pean, and were formerly assumed to be of immemorial antiquity, but recent archaeological work has pushed the dates of most of them down into the late fourth century or later. At Alba the techniques involve the use of smaller blocks and more careful workmanship in successive phases, until finally with the use of cement we reach the 80's B.C. and the age of Sulla. On the northwest, where the hill has the gentlest slope, the circuit is triple, and the outermost is the latest. The loop to the north was the *arx;* it was destroyed by an earthquake in 1915. The wall is pierced by four gates, some with portcullis and bastions. The Via Valeria entered at the northwest, made a right-angled turn, passed the civic center, and emerged at the southeast; that is, it was made to conform to a grid plan within the colony, a grid plan laid down despite the hilly terrain, which made terracing necessary.

Excavating Alba's civic center, the Belgians found a Forum, with altar and miniature temple, buried under many feet of earth. They also found a basilica (a rectangular roofed hall with nave and two side aisles, used as a law court and commercial center), presenting its long side, with three entrances, to a portico facing the Forum. Beside the basilica, a market, with baths on one side and a temple on the other, with early revetments, repeatedly restored. An adjoining street, parallel to the Valeria, was lined with shops, including a fuller's drycleaning establishment and at least one wine shop. The doorsills still show slots for the shutters. In front of the shops ran a portico supported on high pilasters. In the curb were holes where customers might tie their mules. At the corner of the *decumanus,* the excavators found charming statuettes of elephants, used as street signs. Under the market were revealed subterranean chambers accessible only by manholes; the excavators suggest that these are the very dungeons, dark underground *oubliettes,* where prisoners of state like King Syphax of Numidia in 203 B.C., King Perseus of Macedonia in 167, the Gallic chief

Bituitus in 121 were incarcerated, for the Romans often used their colonies as detention points.

Levels, construction techniques, and artifacts assigned various dates to these buildings, but their earliest phases fall in the Republican period, in the age of Sulla or earlier. To the age of Sulla belongs also a handsome rock-cut theater. There is an amphitheater of the early Empire; as we know from a new inscription, its donor was Macro, the notorious informer under the Emperor Tiberius, who brought about the fall of the Emperor's ambitious and scheming favorite, Sejanus.

Walls, grid, civic center, public buildings: these made of Alba a smaller and more orderly replica of Rome. The general layout is repeated so often in so many places that it suggests a master plan made in the censors' office in Rome. By the time Cosa was founded, in 273 B.C., the Romans already could draw on the experience of founding at least eighteen colonies.

Cosa, where the writer did his first excavating, may be used to supply a little more detail on materials and methods in field archaeology. Seven eight-week spring seasons of excavation there (1948-1954), modestly intended as laboratory training for young American classicists, have in fact resulted in a remarkably complete picture of an old-style Latin colony. The site was chosen for excavating because it looked attractive from air photographs, because it was convenient to Rome (ninety miles up the Via Aurelia on the Tyrrhenian Sea), and because its walls were almost perfectly preserved, great gray masses of polygonal limestone looming up as high as a four-story building on a 370-foot hill that rises out of the reclaimed swamplands of the Tuscan Maremma. For Cosa was planted, carved out of the territory of the once proud Etruscan city of Vulci, to mount guard over Rome's newly acquired marches, and to affirm Rome's name and supremacy in a restive neighborhood.

A large assortment of gear is necessary for a modern scientific dig, even a modest one: for surveying and levelling, clinometer (which measures slopes), plane-table (which measures angles), alidade (which shows degree of arc), prismatic compass with front and back sights (for taking accurate bearings; the prism brings the object being sighted, the hair-line of the front sight, and the reading on the compass card all in a vertical line together), leveling staves marked in centimeters (for measuring elevations); templates for recording the curves of moldings; brooms, brushes, and mason's tools for cleaning the architectural finds; zinc plates and sodium hydroxide pencils for electrolysis of coins; measuring tapes of all sizes, mechanical drawing instruments, trowels, marking-pegs, cord, squared paper, large sheets of filter paper for taking "squeezes" of inscriptions, catalogue cards, India ink, shellac, cardboard boxes, small cloth bags, labels, journal books, field notebooks, and a small library of technical manuals. The gear was divided between the villa where the staff lived and an abandoned Italian anti-aircraft observation post on the site itself, whose concrete gunmounts made excellent drying floors for freshly washed potsherds.

Ambitious excavations use a light railway for carting earth to the dump, but at Cosa, which ran on a shoestring budget ($5000 for eight weeks), the vehicle was the wheelbarrow, the track a set of boards bound at the ends with iron to keep them from splitting. Twenty of the local unemployed formed the corps of workmen. The foreman, in better times a master carpenter, used a pick with all the delicacy of a surgeon with a scalpel.

The first step in excavating a site is to lay down a grid—fifty-meter squares are convenient—marked with wooden stakes set in cement and levelled. During the ten months of the year when there was no digging and Cosa was abandoned to the shepherds, they operated on the conviction that the stakes marked the spot where the treasure lay buried. They would overturn them and dig like badgers, and each new season would have to begin with a partial re-survey.

A typical excavating day would begin with the removal of surface earth in wheelbarrows. As large objects came to light—bits of amphora, roof-tile, terracotta revetments— they were placed in shallow yard-square wooden boxes called *barrelle,* equipped fore and aft with carrying shafts, and labelled accurately with the precise designation of the area from which the finds came: Capitolium Exterior South, Level I; Arx North Slope, Surface, and the like. Small objects—bone *styli,* small sherds, loomweights (pierced terracotta parallelepipeds, whose weight held the threads hanging straight down on an ancient vertical loom), lamps, fragments of inscriptions—went into separate marked cloth bags. Thus the horizontal and vertical findspot of each object was precisely known, so that when a dated or datable object was found in a level, the whole level could be automatically dated, and so the whole mosaic painstakingly put together and the history of the site analyzed, or, as the archaeologist says, "read." The meanest potsherd, accurately defining a context, thus becomes more valuable historically than a whole museum shelf full of gold jewelry from an unstratified dig.

When a *barrella* and a set of cardboard boxes had been filled, they were carried to the excavation shack and sorted. Objects that could not be "read"—shapeless bits of rubble, parts of coarse pots without profile of base or rim— were discarded, the rest sent to be washed. After washing and drying, cataloguing began. Every object was painted with a small square of shellac, on which its catalogue number was written in India ink and then shellacked over to preserve it. A letter indicated the dig, another the season, a number showed the place of the object in the chronological sequence of finds. A typical entry might read like the card, p. 101. Leica or plate photographs were taken of all important finds

CC 1487   Capitolium Exterior South
            Level I
Moulded terra-cotta revetment
Width 0.17 (centimeters)
Height 0.14
Thickness 0.03
    Pale pink terra-cotta, much pozzolana. All edges preserved, slight crack lower right corner. Nail-holes each corner. Strigillated cornice moulding above, finishing in a half-round moulding, enriched thunderbolt pattern in field. Thunderbolt runs from upper left to lower right, tapering to points at ends, hand grip in center; enriched on either side of hand grip with seven-point sword-and-sickle palmettes. Photograph.

and separately indexed for ready reference in the final publication.

After the workmen's day (7:00 A.M. to 4:30 P.M., with a half-hour for lunch) was over, there was still much for the staff to do. Pottery, spread out on trestle tables, had to be examined, joins made where possible, types distinguished. (Careful attention at Cosa to plain Roman black glaze has led to an arrangement of types in a dated series which will be useful for future dating on other sites.) Evenings were devoted to writing up the journal, studying the manuals, making drawings, planning the next day's dig, and shop talk. The results of a typical season's work, in 1950 on the *arx* at Cosa (Fig. 4.4), were to isolate a second temple at right angles to the Capitolium, restore on paper the design of several sets of terracotta revetments, follow the line of the Via Sacra from the *arx* gate to the Capitolium, clear the *arx* wall, get down to bedrock beside the Capitolium, discover a terracotta warrior who was part of the pedimental sculpture of an older temple under the excavation shack, and in general get a pretty clear idea of the religious center of the colony as it was, perhaps, in the time of the elder Cato, in the early second century B.C.

In the two seasons preceding the discoveries on the *arx*

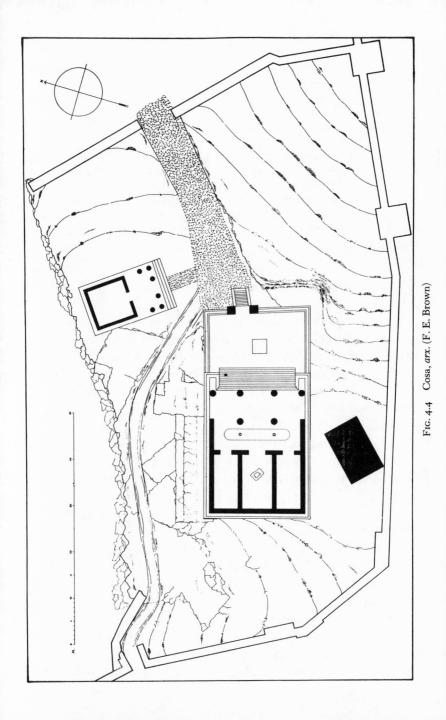

FIG. 4.4 Cosa, *arx.* (F. E. Brown)

just described, much work had been done. In the survey to set up the fifty-meter grid, Cosa's own ancient rectangular grid of streets, with pomerial street running just inside the wall as at Marzabotto, came out clear enough to be plotted on the plan (Fig. 4.5), together with the standard blocks of housing, like the identical "ribbon-development" apartment blocks of a welfare state, which compensated the pioneers for whatever fleshpots they had given up in the

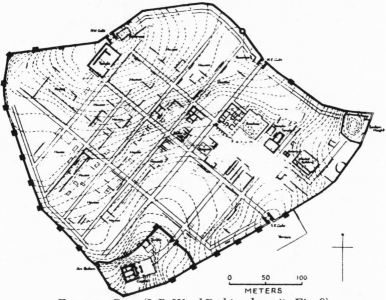

FIG. 4.5   Cosa. (J. B. Ward Perkins, *loc. cit.*, Fig. 8)

metropolis or elsewhere. Housing was found to occupy two-thirds of Cosa's thirty-three acres, while public buildings took just over twenty per cent, and streets the rest. The site, which is waterless, was found to be honey-combed with cisterns: over sixty-five were plotted. The mile-and-a-half of walls, with their eighteen towers, spaced an effective bowshot apart, had been closely examined. They were found to be built with two faces and a rubble fill. The outer face was handsomely finished, with tight mortarless joints, and sloped seven degrees back—this is called "batter" —from the perpendicular; the inner face was left rough. Potsherds of the Etrusco-Campanian style found in the rubble fill were of a period matching Livy's date of 273 B.C. for the colony. It was clear that the walls, which show throughout no difference in technique, were built all at one go, at the time the colony was founded. Those impatient of the Roman reputation for perfect engineering will be pleased to know that the ancient craftsmen, when they came to close the ring of the wall, found they had made an error of from two to four Roman feet. (The Roman foot approximately equals the English.) The three gates were examined, and found to be of two rooms, with the main gate grooved on its inner walls with slots for the rise and fall of the portcullis, as at Alba. Bordering the roads leading from the gates were tombs. The director of the excavations, by skindiving, examined the outworks of the port, built to prevent silting, and established them as Roman. They were parallel jetties 350 feet long, supported on huge piers measuring twenty by thirty Roman feet, and forty-five Roman feet apart.*

---

* Undersea exploration, one of the most fascinating branches of archaeology, has not been carried as far in Italy as in France (see, *e.g.*, P. Diolé, *4,000 Years under the Sea* [New York, 1954]). But this is a convenient place to report a 1950 Italian operation off Albenga, on the Ligurian coast between Genoa and the French border. Along this stretch of the Italian Riviera fishermen's nets had frequently brought up amphorae, presumably from an ancient wreck, which was soon located in twenty fathoms. The use of an iron grab damaged the sunken hull, but an impressive number and variety of objects were recovered. The ship yielded up over 700 more or less intact cork-sealed, pitch-lined amphorae, from a cargo of perhaps thrice that number; their shape was that current in the second and first centuries B.C. Some had contained wine, others still held hazel-nuts. Campanian black-glaze pottery, of a type datable in the last half of the second century B.C., was found in sufficient quantity to enable Professor Nino Lamboglia, who was in charge of the operation, to set up a whole typology of black-glaze ware, based on types, fabric, and glaze, a typology which proved a useful check for dating Cosan pottery, and for which the Cosan results have provided some corrections. Lead pipes and lead sheathing resembled those found in the ships from Lake Nemi (see Chapter 7), and a stone crucible with molten lead

The 1949 campaign concentrated on the Capitolium (Fig. 4.6), situated so that its central *cella* lay over a cleft in the rock, from which some kind of oracular fraud could be perpetrated. Between porch and *cellae*, running the width of the building, was a cistern lined with the waterproof cement called *opus signinum*, made of lime, sand, and pounded bits of terracotta. The temple walls, which stand on the south to an impressive height, visible far out to sea, were built of brick-like slabs of the local calcareous sandstone, set in mortar. On the north, the line worn in the rock by water dripping gives mute evidence of the wide overhang of the roof, Etrusco-Italic style. Some of the terracotta revetments belonged to the older, wooden temple. It must have made a brave show when it was new, covered with brightly painted tiles, its pediment and roof ornaments glittering in the sun.

The last four campaigns of digging attacked the Forum area, thickly overgrown with asphodel, acanthus, and thistles. Here lay the remains of an ungainly but monumental triple arch of about 150 B.C., the oldest dated arch in Italy. It had a central roadway for wheeled traffic, two side arches for pedestrians, and a stone bench attached to the outer face where old men could sit in the sun and gossip. There was a basilica, as big as a New England town hall, like Alba's (but older: about 180 B.C.). It presented its long side to the Forum, had a nave and two side aisles, and a tribune for the presiding judge at the back, with a vaulted cell, perhaps the local lock-up, beneath it. At some time in the early Empire the basilica was abandoned as a legal center, and restored as a festival hall, or intimate theater.

Other buildings turned out to hold fascinating secrets. A

in the bottom suggested that running repairs could be carried out at sea. Fragments of three helmets, of unusual design, may have been intended for Marius' army, which was campaigning in the north against Germanic tribes in the late second century B.C. The finds are on display in the Albenga Museum (see N. Lamboglia, "Il Museo Navale Romano di Albenga," *Rivista Ingauna e Intemilia* [1950] Nos. 3 and 4).

FIG. 4.6   Cosa, Capitolium. (Fototeca)

complex beside the basilica turned out to be an Atrium Publicum, a public hall in the form of the central unit of an Italic house, which was rebuilt as an inn for the patrons of the adjoining festival hall. When, about A.D. 35 (on the evidence of pottery—the "Arretine ware" characteristic of the period), the basilica wall collapsed, it crushed and entombed in place the inn's complete furnishings and equipment. The excavators suddenly found their hands full of tableware, kitchen crockery, and all sorts of household gear, in metal, glass, and stone; decorative pieces, including a lively marble statuette of Marsyas; and objects of personal adornment, including a fine engraved amethyst. For the first time outside of Pompeii an ancient building had yielded not only its structure but its contents.

On the other side of the basilica, excavation of what had been called Building C brought further surprises. When the workmen had stripped the surface humus off the area of the forecourt, the excavators found themselves looking at a perfect circle of dark earth enclosed by a sandy yellow fill. Further digging established this as a circular, theater-like structure, big enough to hold 600 people. There was an altar in the middle. This must have been the Comitium, the colony's assembly-place (Fig. 4.7). Building C, behind it, must have been the Curia, or Senate House. The undisturbed fill under the Curia floor proved completely sterile; hence the curia must have been built at a date near the foundation of the colony. At this stage both Curia and Comitium were apparently of wood, replaced in a second phase, before the end of the third century B.C., with purple tufa from nearby Vulci.

A healthy site, an orderly plan, a water supply, strong walls, housing, provision for political and religious needs: the basic necessities are all here, at Cosa, and all as early as the founding of the colony. By hard work, painstaking accuracy, and intelligent inference, Brown and Richardson, the excavators of Cosa, have given us the clearest possible

picture of the physical structure of a Roman colony well on
in the first intense period of history in the planting of advanced bases. Cosa is clearly the fruit of long practice and
Etrusco-Italic tradition, untouched by Hellenism (no Greek
architectural language in sculptural or ornamental marble)
or by new-fangled techniques (no brick or concrete in the

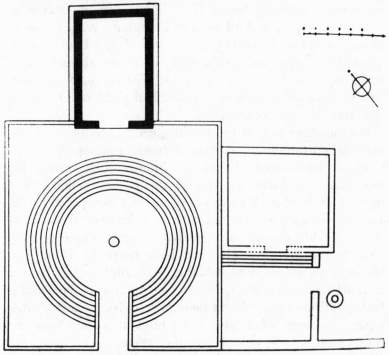

FIG. 4.7   Cosa, Comitium.
(L. Richardson, Jr., *Archaeology* 10 [1957], p. 50)

early phases). When we carry down Cosa's architectural
history to the early Empire, we infer the death of freedom
of speech from the remodelling of the basilica into a theater.
And when freedom of speech and public life died, the colony
lost its sense of community. Its thirty-three acres would
have held 3000 to 3500 settlers comfortably. But the first
draft of settlers numbered probably 2500 families. (We

infer families, not soldiers only, from the discovery of loom-weights, hardly appropriate for Roman legionaries.) 2500 families make a population of at least 7500, and probably more, given Italian philoprogenitiveness. Some of these must have lived well outside the colony; only those whose cen-turiated allotments, explained below, lay nearest the walls would have lived in the colony proper. The holders of more distant plots would come to town only for market, worship, litigation (as long as the basilica lasted), or refuge from raiding parties of Gauls or other enemies. And so, under despotism, the community disintegrated. The temples held on longest. "Only the gods, in the end," writes Professor Brown, "held steadfastly to their ancient seats."

By derivation, a *colonia* is a place where men till the soil. Colonists were assigned centuriated allotments. Since traces of centuriation have been found both at Alba Fucens and at Cosa (Figs. 4.8 and 4.9), as well as at nearly fifty other certain and half as many possible sites in Italy, this seems an appropriate place to discuss the subject. Wherever col-onies were planted, wherever land was captured, confis-cated, redistributed to the poor or to veterans, the surveyor with his *groma,* or plane-table, was on hand. Air photog-raphy is a great help in revealing traces of the Roman sur-veyor at work, for modern land-use has often overlaid the ancient traces, leaving ancient crop-marks as the only clue. The standard surveyor's unit was the *centuria* of 200 *iugera* (the *iugerum,* five-eighths of an acre, being the area an ox could plow in a day), and a side of twenty *actus* (776 yards), its corners marked by boundary stones, some of which survive. There has been too little digging to confirm the results of air reconnaissance, but it seems clear that some centuriation goes back to the late third century B.C. Dr. Ferdinando Castagnoli, the Italian expert, is inclined to date that of Alba and Cosa at least this early, as well

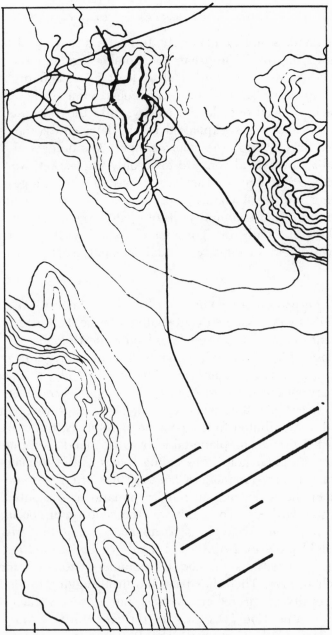

FIG. 4.8   Alba Fucens, centuriation.
(F. Castagnoli, *Bull. Mus. Civiltà Rom.* 18 [1953–1955], p. 5)

as large stretches in the fertile Campanian plain northwest
of Naples.

The surveyor liked to link up his centuriated grid with
a colony plan. Thus at Cosa the *groma,* for siting the allotments, could have been set up in the Porta Romana (the
northeast gate), and at Alba the line of the Via Valeria
inside the walls, if projected, would cut the lines of centuriation at right angles. The four sides of the *centuria*
were usually marked by roads, the inner subdivisions by

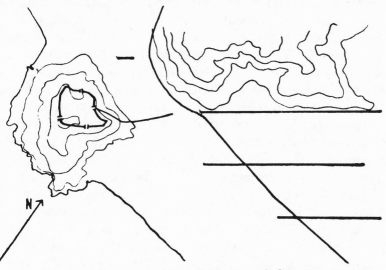

FIG. 4.9   Cosa, centuriation. (F. Castagnoli, *loc. cit.,* p. 6)

narrower roads, trees, hedges, or drainage or irrigation
ditches. Modern land-use often follows the line of the ancient: one stretch recently laid out and now in use at Sesto,
west of Florence, deliberately follows the traces of Roman
centuriation, restored by a classically trained engineer for
modern man to admire. As with the grid inside a colony
wall, the centuriated grid of allotments was laid out from a
basic *cardo* and *decumanus.* The Roman surveyors were
balked by no natural barriers. Bradford cites one line of
centuriation running as high as 1600 feet above sea level

(though within the *centuriae* the furrows might follow the contours) and another, in Dalmatia, continues from a peninsula across to the mainland, spanning an arm of the Adriatic Sea three miles wide. In north Italy, where the flatlands of the Po Valley made the survey easy, one can ride from Turin (Roman Augusta Taurinorum) to Trieste (Roman Tergeste), three hundred miles, through centuriated systems all the way. The same air photographs which revealed neolithic sites to Bradford in Apulia showed Roman centuriation, too, and subsequent digging turned up pottery of Gracchan date (about 133-122 B.C.). A particularly extensive stretch, outside of Italy, is found in Tunisia. It has been traced from the air 175 miles from Bizerta to Sfax, and southwestward from Cape Bon for 100 miles inland. It probably goes back to ambitious plans of Gaius Gracchus, about 122 B.C., to resettle Rome's urban proletariat.

The examples of colonized and centuriated sites mentioned here hardly even scratch the surface of the subject. Dozens of others remain to be explored, on hilltops and headlands, by rivers and crossroads, the length and breadth of Italy. Recent excavation at the Latin colony of Paestum, on the coast fifty miles southeast of Naples, has traced the Roman grid (Fig. 4.10), identified yet another Comitium, and produced over 1,000,000 small finds. And still other colonial sites lie under populous modern towns and cities: examples, in chronological order of planting, are Anzio, Rimini, Benevento, Brindisi, Spoleto, Cremona, Piacenza, Pozzuoli, Salerno, Vibo Valentia, Bologna, Pèsaro, Parma, Modena, and Òsimo. Their foundation-dates span the years from about 338 to 157 B.C., the expanding years of the Roman Republic, the years of "Manifest Destiny." Their continued existence compliments the Roman founders' nice eye for a promising site, but makes large-scale investigation of Roman levels difficult or impossible, for residents of flourishing modern cities naturally resist resettlement in the interests of archaeology. Excavation in these populated

areas must wait upon repair of war damage, urban improvements (as when laying new sewer mains reveals

FIG. 4.10   Paestum: Roman grid of streets (air-photograph).
(Italian Ministry of Aeronautics)

Roman ones that follow the grid of the Roman streets), or
new building to bring new facts to light. No colony has
been completely excavated. At least forty per cent of an-

cient Ostia and Pompeii remains to be dug. But generations of archaeologists of many nations have dealt patiently and intelligently with the evidence. Perhaps, considering the long span of two-and-a-half millennia ·since the earliest tradition of the planting of Roman colonies, the wonder is not that we know so little but that we know so much.

What archaeology has revealed is the story of the exploitation of a frontier, with much that is exciting, and much that is sordid. There are many points of resemblance to the history of the American West, though two differences should be emphasized: the Romans often planted their outposts in the territory not of savages but of their cultural equals, and the Roman frontier was settled not by private but by government enterprise. But the likenesses are striking. Centuriation produces something like quartersections; land grants to veterans resemble grants under the Homestead Act; the Roman grid town-plans were reproduced in our Spanish settlements of the Southwest. And perhaps, on the Roman as on the American frontier, the atmosphere was less democratic than Frederick Jackson Turner thought.

What archaeology digs up in the colonies is material remains, brute facts, but what it infers is men; men marching out in serried ranks under their standards for the formal act of founding (*deductio*); Romans and local Italians living side by side with some degree of amity and equality; Romans impressing their ways and speech on the peoples round about; Roman slum-dwellers given a new chance in the new territory; large estates broken up to give land to the landless; grizzled veterans settled in the quiet countryside after a lifetime of hard campaigning; Romans homesick in strange places; undergoing the rigors of frontier existence; subject to the ferment of success and failure; forging a cultural life (the epic poet Ennius, the dramatist Pacuvius, the satirist Lucilius, all came from Roman colonies).

The grid plans, in town and country, as Bradford has pointed out, show, if not genius, then strong determination and great powers of organization. The grids are, like the Romans themselves, methodical, self-assured, technically competent. They are also regimented, arbitrary, doctrinaire, and opportunist. This was the price the Mediterranean world had to pay for the security of the Roman peace.

But before that peace-without-freedom could be enjoyed, the Roman Republic was to suffer its death throes. That blood-bath was the work of the nabobs of the last century before Christ, who left their stamp, as nabobs will, on the buildings they erected to testify to their glory.

5

Nabobs as Builders: Sulla, Pompey, Caesar

The aftermath of Sulla's second march on Rome in 83 B.C.
was a spate of political murders and confiscations. The
profits were enormous, and Sulla used them for the most
ambitious building program in the history of the Republic.
His motive was in part the desire to rival what he had
seen in the cities of the Greek East, in part his understanding that massive building projects are the outward and
visible sign of princely power. And so he monumentalized
the same Forum in which he displayed the severed heads
of his enemies, planning, in the Tabularium, or Records
Office, a theatrical backdrop for the tragedy which in the
ensuing years was to be played below. He settled 100,000
of his veterans in colonies in central and south Italy. He
built or reinforced walls in Rome, Ostia, and Alba Fucens;
theaters in Pompeii, Alba, Bovianum Vetus, and Faesulae;
he built temples in Tibur, Cora, Tarracina, Pompeii and
Paestum. And this is only a sample of his prodigious building activity. But by all odds the most grandiose of his
completed projects took shape at Praeneste (nowadays
Palestrina), a little over twenty miles east of Rome, where
he sacked the town to punish it for taking the side of his
enemy Marius. He then built or restored there the great,

axially-symmetrical, terraced Sanctuary of Fortune, the most splendid monument in Italy of the Roman Republic.

In 1944 allied bombing sheared off the houses from the steep south-facing slope where the medieval and modern town was built, and revealed the plan of the Sanctuary. Now, after fourteen years of excavation and restoring (reinforcement with steel beams, injecting liquid concrete, loving reproduction of the craft of ancient masons), the plan is clearer than it has been at any time since antiquity. The finds are displayed to advantage in the Barberini Palace at the top of the Sanctuary, splendidly reconstructed as a museum. The site repays a visit perhaps more than any other in Latium.

The archaeological zone of Palestrina falls into an upper and a lower part. In the lower area exciting discoveries were made in 1958. Its southernmost retaining wall, and the monumental ramped entrance, the Propylaea—enlivened in antiquity with jets of water playing—was cleared. Between it and the buildings of the lower zone, excavation seventy years before had shown traces of pools and shaded porticoes. In 1958, also, the façade was removed from the cathedral in the center of the lower zone, revealing behind it an imposing Roman temple with a lofty arched entrance, its *cella* corresponding to the forward (south) part of the nave of the present church. To the left rear (northwest) of this temple was a natural cave, long known as the Antro delle Sorti, where, according to time-honored local lore, the lots were cast which gave this sanctuary of Luck its fame. The cave, the excavators discovered, had been monumentalized into the apse of a building (not shown in the plan), its floor paved with a mosaic representing the sea off Alexandria. The mosaic was sunk a couple of inches below floor level and sloped forward to allow a thin film of water to play over it, which brightens the colors and makes the mosaic fish extraordinarily realistic. The mosaic also portrays architectural elements—an altar, column, and capital

—in what corresponds to the so-called Second Style at Pompeii, dated in the first half of the first century B.C.

Opposite this building in the plan is another with a grotto much like the natural cave on the left. It was from this apse, again at a level a couple of inches below the rest of the floor, that the famous Barberini mosaic (Fig. 5.1) came, a late Hellenistic copy of an original of the early Ptolemaic age in Egypt. It is now handsomely restored and displayed in the museum at the top of the Upper Sanctuary. The mosaic combines a zoological picture-book of the Egyptian Sudan—its real and fabulous monsters labelled in Greek—with a spirited scene of the Nile in flood, with farm-house, dove cote, a shipload of soldiers, crocodiles, hippopotamuses, an elegant awninged pavilion, a towered villa in a garden, a group of soldiers feasting in mixed company (after them, the deluge), more wine, women and song in an arbor nearby, behind the pavilion a temple with statues of Egyptian gods in front, before them a man riding, his servant following afoot with baggage; behind the arbor a straw hut, with ibises in flight above it; in the flood waters, canoes (one loaded with lotus blossoms) and two large Nile river craft with curving prows—altogether the most spirited essay which has come down to us in the art of the mosaic. Interest in Egypt is a striking feature of both Pompeian and Roman wall-painting of the last half-century of the Republic and the early Empire. Examples are the scene from Pompeii of pygmies fighting a rhinoceros and a crocodile, now in the Naples Museum, the cult scenes from the Hall of Isis under the Flavian Palace on the Palatine, and the frescoes of the Pharaoh Bocchoris in the Terme Museum from the villa under the Farnesina. Alexandria was then the intellectual and artistic capital of the world. The Lucullus who founded the Sullan colony at Praeneste appears from an inscription found in the lower area to be not the famous *bon vivant* (who had been in Alexandria, the first foreign general ever to be

FIG. 5.1 Palestrina, Museum. Barberini mosaic. (Museum photo)

entertained by a Ptolemy in the palace) but his brother Marcus. Nevertheless the two brothers were very close, and the more famous of them may have supplied the mosaic, the mosaic-maker, or the idea of using Egyptian motifs.

M. Lucullus' name was carved on a fallen epistyle, a marble block intended to connect two columns. Where did the block belong? Gullini, the excavator, connected it with a building which ran between the two apsidal halls in the lower area. What survives is a back wall, built in the technique called *opus incertum,* a strong lime and rubble wall, studded externally with fist-sized stones of irregular shape. This technique was standard in the age of Sulla. The wall was decorated at regular intervals with two stories of half-columns, ingeniously combining function with decoration: they mask drainage conduits. The pavement in front of the wall shows the marks of two column-bases in two different rows, enough to justify restoring on paper a whole forest of twenty-four columns. Two dimensions are known: the diameter of the bases and the height of the half-columns on the wall behind. Their proportionate relation is appropriate to Corinthian columns, and some Corinthian capitals of a size to fit were found in the area. Working from these finds, the architect Fasolo could restore on paper a two-story basilica (Fig. 5.2, bottom) between the two apsidal halls (only one hall is shown in the reconstruction). The basilica is on a higher level than the newly-isolated temple to the south of it. The difference in level is made most clearly visible by sets of superimposed columns on the southwest side of the basilica (where the lower columns are below the basilica pavement level), by the pavement below the *piazza* of the modern town, and in the façade of the right-hand (eastern) apsidal hall, which is in *opus incertum,* while its lower level, the colony's *aerarium* or treasury, heavily built of tufa blocks, had the difference in construction hidden by a portico with Doric columns.

The terrace marking the transition between the lower

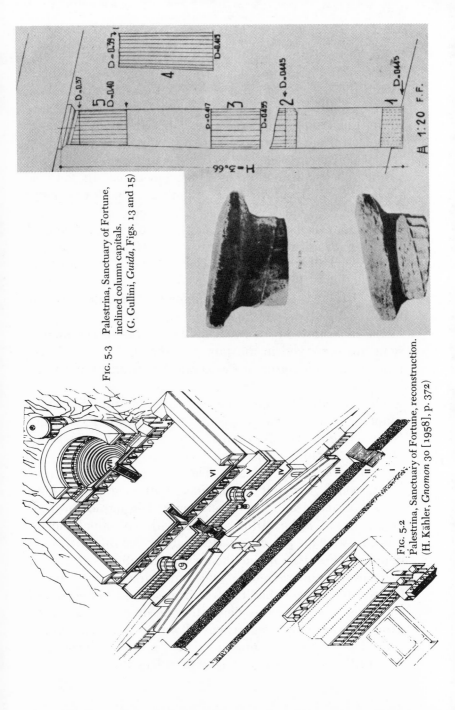

FIG. 5.3 Palestrina, Sanctuary of Fortune, inclined column capitals. (G. Gullini, *Guida*, Figs. 13 and 15)

FIG. 5.2 Palestrina, Sanctuary of Fortune, reconstruction. (H. Kähler, *Gnomon* 30 [1958], p. 372)

area and the Upper Sanctuary used to be covered by houses and shops, all damaged or destroyed by the 1944 bombing. When the debris was cleared away, it was found that the modern buildings had rested on a two-level terrace (I and II in the reconstruction), and had backed against and protected from centuries of weathering 325 magnificent feet of polygonal wall. The wall gives an architectonic front to the cliff and is at the same time functional. Its top was the architect's base line; on it he built his complex, a splendid series of superimposed terraces, which, now that the rubble from the bombing has been cleared away, is revealed in all its magnificence, of ramps (III), Hemicycle Terrace (IV), Terrace of Arches with Half-columns (V), and Cortina Terrace (VI), all leading up to the final stepped hemicycle (VII) with the circular *tholos* for the cult statue at the very top. A draped torso in blue Rhodian marble (now in the museum), of a size to fit the *tholos*—whose dimensions are preserved in the fabric of the Barberini Palace—may be the cult statue of the goddess Fortune: Lady Luck herself.

The next level is approached by a pair of imposing ramps running east and west, converging on an axis. Fasolo and Gullini found that the ramps were supported by a series of concrete vaults, concealed, all but one, by a facing of *opus incertum* (see p. 120). The exception is the central vault, which was left open, lined with waterproof concrete, and made into a fountain-house. The terrace in front of the ramps is beautifully paved with polygonal blocks. A room—perhaps priests' quarters—at the bottom of the left ramp is decorated in the Pompeian First Style—embossed polychrome squares, red, buff, and green, with dado. Houses at Pompeii thus decorated are dated between 150 and 80 B.C., so that this decoration accords with a Sullan date. The decorated room is paved with waterproof cement with bits of white limestone imbedded in it. The technique, called *lithostroton*, was in vogue in Sulla's time.

On the ramps were found three curious column capitals, which at first puzzled the excavators, and then gave the clue to the whole complex on top of the ramps. What is odd about the capitals is that they incline (Fig. 5.3) twenty-two degrees with respect to the axis of the columns. Since this slant corresponds to the grade of the ramp, the columns must have been intended to bear an inclined architrave or beam of stone. This poses a difficult problem in statics; that Sulla's architect solved it is the wonder of his modern successors. The roadway up the ramp shows, on the outboard (south) side of a drain running up its middle, a stylobate (course of masonry on which columns rested) with cuttings for column bases. Reading these stones, Fasolo and Gullini concluded that the outboard half of the roadway up the ramp was roofed, while the inboard half was open to the sky. On the extreme outboard edge of the roadway are preserved the remains, about a yard high, of a wall in *opus incertum*, with the bottoms of half-columns, their fluting laid on in stucco, mortised into it at intervals corresponding to the cuttings in the stylobate. The half-round profile at the bottom of the wall suggests projecting the same profile all the way up. This involves restoring a blank windowless wall (windows would make it too weak to bear the weight of the roof) closing the entire south side of the porticoed roadway, blocking the breath-taking view across Latium to the sea, and forcing the eye upward to the top of the ramp. Architectural members designed to be clamped together in pairs, of a size to fit the tops of the inclined capitals, gave the answer to the question how the portico was roofed. One of the pairs supported a barrel vault, the other a vertical masonry wall designed to mask the spring of the vault. Other architectural members, with an oblique chamfer, found at the top and the bottom of the ramp, suggest that the ends of the vaults were masked with a pediment or gable end, and therefore that the whole vault was covered with a pitch roof. The two ramps debouch at the top in an open space paved in herringbone brick, a sort of balcony with—at last—a splendid view southward. To the north a stair led to the next level, the level of the Hemicycle Terrace.

The Hemicycle Terrace (IV) is planned, Fasolo and Gullini discovered, symmetrically to the axis of the whole composition, at this level marked by a central stair which has suffered a good deal from having had a modern house built on top of it. One can make out, however, that the stair was narrowed at one point (where there may have been a gate) by fountain niches on either side. The play of water is important at every level of the Sanctuary. Under the stair passes a vaulted corridor connecting the two axially symmetrical halves of the terrace. Closest to the stair on each side are four arches; beyond these, the monumental hemicycles which are the architectonic center of each wing. They have vaulted, coffered ceilings, and a concentric colonnade with Ionic-Italic (four-voluted) columns. Before they were restored, these were badly corroded, and covered with verdigris from the acid of the coppersmith's shop which occupied the spot before the bombing. The epistyle carries an inscription, almost illegible, but apparently referring to building and restoring done on the initiative of the local Senate, presumably after the Sullan sack. The outer surface or extrados of the vaults is concealed—as it was on the porticoed ramp—by a story called an attic, in *opus incertum,* divided into rectangular panels by engaged columns with semicircular drums in tufa. At the back of each hemicycle runs a platform approached by two steps, with consoles on which planks could be placed to make more room; this suggests that it was intended for spectators to stand on. The pavement, as in the room at the foot of the ramp, is *lithostroton;* the likeness in the paving justifies the inference that the two terraces (III and IV) were built about the same time. On the far side of each hemicycle are four more arches. In front of the right-hand (eastern) hemicycle is a wishing well, with footings round it from which Fasolo and Gullini have been able to restore to the last detail, with the help of some architectural fragments, a small round well-house, with a high grille above its balustrade, now to be seen in the museum. Coins found in the well, whose heaviest concentration is in the mid-second century A.D., suggest that the well-house is much later in date than the terrace on which it stands. But the well-house stands on the central terrace of seven; it may

FIG. 5.4 Palestrina, Sanctuary of Fortune. Model from southwest, showing buttresses, and ramp from Hemicycle Terrace to Cortina Terrace. (H. Kähler, *Ann. Univ. Saraviensis* 7 [1958], Pl. 39)

have been the spot where, in the early days of the Sanctuary, the lots were cast. From either end of the Hemicycle Terrace ramps (Fig. 5.4) ascended to the Cortina Terrace (VI), the next but one above.

The stair which divides the Hemicycle Terrace leads to the Terrace of the Arches with Half-columns (V), also symmetrically planned on the axis of the stair. There are nine deep arches on either side of the stair. Possibly these were stalls for the various guilds—wine merchants, wagoners, cooks, weavers, garland-makers, second-hand dealers, money-changers—who, as we know from inscriptions, made dedications to Fortune, and had a financial interest in her Sanctuary. Here again close observation has enabled the excavators to tell exactly how the façade of this terrace looked when it was new. The even-numbered arches are narrower and lower than the odd-numbered ones, are left rough within, and are floored with a pebble fill, from all of which it is inferred that they were not meant to be seen. Sills found *in situ,* and uprights, cornices, and volutes, found on the Hemicycle Terrace, where they do not fit into the architecture, and therefore must have fallen from above, can be restored as blind doors set in the walls which closed the even-numbered arches. Small travertine panels, with a molded surround, and a cornice above, found on this terrace, will have been set into the wall on either side of the blind doors, at lintel level. The same decorative motif was found in place on the back wall of the basilica area in the lower zone. The repetition of motif makes an aesthetic link between the two levels. The odd-numbered arches are mosaic-paved and plastered, and were therefore meant to be visible. Enough remains in place to show that the profile of the arch was set with tufa blocks supported on pilasters. These alternating open arches framed with pilasters and closed arches with blind doors all supported an epistyle and cornice which in turn supported the parapet of the Cortina Terrace above.

The Cortina Terrace (VI), nearly 400 feet deep, was a hollow square, open to the south except for a balustrade, closed to the east and west by a three-columned portico, connected at the back (north) with a *lithostroton*-paved vaulted corridor, called a cryptoporticus, which runs under the stair to the semicircular Terrace VII. Again, similarity of plan and décor ties the whole ensemble together. (Nowadays, the approach to Terrace VII is by a double-access stair, but this is of the seventeenth century.) At the back of the terrace, six arches, three on either side of the central stair, gave access to the cryptoporticus. At either end of the three-arch sequence is an arched projecting fountain house in appearance not unlike a Roman triumphal arch, with a pair of narrow windows in its back wall, opening on the cryptoporticus. Heavy deposits of lime on the back wall suggest an arrangement whereby persons passing through the cryptoporticus could look out through a thin sheet of water onto the Cortina Terrace. Enough traces remain to restore on paper the three-columned portico on the east and west. It was roofed with a pair of barrel vaults, coffered like the ones in the hemicycles of Terrace IV (another aesthetic link), and roofed like the great east-west ramps which connect Terraces III and IV. The portico's outer walls were buttressed, and the north-south ramps from the Hemicycle Terrace also helped to counter the outward thrust.

And so we come to the exedra, the seventh of the super-imposed terrace levels, a most holy place, where the priests could appear and offer sacrifice on an altar in full view of the faithful assembled on the semicircular steps. At the top of the exedra there now rises the splendid semi-circle of the Barberini Palace, but plate glass let into the museum's ground floor paving shows the tufa footings of a semicircular series of columns, which must have been the middle set of another double portico answering to the one on the Cortina Terrace below, and, like it, double-barrel-vaulted and pitch-roofed, but of course semicircular in plan instead of U-shaped. Access to the porticoes was not on the central axis of the whole complex, but by a short narrow stair at either end of the exedra. (We shall see how Hadrian, too, centuries later, liked these split-access arrangements.) But, though there is no direct approach, the distance between the columns on either side of the main axis is extra-wide, to give a better view of the circular building (*tholos*) above and behind, the culminating point of the whole plan, where the cult statue was placed.

Such is the careful plan of the complex, justifying this detailed treatment because it is a turning point in the history of Roman architecture, perhaps the most seminal architectural complex in the whole Roman world. Everything (Fig. 5.5) centers on an axis, everything rises, aspires to the apex at the cult-statue, embracing a superb and at each level more extensive view of the plain stretching away southward to the sea. The materials and technique with

FIG. 5.5   Palestrina, Museum. Sanctuary of Fortune, model.
(J. Felbermeyer photo)

which this form is realized and supported are interesting in themselves and for what they contribute to the dating of the Sanctuary. The basic materials are tufa, limestone, and concrete; no marble is used except in statuary. Limestone, which in Roman architecture comes to predominance later than tufa, is used for the facing of polygonal walls and *opus incertum,* for décor (*e.g.,* the Corinthian capitals of tufa columns), for pavements. The limestone spalls or chips left over from the facing of *opus incertum* were used in concrete cores and for fill. Tufa is used for footings, structure in squared blocks (*e.g.*, caissons for concrete), the voussoirs, or wedge-shaped blocks, of arches, column drums, the core of stuccoed decorative elements, cornices, corners. Both materials are subordinate to concrete.

The use of concrete at Palestrina amounts to an architectural revolution, and, as often, the revolution in taste is combined with a revolution in materials and methods. This strong, cheap, immensely tough material enabled the architect to enclose space in any shape; henceforward architects could concentrate on interiors, and the day of the box-like temple was over. The architectural history that culminates in the Pantheon begins here. The architect was clearly more expert in the use of concrete than in the use of stone. Palestrina concrete is hydraulic, a combination of limestone chips and mortar made of *pozzolana* (volcanic sand) and lime. Concrete footings, Fasolo and Gullini found, go down to bedrock everywhere; *e.g.*, each of the three rows of columns of the Cortina Terrace portico rests on a foundation wall of concrete based on bedrock, while the space between is hollow, to relieve weight. For the same reason the whole hollow square of the Cortina Terrace rests on a series of rectangular concrete coffers with a stone fill. The result of this use of concrete is that the whole Upper Sanctuary is structurally a single unit. Each level is planned as a step toward, and a retaining wall of, the level next above. The stresses, Fasolo reports, are never more than about three pounds per square yard for walls and eight pounds per square yard for columns; this in a structure which is in effect a skyscraper 400 feet high. There is repetition of motif throughout, not from paucity of imagination, or because it is the easy way, but of set aesthetic purpose, to emphasize the concealed structural unity and to use the functional parts of the complex to give architectonic unity to the whole. Thus the upper hemicycle stair repeats the two hemicycles of the lower terrace, and the relation between them is a triangle, which repeats in a different plane the triangle of the double converging ramp. The arches are treated as beams to bear the weight of stone construction, and the stone construction is a caisson for the concrete.

Fasolo and Gullini argue ingeniously for a date earlier than Sulla for the Sanctuary, but their arguments have not found general favor. The most that can be said is that certain inscriptions mentioning restoration, reconstruction, or dedications to Fortune earlier than 80 B.C. imply a previously existing and probably much simpler structure, centering on the east half of the Hemicycle Terrace, but nothing in the technique or materials now visible or inferred requires other than a Sullan date for any part of the Sanctuary.

In materials and methods, in massiveness and axial symmetry, the Sanctuary of Fortune bears a Roman stamp. But when we recall the experience of Sulla and his lieutenants, the Luculli, in the Greek East, Greek influence is very likely. Of the many Hellenistic Greek complexes available for comparison, the closest in spirit to Palestrina is the Sanctuary of Asclepius on the island of Kos in the Dodacanese, in the southeast Aegean Sea, where the major temple, built in the mid-second century B.C., is the focal point of a grandiose composition (Fig. 5.6). Placed on the highest of three terraces, it is framed by a three-sided colonnade like the Cortina Terrace at Palestrina, and approached by three successive monumental stairways leading up the lower terraces, which are arched as at Palestrina. A few standard architectural ingredients, arches, colonnades, monumental stairways, are grouped as a clearly defined composition, easy to grasp, simple, bold, plastic, the few standard elements firmly juxtaposed. Contrasts of scale, an elevated and central position, an axial approach, all make of the temple the focal, culminating point of the composition. It is exactly so at Palestrina, and in scores of other Hellenistic sanctuaries. Also noteworthy in both places is "the same outspoken taste for vista. Not only is the triple-terraced

FIG. 5.6   Kos, Sanctuary of Asclepius, reconstruction.
(R. Herzog and P. Schatzmann, *Kos* 1, Pl. 40)

FIG. 5.7   Tarracina. View toward Circeii from Temple of Jupiter Anxur.
(H. Kähler, *Rom und seine Welt*, Pl. 49)

sanctuary visible from afar, not only is the crowning ele-
ment, a temple, a beacon toward which visitor and wor-
shipper alike are drawn by the now familiar devices of
setting, frontality and access, but again, once we have
reached the summit, a scene of breathtaking beauty, of
unexpected amplitude, of mountain, sea and plain confronts
us." The words are those of Phyllis Lehmann, from whom
the description of the site at Kos draws heavily, but they
were reinforced by a visit made by the present writer to
the island in September, 1956, expressly to compare the
site with Palestrina. Mrs. Lehmann goes on, "Although
many factors, notably the sanctity of a cult spot, were involved in the choice of such sites, their architectural treatment attests a keen awareness of landscape setting as a
prime aesthetic ingredient in the total effect." The unknown
architect-genius who planned Palestrina probably knew the
Greek Sanctuary at Kos; he was certainly in touch with
the main movement of mind of his age. But the final impression of this dynamic, utterly functional, axially symmetric complex is not Greek but Roman, a great memorial
façade to celebrate the end of a Civil War. Italy as well
as Greece can provide ground-plans by which parts of the
Sanctuary at Palestrina might have been inspired, notably
one in Cagliari in Sardinia, and another at Gabii, near Rome.

This Roman classical masterpiece has, then, ancestors;
what about its descendants? They are many: from the
Sanctuary of Fortune contemporary and later architects
learned much. An example of this influence is the Temple
of Jupiter Anxur at Tarracina, above the Via Appia where
it touches the coast sixty-seven miles south of Rome. Here
the use of concrete, of *opus incertum,* of arch and vault,
of setting and landscape, is in the unmistakable idiom of
Sulla's architect. It is an architectural complex and a seascape which mediates, as Palestrina does, between man
and nature. It is designed to capture attention from the
colony below, to become more impressive as one approaches,

and to give a gradually widening view of the sea as one ascends. The temple was oriented north and south, with a portico behind (Fig. 5.8). It is set at an angle upon a

FIG. 5.8   Tarracina. Temple of Jupiter Anxur, reconstruction.
(F. Fasolo and G. Gullini, *Il Santuario di Fortuna Primigenia*, Pl. 25)

tremendous concrete podium, with arched cryptoporticus as at Palestrina. On the seaward side the play of light and shadow on the podium arches is enormously impressive; on the side toward Sperlonga the sturdy blind buttress arches are again strongly reminiscent of what we have seen on the Terrace of the Half-columns. Within the crypto-porticus (the vaults under the Temple platform) the play of light and shadow is again very satisfying, and yet the structure is functional as well: the cryptoporticus lightens the huge weight of the concrete, and the sturdy concrete construction has stood the test of time.

Another Sullan descendant is the Tabularium (Public Records Office) in Rome (Fig. 5.9), finished in 78 B.C. by Quintus Lutatius Catulus, to whom Sulla's veterans transferred their allegiance after Sulla's death. It was a part of Sulla's plan for monumentalizing the Forum, to provide, as it were, a scenic backdrop for it, which serves at the same time as a terrace-level to give order to the Capitoline Hill above. Its plan, its frontality, and its use of arch, vault and concrete is in the Palestrina tradition. There is a crypto-porticus in concrete, fronted by arches framed in half-columns placed at points in the wall which required extra strength. The upper levels of the Tabularium were removed by Michelangelo when he designed the Palazzo del Senatore, Rome's city hall. Perhaps this may be taken as a symbol of the extent and the limits of the influence of Palestrina's architect on Renaissance masters. One archeologist, Heinz Kähler, has argued, ingeniously but without carrying conviction, for an influence of the Cortina Terrace and the exedra above it upon the design of Pompey's theater in Rome: one nabob borrowing architectural effects from another.

Finally, about the time of Cicero's consulship (63 B.C.), Palestrina influenced the Sanctuary of Hercules Victor at Tivoli, well-known to many from Piranesi's etching as the Villa of Maecenas. Like Kos and Palestrina (Cortina Terrace), it had a portico on three sides, and a temple against the back wall. Nowadays it houses a paper-mill, but forty years ago the portico was uncluttered. There was an approach by ramp and semicircular stair (Fig. 5.10), very

FIG. 5.9   Rome, Tabularium. (Fototeca)

theatrical, like Palestrina and the Tabularium; the material is again concrete faced with *opus incertum*. The podium is again supported on concrete vaults, and lightened by a complicated arrangement of subterranean rooms. A vast cryptoporticus pierces the whole podium to carry the Via

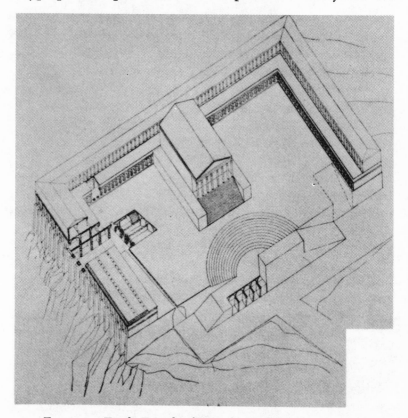

Fig. 5.10   Tivoli, Temple of Hercules Victor, reconstruction. (Fasolo and Gullini, *op. cit.*, Pl. 27)

Tiburtina, the main road from Rome to Tivoli. The famous terraced gardens of the Villa d'Este nearby, with their plays of water, felt the inspiration of Palestrina; their architect, Pirro Ligorio, has left sketches of our site made by him on the spot. Pietro da Cortona, Bramante, Raphael, Palladio and Bernini also knew and sketched Palestrina. Another successful terrace plan inspired by Palestrina is Valadier's treatment in the 19th century of the steep slope up the Pincio from the Piazza del Popolo in Rome.

Palestrina inspired the architects of the Roman Empire, too: for example—one among many—it influenced to some extent (see also p. 267) the architect of Trajan's Market in Rome, who uses terracing, concrete, and framed arches (but the arches are flat, the framing is pilasters instead of half-columns, and the façade is brick instead of *opus incertum.*) The inspiration does not stop here: it is to be found on the Palatine, in Hadrian's villa near Tivoli, Diocletian's Baths in Rome, and his palace at Spalato, and the Basilica of Maxentius in the Roman Forum.

From his building, from which the history of Roman architecture really begins, we can reconstruct the personality of the architect. It makes the whole history of Roman architecture come alive, when we really know one complex. The architect was a master of the manipulation of surface, of light and shade, of counterthrust, controlled views, the unitary plan, of space both full and empty. For him, organic function is also decorative; the stylistic fact is the constructive solution; his organization is clear, his use of the classical "orders" of Graeco-Roman architecture, Tuscan and Ionic, in stone as bearing walls is classical in its combination of beauty and function. The plan of his Sanctuary imposed itself as well on the secular plan of the colony below. He is a real genius, one of the greatest architects of all time. He achieves his magnificent results by creative imitation of earlier models, and in this he is Roman. Because his imitation is creative, it does not peter out in formalism, but has a seminal effect upon other architects of the Republic, the Empire, the Renaissance. A detailed study of his masterpiece not only leaves us profoundly impressed with the patience, thoroughness and imagination of Italian archaeologists; it reinforces again the lesson of the continuity of history and the cultural importance for the whole western world of the Roman Republic.

Sulla went into voluntary retirement and—a rare achievement in his time—died in bed. The next nabob to equal him in stature, violence, and unconstitutionality was a man who had begun his career as Sulla's lieutenant, Pompey the Great. Victories in Sicily and Africa, against slaves, pirates, and Mithridates, brought him enormous spoils; he too turned his mind to buildings to monumentalize his glory. The result was Rome's first stone theater, in the Campus Martius, dedicated in his third consulship (52 B.C.) but begun in his second (55 B.C.), in a great show involving 500 lions and seventeen to twenty elephants. What survives of it is little more than a curve in a Roman street, some blocks of tufa beneath a Roman square, and a memory. Beneath the curve of the Via di Grotta Pinta, which perpetuates the outline of its *cavea*, one may visit today, in the lower regions of a Roman restaurant, the underpinnings of the great building, which once held 12,000 spectators. The technique of these vaults, a development of *incertum* called *opus reticulatum*, involves setting pyramidal bricks, point inward, in a lozenge pattern into a cement core. But though the entire superstructure has disappeared, an ancient plan survives. In the late second century A.D. the Emperor Septimius Severus caused to be placed on the wall of the library in Vespasian's Forum of Peace a marble Plan of Rome, the *Forma Urbis*, which has come down to us in over 1000 fragments. The ingenuity with which these have been pieced together (work still going on in 1959) would make a story in itself, but for our present purpose only four fragments (Fig. 5.11) are relevant. The two parallel walls to the right (which is west; north is at the bottom) give a fascinating insight into the puritanical Roman mind at work. Straitlaced Romans objected to theaters as immoral. Pompey's architect therefore

designed at the top of the theater's *cavea* a temple of Venus
Victrix, represented by the two parallel walls in the plan.
The theater seats might then pass as a hemicycle approach
to a temple (compare the hemicycle approach to the
tholos at Palestrina). Puritanism was appeased.

Behind the stage the marble plan shows a great rectangular portico, with a double garden-plot in the middle,
where we may restore in imagination trees planted, foun-

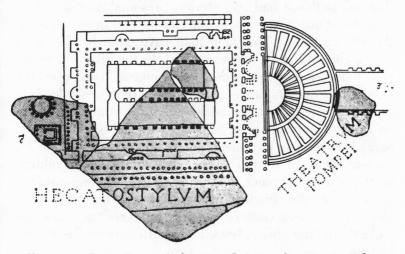

Fig. 5.11   Rome, Pompey's theater and portico, from *Forma Urbis*.
(G. Lugli, *Mon. Ant.*, 3, p. 79)

tains playing, and works of art displayed. At a Senate meeting in a building associated with the portico, on the Ides
of March, 44 B.C., Caesar fell at the base of Pompey's
statue, pierced by twenty-three daggers. What may be the
tufa blocks of this very building are visible today through
a sheet of plate glass in a pedestrian underpass in the Largo
Argentina. (Temples A and B of the Largo Argentina appear to the left in the plan.)

Caesar was a greater man than Pompey. His spoils of
victory, after eight years in Gaul, were richer, and so was

his building program. The most impressive surviving evidence of it is the ground plan of his basilica, the Basilica Julia in the Republican Forum, and, north of the old Forum, which Rome and his own grandeur had outgrown, a grandiose new one, the prototype of an Imperial series.

The Basilica Julia was planned and executed at Caesar's direction between 54 and 46 B.C., to balance the second-century Basilica Aemilia opposite. All that remains is pavement and piers, but the size of the piers is enough to show that the building had two stories, presumably with a balcony to afford a view of spectacles in the open space of the Forum below. Time and man have dealt harshly with the basilica. When it was excavated, in the 1840's, a medieval limekiln was found on the pavement. This, plus the knowledge that its stone was sold by the oxcart load in the Middle Ages for the benefit of a hospital which rose on the site, explains what happened to the superstructure. Scratched on the pavement are rough sketches, done by ancient idlers, of statues which once adorned the building or the Forum adjacent, and over eighty "gaming-boards," scratched circles divided into six segments on which dice were thrown and counters moved. Lawyers' speeches apparently did not always hold the full attention of the Forum hangers-on.

Caesar's Forum has left more impressive remains. It cost him a fortune, since his enemies, owners of the expropriated houses, charged him 100,000,000 sesterces, five million uninflated dollars, for the land. Its excavation was begun in 1930, and finished in three years, by Corrado Ricci, as a part of Mussolini's (Fig. 5.12) grandiose plan for systematizing the center of the city and restoring the ancient dictator's Forum to set off a modern dictator's monument, a new street, the Via dell'Impero, driven through slums and ancient monuments to connect the Coliseum with his headquarters in the Palazzo Venezia. The excavation exposed the southern two-thirds of Caesar's Forum; the rest

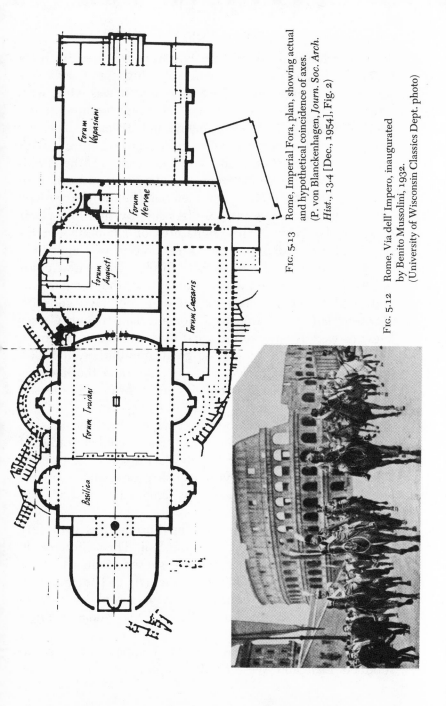

Fig. 5.13 Rome, Imperial Fora, plan, showing actual and hypothetical coincidence of axes. (P. von Blanckenhagen, *Journ. Soc. Arch. Hist.*, 13.4 [Dec., 1954], Fig. 2)

Fig. 5.12 Rome, *Via dell' Impero*, inaugurated by Benito Mussolini, 1932. (University of Wisconsin Classics Dept. photo)

Forum Vespasiani

Forum Nervae

Forum Augusti

Forum Caesaris

Forum Traiani

Forum Caesaris

Basilica

lies under the new street. The Forum as revealed by Ricci is another example of axial symmetry (Fig. 5.13), a narrow porticoed rectangle, over twice as long as it was wide, with a temple set in the Italic fashion on a high podium at the back. Working with great patience and delicacy, Ricci set up three of the temple's fallen columns (Fig. 5.14), with their architrave, frieze, and cornice. Some of the architectural blocks leave between the dentils—a row of projecting tooth-like rectangular members below the cornice —two small distinctive marble disks side by side like a pair of spectacles. This is the "signature" of Domitian's architect Rabirius, and prove that a restoration of the temple was planned during his reign (A.D. 81-96). There are Cupids in the interior frieze, which prove that the temple was dedicated to Venus, Caesar's ancestor. To have gods for ancestors lent distinction to a Roman clan, though Caesar knew as well as any skeptic what it really meant. He knew his pedigree back to an ever-so-great grandfather, and God knew who *his* ancestor was. In the *gens Iulia* the line was traced back to Iulus the son of Aeneas, who was the son of Anchises and Venus.

The portico, like that behind Pompey's theater, was an art museum. Ancient authors mention a golden statue of Cleopatra (one of the dictator's few sentimental gestures?), a golden breastplate set with British pearls, and a bronze equestrian statue of Caesar on his famous horse which had human front feet!

The ground to the south of the Forum rises over fifty feet to the slopes of the Capitoline Hill. This difference in level was filled with three setback stories of luxury shops in massive rectangular blocks of *peperino*. The Street of the Silversmiths, the *Clivus Argentarius,* ran above and behind the shops at the Forum level. This whole complex survives.

Three men on horseback, Sulla, Pompey, and Caesar, subdued East and West for Rome, and used part of the

FIG. 5.14 Rome, Forum of Caesar. (Fototeca)

profits to change the face of Rome in forty years. They would have said that they did it out of what the Romans called *pietas*, a threefold loyalty to family, state, and gods. Each, to reflect credit on his family which ruled the state, on the gods his ancestors, and on the state his perquisite, erected great public buildings in the city to be his monument. Sulla's dramatic revamping of the old Forum, Pompey's theater and portico, and Caesar's new Forum made of a shabby civic center a metropolis almost worthy to vie with the cities of the Greek East. Almost, but not quite, for the building material was still local stone, stuccoed tufa or the handsome limestone from Tivoli called travertine, which weathers to a fine gold, and has ever since been Rome's characteristic building material. It was considered worthy in the Renaissance to build the fabric of St. Peter's. For its next transformation, this time into a city of marble, Rome had to wait for the rise to power of the greatest nabob of them all, Caesar's adopted son and successor, Octavian-Augustus.

6

Augustus: Buildings as Propaganda

In 1922, after the success of the Fascist march on Rome, Benito Mussolini felt acutely the need for an aura of respectability to surround his upstart régime. Another swashbuckling *condottiere*, 1965 years earlier, Caesar's heir Octavian, had felt the same need. Both resorted to the same method: an ambitious building program, and a vigorous propaganda campaign designed to substitute for dubious antecedents a set of more or less spurious links with the heroes of the glorious past. About Fascist architecture the less said the better; the other point will be the subject of this chapter. In fourteen years (1924-38) Italian archaeologists changed the face of central Rome, and in the process of glorifying *Il Duce*, added more to our knowledge of Augustan Rome than the previous fourteen centuries had provided.

Octavian's building activity, both before and after he took the title Augustus, was prodigious. In his autobiography he boasts of restoring no less than eighty-two temples. He built many new ones besides, and embellished Rome, and his own glory, with his new Forum, a portico, his arch, his grandiose mausoleum, an Altar of Peace, and, in addition, parks and gardens, baths, theaters, a great library, markets, granaries, docks, and warehouses. Meanwhile he himself lived in ostentatious simplicity in a modest house on the Palatine, and encouraged the cult of antique austerity by restoring the hut of Romulus. At his death Rome was at last an Imperial metropolis: the city of brick had become a city of marble. Rome had gained grandeur and lost freedom in the process. Toward the assessment of the gains and losses, the excavators' discoveries in Augustus' Forum, at his arch, in his mausoleum, and particularly in the difficult and ingenious recovery and reconstruction of his Altar of Peace have made the most important contributions.

Ever since 1911, Corrado Ricci had dreamed of excavating the site of Augustus' Forum (see Fig. 5.13), known to lie to the northeast of and at right angles to Caesar's, overlaid by modern construction. In 1924 Mussolini gave him his chance, and by 1932, when the Via dell' Impero was opened with Fascist pomp (see Fig. 5.12), the Fora of Caesar, Augustus, Nerva, and Trajan had all yielded up secrets to the archaeologist's spade.

Of Augustus' Forum, when Ricci began to dig, the most conspicuous part was the firewall at the back, separating it from the fire-trap slums of the Subura, ancient Rome's red-light district. The firewall is over 100 feet high, the exposed parts in travertine, the rest in *peperino* and *sperone*, the traditional Italic building stones of the period. This use of local materials, combined, as Ricci was to discover, with marble, is the symbol of the compromise, the amalgam of Italic and Greek materials, methods, and forms, which is the hallmark of the Augustan Age.

When the buildings cluttering the site had been cleared away, the plan (Fig. 6.1) was found to be based upon that of Caesar's Forum: a rectangular portico with a temple at the back. But the rectangle was enriched at the sides with curves, as at Palestrina earlier and in Bernini's portico in front of St. Peter's later. Each of the hemicycles had, let into

FIG. 6.1 Rome, Forum of Augustus, model by I. Gismondi. (Mostra Augustea della Romanità, *Catalogo*, Pl. 35)

the walls on two levels, niches two feet deep, big enough to hold statues of half life size. Excavations in the area of the south hemicycle as early as 1889 had turned up fragments of drapery in Carrara marble, and bits of inscriptions which, in combination with literary evidence, gave to the great Italian epigraphist Attilio Degrassi the clue to the subjects of the statues. The inscriptions, called *elogia*, recorded the *cursus honorum*, or public career, of a set of heroes, triumphing generals, or others who had deserved well of the Republic. Three examples are Aulus Postumius, who, with the help of the Great Twin Brethren Castor and Pollux (the household gods of the Julian clan), beat the Latins at the battle of Lake Regillus in 496, and built his divine helpers a temple in the Forum; Appius Claudius the Blind, who built the Appian Way (312 B.C.) and an aqueduct; and Sulla—nabobs and builders all. But there was space in the two levels of hemicycle niches, and in others hypothetically restored in the portico's rectilinear wall, for over fifty statues with *elogia*. So Degrassi made a search for other stones similarly inscribed, some of which turned up in the most unlikely places.

One had been used as a marble roof-tile of Hadrian's Pantheon; it was in the Vatican collection. Another was found in a vineyard near Rome's north gate, the Porta del Popolo. The former immortalized one Lucius Albinius, who took the Vestal Virgins in his wagon to Caere for safety when the Gauls were threatening Rome in 390 B.C. The latter was of Sulla's great rival Marius, the friend of the people. The dimensions, letter-heights, and letter-styles of both made their origin in Augustus' Forum extremely likely. A set of seven more had been known since the seventeenth century or earlier as coming from the site of the Forum of Arezzo, ancient Arretium, in Tuscany. The texts of some of these turned out to be copies of *elogia* from the Forum of Augustus. This justified the inference that in this matter of a Hall of Fame, provincial cities imitated the metropolis.

Thus those *elogia* from Arezzo for which no Roman prototype had been found might yet give a clue to what the
Roman collection had once contained. This inference en-
riches the list by the names of Manius Valerius Maximus,
conciliator of class struggles, and Rome's first dictator
(494 B.C.); Lucius Aemilius Paullus, one of the greatest
triumphatores of them all, who beat the Macedonians at
Pydna in 168 B.C., and symbolized the union of Roman traditions with Hellenism, as Augustus aspired to do; Tiberius
Sempronius Gracchus, father of the reforming Gracchi; and
Sulla's lieutenant Lucius Licinius Lucullus, whose brother
was responsible for the terraces and hemicycles at Palestrina.

The south hemicycle and portico, then, ingeniously connected Augustus' name with a set of nabobs, builders, successful generals, philhellenes, and men remarkable for piety
to the gods or popularity with the masses. What of the
north hemicycle? Here Ricci discovered the *elogium* of
Rome's and Augustus' legendary ancestor, *pius Aeneas* himself, who also appears on the Altar of Peace; a set of the
Kings of Alba Longa; Romulus, also probably on the Altar of Peace; Caesar's father; Marcus Claudius Marcellus,
Augustus' much beloved heir, whose untimely death Vergil
movingly mourns in the *Aeneid,* and whose ashes lay in
Augustus' mausoleum; and Nero Claudius Drusus, Augustus'
stepson, who also is figured, like Aeneas and Romulus, on
the Altar of Peace. It looks very much as though the Hall
of Fame on this side of the portico was intended to connect the legendary Kings of Alba and Rome with the Julio-
Claudian dynasty. And the climax of it all was yet to come.
At the end of the north portico Ricci excavated a square
room with a pedestal at the back. On the pedestal he found
a cutting for a colossal foot, seven times life size. Forty
feet up the back wall were the put-holes for the struts of a
huge statue. Whose? The Forum's temple was dedicated
to Mars, but the place for the god is in his temple. The
most likely candidate is the *Dux* himself, Augustus, father

of his country, in whom Roman history came, in more senses than one, to a full stop.

Medieval limekilns tell, as usual, how the rich marbles which decorated both portico and temple were broken up and melted down into whitewash, but three marble Corinthian columns sixty feet high give some idea of the temple's grandeur. Its podium, lofty in the Italic fashion, was not solid marble, simply tufa revetted or veneered with thin marble slabs, an economical, and, some might say, dishonest way of making a city of marble of the desired Hellenic appearance. The statue-base at the back of the temple (which was apsidal to match the hemicycles in the porticoes) is too wide for a single figure. The cult statues must have been of Mars and Venus, another delicate reference to the ancestry of Augustus' adoptive clan. The temple itself was vowed, the literary sources tell us, at the battle of Philippi (42 B.C.) to Mars Ultor, avenger of the murder of Julius Caesar, and Caesar's sword was piously preserved as a relic in it. The Forum did not neglect the arts. Like Caesar's, and like Pompey's portico, it was a museum. It did service also for literature: we are told that lectures were delivered in the hemicycles. Begun in 37 B.C., the Forum took thirty-five years to finish. By 2 B.C. other propaganda devices—especially the arch, the Altar of Peace, Vergil's epic, Livy's history, and Horace's lyric—had, as we shall see, given the desired respectability to Augustus, the Prince of Peace.

It was the victory of Actium (31 B.C.), over the combined fleets of Antony and Cleopatra, that enabled Octavian to pass as the Prince of Peace. In 1888-89, in the old Forum, between the Temples of the deified Julius and of Castor, were excavated the footings of an arch, originally with a single passageway, later enlarged to three. This arch was identified from literary sources as the one erected by Augustus to commemorate that victory, enlarged later when another occasion for propaganda arose. The arch itself is a routine affair, with plenty of precedent, though one might ponder the propriety of thus gloating over Antony, a former colleague and a Roman citizen. (Gamberini, the excavator, even found, in the bottom of square stone receptacles beside the arch, laurel seeds which suggest that the tree of victory was prominent in the landscaping of the arch.) But, given the Roman propensity in general, and Augustus' in particular, for propagandizing in stone, the question naturally arose what opportunity for self-advertisement the arch offered. The answer was not given until Degrassi published another book in 1947.

For many years archaeologists had believed that on the walls of the nearby Regia had been engraved the *Fasti Consulares* (lists of Roman consuls from the founding of the Republic and probably of the kings as well), and the *Fasti Triumphales* (lists of triumphing generals from Romulus to 19 B.C. I have remarked in another book° how much one can learn of a people by what they make lists of: Greeks, of Olympic victors; Americans, of baseball averages; Romans, of statesmen and military heroes). But in 1935 a careful study of the Regia by the American F. E. Brown proved that the part of its wall where the *Fasti* must have begun was masked in the rebuilding of 36 B.C. by another structure, and that the space available, carefully measured for the first time by Brown, did not fit the surviving *Fasti*, which were discovered in 1546 and are still preserved in the Conservatori Museum. Clearly the Regia was not the place where the *Fasti* were inscribed. Since two-thirds of the extant fragments were found between the Temple of the Deified Julius and the Temple of Castor, and since their dimensions suited those of the footings of the Arch of Augustus, the inference was clear. It was on the arch (Fig. 6.2) that the consular *Fasti* were carved, and this is now the universally accepted opinion.

° *The Roman Mind at Work* (Van Nostrand, Princeton, 1958).

They were displayed on either side of the lateral passage-way, where pedestrians could read them, the consular lists framed by pilasters with a pediment above (reconstructed in the museum by Michelangelo), the list of *triumphatores* on the corner pilasters of the enlarged arch. The result of this display was again, as in Augustus' Forum, to connect the upstart Octavian with a more respectable or heroic past. His name appears twice among the *triumphatores* (the slab that referred to Actium is unfortunately missing) in a list that began with Romulus and contained the names of the greatest heroes of Roman history; in the consular lists his name figured twenty-four times. This collocation and repetition could do him no harm.

In the consular lists the names of Mark Antony and his family have suffered *damnatio memoriae;* that is, they have been first inscribed and then chiselled out. In the list of *triumphatores,* on the contrary, Antony's name is allowed to stand. What is the legitimate inference from this? Clearly it is that the two lists were inscribed at different times, and that on the first occasion our *condottiere* felt a certain insecurity, which by the time of the second had disap-peared. Literary sources date the second occasion in or shortly after 19 B.C., after the Roman standards disgrace-fully lost by Crassus at Carrhae had been recovered from the Parthians. In these eleven years or so the *condottiere* Octavian had become Augustus, the Revered One, Ex-pander of Empire, Father of his Country, Prince of Peace. Within those years Vergil's *Georgics* had cast an aura of beauty over Octavian's resettlement of veterans on the land; the *Aeneid* had connected this modern Aeneas, the pious one, the bearer of burdens, with his legendary an-cestors; Horace's Roman Odes had praised Augustus' re-ligious and moral reforms; and Livy's history had put into Augustan prose the lays of ancient Rome. Augustus could afford to be magnanimous to his enemies: he had seen to it that most of them were dead.

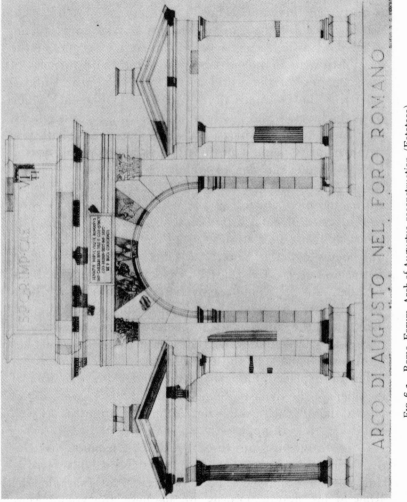

FIG. 6.2 Rome, Forum. Arch of Augustus, reconstruction. (Fototeca)

But it was not enough that the past be controlled and rewritten, and connected with the present on splendid monuments. Augustus must control the future, too; even after his death men must admire and worship him and his dynasty. To this end he began (literary sources tell us it was in 28 B.C.) in the Campus Martius a massive mausoleum (Fig. 6.3), which should be reminiscent in shape of the great Etruscan *tumuli* of centuries before, and in mass of such wonders of the world as the Mausoleum at Halicarnassus or the pyramids of Egypt. This monument, which through the centuries has been successively fortress, circus, park for fireworks displays, bull-ring, and concert-hall, was stripped to its gaunt core in 1935, as another part of the Fascists' Augustan plan to attach themselves to the memory of Augustus. The excavators, Giglioli and Colini, found within the circular ring of the mausoleum's vertical outer wall a series of concentric vaulted corridors (Fig. 6.4) in concrete, rising four stories or 143 feet, surrounding a central hollow cylinder where Augustus' ashes were to lie. A statue of the great deceased would have surmounted the cylinder, and the whole massive structure would have been heaped with earth and planted with cypresses. Before the door stood the bronze tablets bearing Augustus' autobiography—a calmly audacious fabrication of history, it has been justly called. In the corridor around the central cylinder were placed the marble containers for the urns of members of the dynasty. Some of the containers were found *in situ,* though their ashes—and, ironically, Augustus' as well —had long ago disappeared.

It was Augustus' fate to outlive his lieutenants, his relatives (see the family tree, Fig. 6.5), and all his favorite candidates for the succession. There lay, for example, the ashes of his stepson Drusus, his nephew, the young Marcellus, and his grandchildren, Lucius and Gaius; his lieutenant Agrippa; his sister Octavia, once given in a dynastic marriage to Mark Antony; his stepson Tiberius' one-time

FIG. 6.3   Rome, Mausoleum of Augustus. (Fototeca)

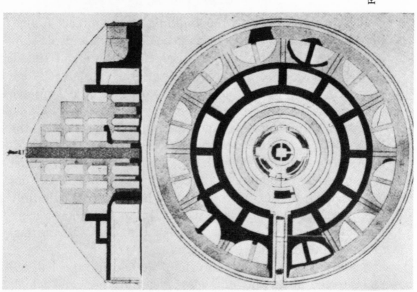

FIG. 6.4   Rome, Mausoleum of Augustus, plan and elevation.
(G. Lugli, *Mon. Ant.*, 3, p. 197)

wife Agrippina, divorced to give place to Augustus' daughter. Agrippina survived Augustus; who knows what palace intrigue brought her ashes here? Her one-time husband's ashes rested here, too, and those of Germanicus, Tiberius' adopted son, also those of the mad Emperor Caligula, of Claudius, Vespasian, Nerva, and Septimius Severus' consort Julia Domna (for the Severan dynasty, too, had need of respectability).

In stripping the mausoleum to its core, and building a deplorable neo-Fascist *piazza* on one side of it, an equally deplorable concrete shed for the reconstructed Altar of Peace on the other, the archaeologists of the '30s stripped Augustus, too, of his pretensions. Yet the decayed grandeur, the disappointed hopes, the inevitable passing of régimes, strike their own note of pathos and mortality:

> "My name is Ozymandias, King of Kings:
> Look on my works, ye mighty, and despair."

However unfortunate the building that protects it may be, the reconstructed Altar of Peace in the Field of Mars must be recognized as one of the great triumphs of Italian archaeology. Sculptured reliefs from this structure were first discovered, though not recognized as such, as long ago as 1568, in the underpinnings of what is now the Palazzo Fiano, on the Corso, Rome's *cardo*, which overlies the ancient Great North Road, the Via Flaminia. Other soundings were made in 1859 and 1903, and the reliefs were first recognized as belonging to the altar in 1879. But it was not until 1937-38 that G. Moretti carried through the incredibly ingenious and patient work which led to the almost complete recovery and reconstruction of the altar and the historic sculptured frieze surrounding it.

A colossal engineering problem arose because the Palazzo Fiano rested upon wooden piles driven into the water which

FIG. 6.5 GENEALOGICAL TABLE OF THE JULIO-CLAUDIAN CAESARS

NOTICE that Julius Caesar left no descendants, but adopted his great-nephew Augustus. Connections with Augustus were later traced by descent from his daughter Julia, his stepsons Tiberius and Drusus, or his sister Octavia. The names of emperors are in capitals. Numerals in parentheses show the order of marriages. Single lines indicate blood relationship; double lines, marriage; the dotted line, that the Cn. Domitius is the same person.

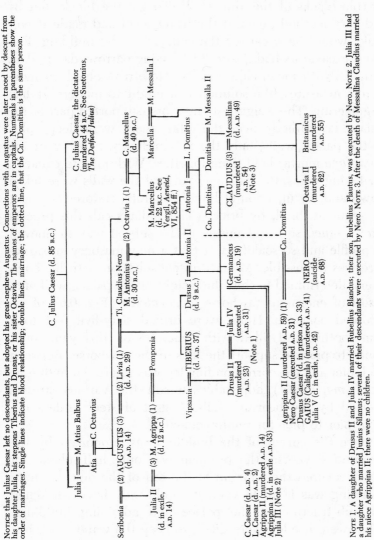

NOTE 1. A daughter of Drusus II and Julia IV married Rubellius Blandus; their son, Rubellius Plautus, was executed by Nero. NOTE 2. Julia III had a daughter who married Junius Silanus; several of their descendants were executed by Nero. NOTE 3. After the death of Messalina Claudius married his niece Agrippina II; there were no children.

FIG. 6.5   Family tree of the Julio-Claudians.
(P. MacKendrick and H. Howe, *Classics in Translation*, 2, p. 370)

in this part of Rome underlies most of the buildings. These piles, and reinforcements to them, pinned down some of the marble blocks of the altar itself. To get the blocks out by ordinary methods, even if the water level had made it possible, would have caused the collapse of the building. Previous excavators had resorted to driving narrow, damp, dark tunnels, with incomplete results. Moretti resolved on more heroic measures; the solution is a credit to modern Italian engineering. The weightiest and worst-supported part of the palace lay directly over the altar; there were deep splits in the palace walls; only the extraordinary tenacity of the *pozzolana* mortar held them together. With infinite capacity for taking pains, the damaged parts of the walls were taken down and, by injection of liquid concrete, restored segment by segment, brick by brick. (The Italians call this process *cuci e scuci,* sew and unsew.) The subsoil was so uneven in profile and so soaking wet that a new masonry substructure was impossible. Moretti, in consultation with his engineers, determined to shift the weight of the palace wall onto a sort of enormous sawhorse or *cavaletto* (Fig. 6.6) of reinforced concrete. Holes were drilled sixty-five feet to a firm footing and filled with concrete; on this were built concrete piers to support the legs of the sawhorse. Between each pier and the corresponding leg was inserted a hydraulic jack (*martinetto*) adjustable to suit the various stresses exerted by the bearing walls. A grid of steel girders ran from pier to pier for reinforcement.

Once the corner of the building was supported by the concrete sawhorse, the problem was only half-solved, for water covered the altar up to the top of the outside steps. Pumping was labor in vain; it would only have weakened the substructure of the palace and adjoining buildings. What were needed were dikes, to keep the water out while the area inside them was emptied. But a cement dike was impossible, because of the maze of water, gas, and sewer mains, heat, power, and light conduits which, at all levels

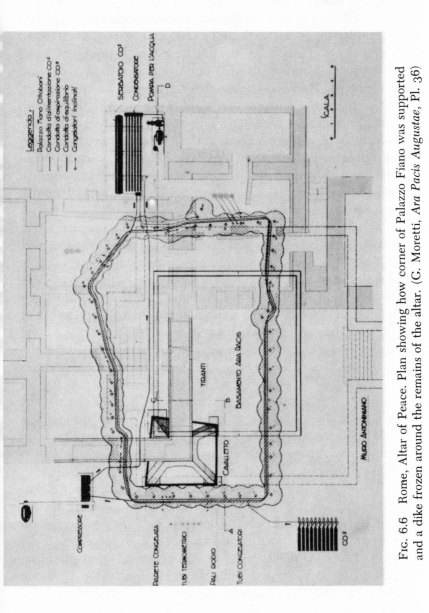

FIG. 6.6   Rome, Altar of Peace. Plan showing how corner of Palazzo Fiano was supported and a dike frozen around the remains of the altar. (G. Moretti, *Ara Pacis Augustae*, Pl. 36)

and in all directions, crisscrossed the subsoil of this busy part of modern Rome. A trench about five feet wide was dug, with a 230-foot perimeter. From a horizontal pipe laid in it, fifty-five three-inch pipes ran down vertically at equal intervals to a depth of twenty-four feet. Into these pipes was pumped carbon dioxide under a pressure of eighty atmospheres. Radiation from the refrigerant in the vertical pipes froze the surrounding muddy earth, and the impenetrable dike was a reality. The water inside covering the altar was then pumped out, and all the architectural blocks and fragments could be removed. Thus succeeded one of the most difficult and delicate excavations ever made. All was finished to meet a deadline, the bimillennary of Augustus' birth, September 23, 1938.

What Moretti now had to work with in his reconstruction was not only the slabs and fragments he had just extracted, but also the finds from previous excavations going back to 1568 (Fig. 6.7). Over the intervening years these had been scattered. Most of the 1568 finds had been sawn into three lengthwise (for the slabs were over two feet thick, too heavy for easy transport) and shipped to Florence to the Grand Duke of Tuscany, who then owned the Palazzo Fiano site in Rome. One slab was in the Vatican Museum, another in the Villa Medici (seat of the French Academy in Rome), still another in the Louvre. The finds from the 1859 dig had also been kept unrestored . in the palace, and then transferred to Rome's Terme Museum. One slab was found in re-use face down as a cover for a tomb in Rome's Church of the Gesù.

These were all decorative elements. Under the Palazzo Fiano still remain the tufa footings and some of the travertine pavement (Fig. 6.8). These, though they were not removed, made it possible to visualize and reconstruct the plan. The altar itself, in the center of its enclosed platform, proved to be U-shaped, with the open end of the U facing west, toward the Campus Martius, and approached by a

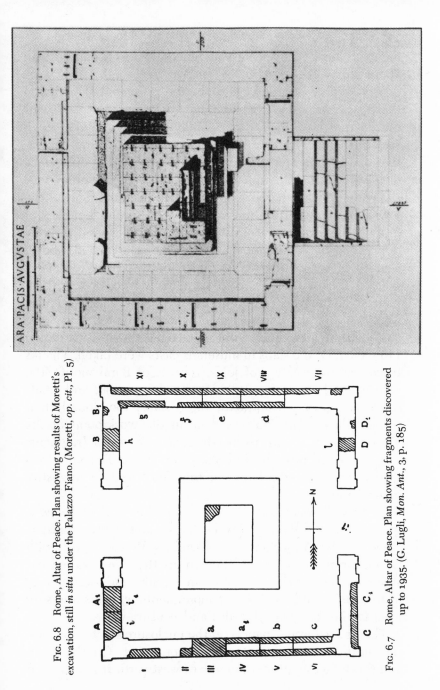

ARA·PACIS·AVGVSTAE

Fɪɢ. 6.8   Rome, Altar of Peace. Plan showing results of Moretti's excavation, still *in situ* under the Palazzo Fiano. (Moretti, *op. cit.*, Pl. 5)

Fɪɢ. 6.7   Rome, Altar of Peace. Plan showing fragments discovered up to 1935. (G. Lugli, *Mon. Ant.*, 3, p. 185)

flight of steps. The whole was fenced off by a marble wall
about thirty feet square and sixteen feet high, with wide
doorways on east and west. Since the pavement sloped, and
there was provision for drainage, the inference was warranted that the altar was originally open to the sky. Each
face of the enclosure wall bore two wide horizontal decorative bands separated by narrower bands, on the outer face
of meanders, on the inner, of palmettes. On the outer face
the wide upper band bore a frieze with over 100 figures; the
lower one motifs from nature: acanthus scrolls, bunches of
grapes, the swans of Augustus' patron Apollo, and a lively
population of small animals. The inner face carried, above,
a motif of swags of fruit festooned between ox-skulls (*bucrania*); below, a series of long, narrow, recessed, vertical
panels, giving the effect, in marble, of a wooden fence.
Many of the slabs were found where they fell and were
easily fitted into their proper place in the reconstruction
(Fig. 6.9). Of the slabs in museums casts were taken. Thanks
to careful observation of joins, repeats of floral motifs, the
identity of historic figures, veins in the marble, and treatment of unexposed surfaces, these slabs, too, found their
proper places. The job was done in the workrooms of the
Terme Museum, with twenty-four large cases of fragments
to work with, plus the full slabs and casts. The altar was
finally rebuilt on the banks of the Tiber next to Augustus'
mausoleum.

The result was worth the effort, for the Altar of Peace is
universally acknowledged to be the greatest artistic masterpiece of the Augustan Age, blending Roman spirit with
Greek forms, occupying in Roman art the same exalted position as the Parthenon frieze in Greek, and destined to
inspire, as we shall see, many monuments with historic subjects in the following decades and centuries.

The figured upper panels on the enclosure's outer face are
the most interesting part of the monument. On the north
and south faces a procession moves westward. It is imagined

FIG. 6.9　Rome, Altar of Peace, G. Gatti's reconstruction. (MPI)

FIG. 6.10　Rome, Altar of Peace, frieze with portrait of Augustus. (MPI)

as turning the corner of the enclosure and entering the west doorway to sacrifice at the altar. The heads on the north side were heavily restored in the Renaissance, but the fasces, the laurel crowns, the senatorial shoes and rings, the cult objects carried make it clear that the procession is of magistrates and priests. The south side, which faced the city, must have been considered the most important half, and here, indeed, many historical figures of Augustus' family and court have been identified. It is noteworthy how the division of the friezes into dynastic and non-dynastic halves parallels the arrangement of the Hall of Fame in Augustus' Forum.

The face in the upper right corner of the fragmentary left panel in Fig. 6.10, though cracked badly across the eye (for the whole weight of the Palazzo Fiano rested upon it for centuries), is recognizable from other portraits, from what remains of the profile, and from the treatment of the hair, as Augustus himself. The figures in the spiked caps to the far right are *flamines,* priests of Jupiter and Mars. The figure second to the left of the first *flamen,* all by himself in the background, is a spectator, the very type of the old Republican Roman. Lictors with the fasces precede the figure to the spectator's left of Augustus. This figure, then, must be the consul of the year, with the other consul on the other side of the Emperor.

But of which year? The consuls of the year 13 B.C., when the building of the altar was officially decreed, were Varus (who fell in the Teutoberg forest twenty-two years later) and Tiberius. Those of the year 9 B.C., when the altar was consecrated, were Drusus and Quinctius Crispinus. Now the slab pictured in Fig. 6.11 contains on its left edge, on either side of the veiled background figure with her finger on her lips (who is Augustus' sister Octavia) a family group. This has been almost certainly identified as Drusus (in uniform, with short tunic), and his wife, Antonia Minor, holding their son Germanicus by the hand. Drusus can hardly be in two places at once. Therefore the consuls on the earlier slab are those of 13 B.C., and the whole procession is imagined as that of the altar's *constitutio*, when the marble version was not yet finished, not yet, perhaps, even begun. This hypothesis explains the treatment of the enclosure's inner face, where the recessed panels represent a temporary wooden fence. The swags in marble relief, of barley, grapes, olives, figs, apples, pears, plums, cherries, pine cones, nuts, oak leaves, ivy, laurel, and poppy—all the riches of a fertile Italy at peace—were originally painted, like Della Robbia terracottas, against a blue background. They must have been intended to render the natural festoons swinging in the open air against the blue sky. The *paterae*, or sacrificial bowls, in two alternating patterns of gilded marble, which hang above the swags, must be imagined as suspended from an upper crossbar.

The persons in Fig. 6.12 are of the greatest historical interest. The tall man with a fold of his toga over his head, whose careworn face and pronounced Roman nose make a recognizable portrait, can be identified from other likenesses as Augustus' lieutenant Agrippa, acting as Pontifex Maximus. The child clinging to his toga is then one of his sons, Gaius or Lucius. Gaius, the elder, born in 20 B.C., would have been, in 13, of the age represented here; a modern symbol of Aeneas' son Ascanius, or Romulus, the son of Mars. The woman in the background with her hand on his head would then be Gaius' mother Julia, Augustus' daughter, whom he was later to banish for her immoral conduct. The older woman in the foreground, the most carefully wrought female figure in either frieze, would then be Julia's stepmother, the redoubtable Empress Livia.

The family group to the right of Drusus in Fig. 6.11 is also pregnant with history. The shapely woman with her hand on the small boy's shoulder is identified as Antonia Major, Mark Antony's daughter by Octavia. The small boy grasping a fold of his uncle Drusus' cloak grew up to

Fig. 6.11   Rome, Altar of Peace, frieze with family group
of Julio-Claudians. (MPI)

Fig. 6.12   Rome, Altar of Peace, frieze probably portraying Agrippa,
Julia, and Livia. (MPI)

father the Emperor Nero. The girl to the spectator's right of the small boy is his sister Domitia; her father, Lucius Domitius Ahenobarbus, later commander of the Roman army in Germany, has his hand raised over her head. The elderly background figure with the kindly, lined face is perhaps Maecenas, Augustus' secretary of state for propaganda, the patron of Vergil and Horace.

The whole atmosphere of the procession is very Italian, quite intimate and informal, without central focus. Its members face in all directions, and are so incorrigibly chatty that Octavia must command silence, finger to lips. Here, in these realistic groups, are the living likenesses of some of the men and women whose ashes later lay in Augustus' mausoleum, of some of the men and women who made a Golden Age. Here are the pages of history made flesh, and here are all the basic ideas of the Augustan program: the pretense of the revived Republic, in the consuls and lictors; the emphasis on religion, in the *flamines* and the veiled Pontifex; the dynastic hopes, in little Gaius; the subvention of literature, in Maecenas.

The east and west ends of the enclosure each contain, on either side of the doorways, a figured panel, four in all, of which two are well preserved. The one to the right of the main (west) entrance portrays a grave, bearded figure (Fig. 6.13) offering sacrifices, with the aid of two acolytes, upon a rustic altar before a small temple containing tiny figures of the Penates as Castor and Pollux, whose connection with the *gens Iulia* we have already noted. The sow in the lower left corner is the famous one with the thirty piglets, whose discovery was to tell Aeneas where to found his city. (What purported to be the original sow and all the piglets, pickled in brine, was on display in a Latin town in Augustus' age.) From the sow the inference is that the bearded figure is Aeneas; he symbolized the past of Rome, and the ancestry of Augustus.

The panel to the left of the east entrance (Fig. 6.14) has as its central figure a full-breasted woman, whose face closely resembles the Livia of the south frieze. She has fruits in her lap, chubby naked babies in her arms, a miniature cow and a sheep at her feet, grain and poppies behind her. She is flanked by obviously allegorical figures of Air (riding a swan), and Water (riding a sea monster). Fresh water gushes from an amphora in the lower left corner; a salt-water harbor (indicated by waves, and perhaps the arch in the background) is at the lower right. Surely this is *Saturnia Tellus,* the fruitful earth of an Italy at peace, that Vergil sang of in the *Georgics,* rich in crops, flocks, and herds, but fruitful most of all in *men.* Of the two fragmentary panels, the west one is restored as a scene of Mars, the shepherd, the wolf, and the twins Romulus and Remus. (The Mars was acquired from a private owner in Vienna, whose Roman art dealer had told him it came from the Palazzo Fiano.) The east one, the least well preserved of all, probably represented the goddess Roma seated upon a trophy of arms, like Britannia on an English penny. Thus one pair of end panels is symbolical, while the other is mythological; the processional frieze deals with contemporary history. The whole makes a tripartite arrangement which is artistically very satisfying. At the same time, victorious Rome, fruitful Italy, the remote founder, and the first king, are all symbolically related here, as in other Augustan monuments, to the contemporary scene and the fortunes of the dynasty.

After the grandeur of the enclosure, the decoration of the altar itself seems modest and unpretentious, perhaps deliberately so. Winged sphinxes support rich volutes, the graceful S-curves which bound the altar table on either side. Beneath, there is a sacrificial scene, with the six Vestal Virgins neatly arranged in order of size. In the sacrificial scene itself, the victims are a steer, a heifer, and a fleecy sheep. The attendants carry the sacrificial knives, platters,

FIG. 6.13   Rome, Altar of Peace. Aeneas sacrificing. (MPI)

FIG. 6.14   Rome, Altar of Peace. Tellus or Italia. (MPI)

pitchers, and other paraphernalia. One twists the horns of
the steer, another the tail of the heifer, to keep them moving. Altar and enclosure together provide our most complete visual record of a Roman state religious ceremony.
And the whole complex, with its religiosity and historicity,
is prolific of descendants: the Arch of Titus, the Cancelleria
reliefs (to be discussed in Chapter IX), Trajan's Column
(to be discussed in Chapter X), his arch at Beneventum,
the Arch of Constantine, the Column of Marcus Aurelius,
the Arch of Septimius Severus. It is the prototype of them
all, and the most masterly: tranquil, unpretentious, stately
yet intimate, delighting in nature, perfectly balanced between country and city, perfectly symbolizing the Augustan
Peace, when men would beat their swords into plowshares,
and study war no more. But within 100 years the altar began
to be neglected. Perhaps, looking behind the façade, some
old Republicans were moved to ask, "Where is the Altar
of Liberty?"

A Forum, an arch, a tomb, an altar: taken together, as
recent archaeology has revealed them to us, they epitomize
the Augustan Age. In the Forum and the arch, the past
recaptured, and pressed into the service of the régime. In
the altar, the heroic and warlike past implicit in the orderly
and peaceful present. In the tomb, posterity, the future
generations, invited to marvel at the dynasty and what it
has wrought. Behind all this, we can see that Augustus, the
most ruthless power politician of them all, was simply continuing the careers of the great captains and dynasts of the
past, like Caesar, Pompey, and Sulla. The refulgence of
the monuments but reflects his monolithic control of the
state, his cracking open of the seams of the old régime. In
the history of art and architecture, Augustus' contribution
is the applying of a standardized scheme of décor, as he
applied a standardized scheme of administration, to the
whole Empire. Henceforward Rome is the producer. She

crystallized the styles and re-exported them to the world that lay at her feet. Next we shall see how the Julio-Claudian Emperors, from Tiberius to Nero, exploited what Augustus had begun.

7

Hypocrite, Madman, Fool, and Knave

Roman historians branded the Julio-Claudian successors of Augustus—Tiberius (A.D. 14-37), Caligula (37-41), Claudius (41-54) and Nero (54-68)—as a hypocrite, a madman, a fool, and a knave. The hypocrite spent millions rehabilitating Asia Minor after an earthquake, the madman provided Ostia with a splendid aqueduct, the fool built for the same city a great artificial harbor, the knave rebuilt Rome—after burning it down first, his enemies said—with a new and intelligent city plan. But it would be easy to interpret the Julio-Claudian age as one of conspicuous consumption and conspicuous waste: there were many who fiddled before Rome ever burned. Thus both Tiberius and Caligula built on the Palatine grandiose palaces, and Nero's Golden House, as we shall see, outdid them all. Tiberius' monstrous barracks at the city wall for the praetorian guard introduces a sinister note. Claudius' Altar of Piety, modelled on Augustus' Altar of Peace, shows how derivative official art can be. Out of the complexity of this half-century, as archaeology reveals it to us, I have chosen four examples, one from each reign: a stately pleasure-dome of Tiberius by the sea at Sperlonga; a pair of extraordinary houseboats, probably Caligula's, from the Lake of Nemi; the curious subterranean basilica at the Porta Maggiore in Rome, which flourished briefly and mysteriously in the reign of Claudius; and Nero's fabulous Golden House.

In August, 1957, road improvements near Sperlonga, on the coast, about sixty-six miles southeast of Rome, offered G. Iacopi of the Terme Museum the opportunity for partially restoring, and closely examining, the ruins of a well-known villa there, commonly called the Villa of Tiberius. Making soundings near the villa in a wide, lofty cave fronting on the beach (Fig. 7.1), partly filled with sea-water, Iacopi discovered that the natural cave had been made over into a *nymphaeum* or *vivarium,* a round artificial fish-pool, with a large pedestal for statuary in the middle, and artificial grottoes opening behind (Fig. 7.2). In the pool and the grottoes, buried under masses of fallen rock, Iacopi and his assistants found an enormous quantity—at last accounts over 5500 fragments—of statuary. The fallen rock gave a clue for dating at least one phase of the cave's existence, and a possible confirmation of the popular name for the adjoining villa. For the historian Tacitus mentions that in A.D. 26, Tiberius, dining in a natural cave at his villa at Spelunca, was saved from being crushed under falling rock by the heroism of his prefect of the praetorian guard, Sejanus, who protected him with his own body. This is very likely the actual cave which Iacopi explored, though his discoveries suggest that there were additions after Tiberius' time.

The exploration was carried on under difficulties of several kinds. The Italian budget for archaeology is notoriously inadequate; the cave was subject to flooding from springs, and lashing by winter storms; and it contained a dangerous quantity of ammunition and explosives stored there in World War II. The first difficulty was temporarily overcome by the generosity of the engineer in charge of the road-building

FIG. 7.1   Sperlonga, Cave "of Tiberius." (G. Iacopi, *I ritrovamenti*, etc., Fig. 8)

FIG. 7.2   Sperlonga, Cave "of Tiberius," reconstruction. (G. Iacopi, *op. cit.*, Fig. 18)

nearby; the second by installing three pumps and building a dike; the third by keeping an ordnance expert constantly on duty.

When the finds from the cave were first reported in the press, great excitement was caused by the announcement —premature, as it turned out—that among the fragments of sculpture were some resembling the Laocoön group. The original Laocoön group had been described by Pliny the Elder as carved out of a single block, probably with the sculptors' names on the base, whereas the famous Vatican Laocoön is not monolithic and is unsigned. Among the Sperlonga finds, on the other hand, were fragments of a Greek inscription giving the names of the three Rhodian sculptors mentioned by Pliny (but not in the precise form transcribed by him: in the Sperlonga inscriptions, their fathers' names are recorded, in Pliny not), plus some colossal pieces (the central figure would have been nineteen feet eight inches tall) including parts of two snake-like monsters, presumably the serpents sent by Athena to punish Laocoön and his sons for resisting the proposal to drag the Wooden Horse within the walls of Troy. This great group, much larger, earlier (according to Iacopi, on the somewhat doubtful evidence of the letter-styles of the Greek inscription, which he would date in the second or first century B.C.) than the Vatican version, and different in conception, fits the pedestal in the middle of the circular pool.

Another inscription goes some way to explain both the quantity and the arrangement of the sculpture in the grotto. In ten lines of Latin verse it describes how a certain Faustinus adorned the cave with sculpture for the pleasure of his Imperial masters, choosing subjects which, Vergil himself would admit, outdid his own poetry. One of the subjects mentioned is Scylla, the fabulous cave-dwelling sea-monster, with a girdle of dogs' heads about her loins, who guarded the straits of Messina. Now in the cave, carved in the living rock, at the right of the entrance, is the prow of a ship, set with blue, green, yellow, and red mosaic, and presenting some evidence of having once had a marble superstructure. To this ship Iacopi would assign some of his key figures: a bearded Ulysses in a seaman's cap, his face expressing horror; a lovely archaic statuette of Athena (Fig. 7.3), grasped by a huge hand (Athena might be the figurehead); Scylla's gigantic hand seizing a seaman by the hair, and a terrified mariner who has taken refuge from Scylla at the ship's prow. A niche carved in the rock above the ship would be an appropriate vantage-point for Scylla herself: in one fragment one of her dog's heads has bitten deep into a sailor's shoulder. It is true that the mosaic names the ship *Argo*, but Iacopi explains this as a generic name for a ship, not necessarily referring to the one that bore the Argonauts.

If Iacopi is right about this group, it was a baroque or even rococo effect that Faustinus arranged for his Imperial masters. But the Laocoön and Scylla groups by no means exhausted his fancy or his pocketbook: there was Menelaus with the body of Patroclus, Ganymede borne to heaven by an eagle (carved so as to be seen to best effect from below, and therefore possibly belonging to a pedimental treatment of the cave façade). There are heads of gods and heroes, satyrs and fauns, a charming Cupid trying on a satyr's mask, a delightful head of a baby with ringlets over the ears—all in the fanciful, complex, sometimes tortured baroque style of Hellenistic Pergamum and Rhodes. These are all of fine crystalline Greek island marble, so that they may be Greek originals. The soapy native Carrara stone is normally used in Roman copies—and in too much modern American church sculpture.

At the present writing the Sperlonga cave cannot be said to have yielded up all its secrets. It is not even certain that the equipping of Tiberius' outdoor dining-room as a lavish baroque museum took place in Tiberius' lifetime, for the

FIG. 7.4   Lake Nemi, Braschi finds (1895) from ships. (G. Ucelli, *Le navi di Nemi*, p. 19)⁻

FIG. 7.3 Sperlonga, Cave "of Tiberius." Head of archaic statuette of
Athena. (Iacopi, *op. cit.*, Fig. 11)

donor, Faustinus, may be the rich villa-owner of that name who was a friend of the poet Martial, and therefore of Domitianic date. The residents of Sperlonga want the sculpture kept where it was found, to entice tourists; the archaeologists want to take it to Rome for analysis and reconstruction. Meanwhile, definitive conclusions are impossible. But one thing is certain: the bizarre taste of the place, whether Tiberius' or Domitian's, is characteristic of the first century of the Empire, and reflects the gap between the ostentatious rich and the church-mouse poor which was one day to contribute to the Empire's fall.

The same fantastic extravagance marks our next finds. Seventeen miles southeast of Rome, cupped in green volcanic hills, lies the beautiful deep blue Lake of Nemi, the mirror of Diana. Here divers, as long ago as 1446, reported, lying on the bottom in from sixteen to sixty-nine feet of water, two ships, presumably ancient Roman. A descent was made in a diving bell in 1535. Another attempt in 1827 used a large raft with hoists and grappling irons, and an art dealer tried again in 1895, but all three efforts were chiefly successful in damaging the hulls, tearing away great chunks without being able to raise the ships to the surface. The 1895 attempt did, however, produce a mass of tantalizing fragments (Fig. 7.4): beams; lead water-pipe; ball-bearings; a number of objects in bronze, including animal heads holding rings in their teeth, a Medusa, and a large flat hand; terracotta revetment plaques, a quantity of rails and spikes, and a large piece of decking in mosaic. This treasure-trove, displayed in the Terme Museum, naturally whetted appetites, not least Mussolini's. He determined to get at the ships by lowering the level of the lake, a colossal task undertaken eagerly by civil and naval engineers enthusiastic about classical civilization. The job was made easier, but no less expensive, because there existed an ancient artificial outlet, a tunnel a mile long, dating from the reign of Claudius, which could be used to carry off the overflow. The pumps were started on October 20, 1928, in the presence of the *Duce*. After various vicissitudes over a space of four years, the lake level was lowered seventy-two feet, and by November, 1932, the first ship was installed in a hangar on the shore, and the second (Fig. 7.5) lay exposed in the mud.

The ships proved to be enormous by ancient standards, of very shallow draft, very broad in the beam (one was sixty-six feet wide, the other seventy-eight) and respectively 234 and 239 feet long (Fig. 7.6). They were larger than some of the early Atlantic liners. Their 1100 tons burden gave them ten times the tonnage of Columbus' largest ship.

The task of freeing the ships of mud and debris, recording the finds level by level, reinforcing the hulls with iron, shoring them up, raising and transporting them to the special museum built for them on the lake shore proved in its way to be as great a challenge to Italian patience and ingenuity as the job of excavating the slabs and fragments of the Altar of Peace from under the Palazzo Fiano. There was always the danger of the ships' settling in the mud in a convex curve, springing the beams. The excavating tools used were made entirely of wood; iron would have damaged the ancient timbers. As each section of the hull emerged from the water that had covered it for so many centuries, it was covered with wet canvas to keep it from deteriorating.

The hulls proved to be full of flat tiles set in mortar. These overlaid the oak decking, and over these again was a pavement in polychrome marble and mosaic. Fluted marble columns were found in the second ship, suggesting a rich and heavy superstructure (Fig. 7.7). A round pine timber from the first ship, thirty-seven feet long and sixteen inches in diameter, with a bronze cap ornamented

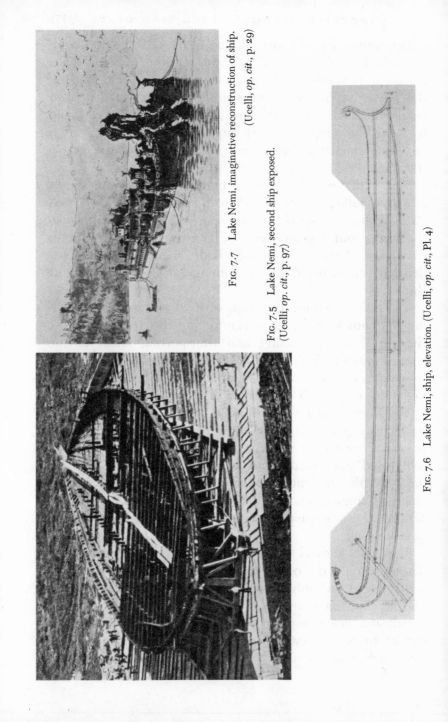

Fig. 7.7 Lake Nemi, imaginative reconstruction of ship. (Ucelli, *op. cit.*, p. 29)

Fig. 7.5 Lake Nemi, second ship exposed. (Ucelli, *op. cit.*, p. 97)

Fig. 7.6 Lake Nemi, ship, elevation. (Ucelli, *op. cit.*, Pl. 4)

with a lion holding a ring in its teeth, proved to be a sweep rudder, one of a pair. It showed that these enormously heavy vessels (the decking material alone must have weighed 600 or 700 metric tons) were actually intended to be practicable, and to move about in the waters of the lake.

Clay tubes, flanged like sewer-pipe to fit into each other, were arranged in pairs to make an air-space between one level of deck and another. This suggests radiant or hypocaust heating, as in a Roman bath: these floating palaces, or temples, or whatever they were—perhaps both—had bathing facilities. Wooden shutters warrant the inference that the ships were provided with private cabins. A length of lead water-pipe stamped with the name of Caligula has been used to date the ships to that reign (and indeed in some ways they accord well with Caligula's reputation for madness), but of course there is nothing to prevent lead pipe of Caligula's short reign (A.D. 37-41) from being used in Claudius', and many scholars, on the evidence of the art objects found, would date the ships in the latter reign.

Boards in the bottom of the hold were removable to facilitate cleaning out the bilge. This was done with an endless belt of buckets, some of which were found, and are on display, restored, in the museum. Over the ribs of the hull was pine planking, then a thin coating of plaster, then a layer of wool treated with tar or pitch, finally lead sheathing clinched with large-headed copper nails.

The second ship had outriggers supporting a platform for the oarsmen, and a bronze taffrail decorated with herms—miniature busts tapering into square shafts. A number of mechanical devices of great technical interest was found: pump-pistons; pulleys; wooden platforms (use unknown), one mounted on ball-bearings, another on roller-bearings; a double-action bronze stem-valve (perhaps for use in pumping out the bilge), which had been welded at a high temperature (1800° Fahrenheit); anchors, one with the knot tied by a Roman sailor still intact, another with a moveable stock, anticipating by over 1800 years a similar model patented by the British Admiralty in 1851. Its use is to cant the anchor, giving it a better bite in the mud.

In 1944 the retreating Germans wantonly burned the ships in their museum. Their gear, stored in a safe place, survived. From careful drawings made at the time the ships were raised, models were made to one-fifth scale. They are now on display in the restored museum.

The ships did not contain within themselves clear evidence about what they were used for. Whether they had some religious purpose in connection with the nearby Temple of Diana, or were used as pleasure-craft, or both, they reflect, like the cave at Sperlonga, the mad extravagance which increasingly characterized the Roman Empire on its road to absolutism.

In 1917, on Rome's birthday, April 21, a landslip beside the Rome-Naples railway line outside the Porta Maggiore revealed, forty-two feet beneath the tracks, a hitherto unsuspected and most remarkable underground, vaulted, stucco-ornamented room, the so-called "basilica," which will serve as a third example of archaeology's contribution to our knowledge of the Julio-Claudian age. To protect the basilica against damage from seepage and vibration from trains—240 a day pass directly above it—it was enclosed in 1951-52, at a cost of over $500,000, in a great box of waterproof reinforced concrete with footings anchored nearly twenty-four feet beneath the level of the basilica pavement.

One entered the chamber in antiquity—it was always underground—down a long vaulted ramp which made a right-angle turn and emerged in a little square vestibule, whose skylight provided the basilica's only natural light. Beyond the vestibule was a vaulted nave (Fig. 7.8) ending in an

FIG. 7.8 Rome, subterranean basilica at Porta Maggiore, general view.
(Fototeca)

apse, and two side aisles. The profiles of the piers upholding
the vaults, and of the arches connecting the nave with the
side aisles, are irregular; and the piers are set at eccentric
angles (Fig. 7.9): this suggests a curious method of construction. A trench must have been dug through the surface
tufa corresponding to the desired perimeter of the building.
Then six square pits were dug, one for each pier, and the
outline of the arches and doorways formed in the virgin
soil. Then mortar was poured in. When it had set, the
entrance corridor was dug and the interior of the basilica

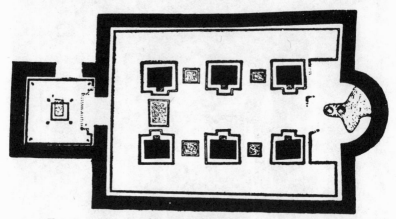

FIG. 7.9   Rome, subterranean basilica at Porta Maggiore.
(*Legacy of Rome*, p. 407)

emptied of earth through the skylight in the vestibule. Then
vault, piers, and walls were stuccoed. In the late Republic
and after, Roman artisans showed great skill in ornamental
stucco-work, a far cry from the wattle-and-daub, in the
primitive huts, which is the remote ancestor of the refined
work in the basilica, and a symbol of how far on the road
to sophistication Rome had traveled from her humble
beginnings.

In the basilica the stucco-work is divided by moldings
into squares, rectangles, and lozenges, filled with figures in
low relief of great delicacy and elegance. Some are simple

scenes of daily life, and many others are part of the standard repertory of Roman art, but the key motifs will bear,
as we shall see, a single, serious interpretation. The apse,
the focal point of the whole structure, was reserved for a
special scene of central importance.

The central panel of the central vault shows a naked
human figure, a pitcher in his hand, carried off by a winged
creature. (The interior of the figure is eaten out; this is
due not to vandalism but to the depredations of a parasitic
insect related to the termite.) In the four surrounding
panels are four other motifs. A hero wearing a lion's skin
shoots with a bow a monster guarding a maiden chained
to a rock. A beautiful, seated, half-naked woman cradles a
statuette in her left arm; a bearded middle-aged man stands
before her. A young man in a short tunic, carrying a leafy
branch or a shepherd's crook, leads off a woman by the
hand. A veiled female figure takes from a tree guarded by
a serpent a fleecy object to give to a man kneeling on a
table nearby. How are these scenes to be interpreted? Do
they share a common motif? According to the French Professor Jérome Carcopino, they do.

The central subject is Ganymede borne heavenward to
be Jupiter's cup bearer. The hero with the lion's skin is
Hercules rescuing Hesione. The woman with the statuette
is Helen with the Palladium, the ancient image on which
Troy's safety depended; the wise Ulysses stands before her.
Or it might be Iphigenia, in faraway Tauris, about to bear
past the Thracian King Thoas the statuette of Artemis
which will release her brother Orestes from torment by
the Furies. In the next panel, if the young man is carrying
a branch, he is Orpheus bringing Eurydice back from
Hades; if he is carrying a shepherd's crook, he is Paris kid-
naping Helen. The veiled female is of course Medea getting the Golden Fleece for Jason. The common theme is
deliverance. Ganymede, liberated from earthly ties, is
borne on wings to the bliss of Heaven. Hercules can free

Hesione because, according to some versions of the myth, he has been initiated into the mysteries. The statue, whether of Athena or of Artemis, guarantees the safety of the city or person who possesses it. Helen, in some accounts, can read the future and assuage men's pain; or, if the theme is Orpheus and Eurydice, we may recall that in an early ver-

FIG. 7.10   Rome, subterranean basilica at Porta Maggiore, apse.
(Fototeca)

sion of the myth the ending was happy. Jason and Medea are freed from fear of the dragon through rites of magic initiation.

Does the great scene in the apse (Fig. 7.10) harmonize with the interpretation? In it, on the right, a graceful veiled woman, holding the lyre of a poetess, descends a cliff into the sea. She is pushed by a baby winged figure standing behind her. Beneath, waist deep in the water, a figure with a cloak outspread stands ready to receive her and escort her to the opposite shore. There, on another cliff, stands an imposing naked male figure, in his left hand a bow, his right outstretched in blessing. Behind him sits a young man thoughtfully supporting his head on his hand. Below in the sea yet another figure holds an oar and blows a horn in greeting. Any Roman intellectual would recognize the scene: it is Sappho, encouraged by Cupid, received by Tritons, blessed by Apollo, making the lover's leap to join her beloved Phaon for eternity. This is not suicide, but liberation from earthly love into an eternity of perfect harmony of the senses with the sublime and the supernatural. The scene is consistent with the others, and provides a further clue to the interpretation of the whole, for Pliny the Elder, in his encyclopaedic *Natural History*, says that the myth of Sappho and Phaon was made much of by a sect called neo-Pythagoreans, inspired by the number-mysticism, and the belief in immortality, of their founder, Pythagoras of Samos, who flourished in the late sixth century B.C. These beliefs were refined in the Hellenistic Age, and taken up by heterodox Roman intellectuals.

This elegant underground chamber, so restrained and literary in décor, so small in size (it measures less than thirty by thirty-six feet) is just the place for a chapel for such an élite and aristocratic sect of ancient freemasons. The hypothesis is borne out by the discovery beneath the floor of the bones of a puppy and a suckling pig, the preferred *pièces de résistance* for a neo-Pythagorean cult meal, perhaps the meal that inaugurated the chapel.

And still other motifs in the stucco decoration strengthen the hypothesis, by stressing redemption, salvation, initiation: a winged victory; a soul arriving in the Isles of the Blest; a woman with a flower, symbolizing Hope; a scene of Demeter, the earth goddess, and Triptolemus, the hero of agriculture, of whom much was made in the Eleusinian mysteries. Other reliefs show the reverse of the coin: the punishment of the uninitiate. The satyr Marsyas is flayed alive for presuming to challenge Apollo to a competition in music. The Danaids, for the crime of murdering their husbands, perform forever the useless labor of drawing water in perforated jars. There are other sinners: Medea with her slain sons: Pasiphaë, the monstrously adulterous Cretan queen; Phaedra, trying her wiles on her sinless stepson; Hippolytus, over-chaste votary of the maiden-goddess Artemis; King Pentheus murdered, for scoffing at the Dionysiac mysteries; his mother, Agave, carries his severed head aloft in Bacchic frenzy. To these has not been given the true neo-Pythagorean vision of the truth; they are portrayed here to symbolize their doom to a private Hell of their own making.

Two long panels on either side of the spring of the central vault reinforce the general intellectual tone. In one, schoolboys recite their lessons before a seated schoolmaster with a ferule in his hand. In the other, the Muse of Tragedy attends the coming-of-age ceremony of a Roman adolescent. (Some interpret this scene as a marriage; if so, the sect will have allegorized it in some way.) We know that the sect was open to both sexes; reliefs in the wall-panels of the basilica show men and women making offerings.

The stuccoes of the vault were in excellent condition when found. (They have since suffered from dampness, now being corrected by air-conditioning.) Also, they show no traces of addition or repairs, but the wall-panels were desecrated in antiquity by vandals, the consoles for offerings ripped off, the lamps and chapel gear carried away. It looks as though the chapel had had a short life, and the cult a violent end. Will history provide a date? Tacitus mentions in his *Annals* a rich Roman, Titus Statilius Taurus, known to have owned property near the basilica, who fell foul of Claudius, was accused of practicing *magicas superstitiones*, and escaped his sentence by committing suicide in A.D. 53. The style of the stuccoes fits this date, the décor of the basilica fits the cult, its state when found fits Tacitus' story. We may suppose that everything within reach was looted, the chamber filled in, and probably never seen again until the spring day 1864 years later when the landslide by the railway revealed its existence.

In 1907 the German archaeologist F. Weege, following in the footsteps of Renaissance explorers of 1488, made his way through a hole in the wall of the Baths of Trajan, near the Coliseum, to find himself in a labyrinth of underground vaulted corridors and rooms partly filled with rubble, which had once been part of an Imperial palace, the Golden House of Nero. Setting lighted candles at every turning to guide his way back, he explored as many as he could of the eighty-eight rooms of this small part of the palace-complex, sometimes crawling with lighted candle over rubble that filled a room nearly to the vault, while spiders and centipedes, and other nameless creatures scuttled away from him into the darkness.

The rooms had been filled with rubble by Trajan, with a twofold purpose: to make a firm substructure for his baths, and to continue the work of the Flavians in damning the memory of the conspicuous consumption and conspicuous waste of the hated Nero. Thirteen hundred and eighty-four years later, when the underground rooms were rediscovered, among the visitors was Raphael, who decorated a loggia in the Vatican Palace in the style of the fantastic paintings on Nero's walls. Since the buried rooms were grottoes, the paintings were "grotesques"—as often, the word has survived, while its history has been forgotten. Other visitors were Caravaggio, Velasquez, Michelangelo, and Raphael's teacher, Perugino. The names of many a famous artist are scrawled right across the face of the ornaments of the vaults. An Italian poem, written not long after the discovery of America, speaks of artists' underground picnics in the Golden House. The picnickers crawled on their bellies to enjoy their subterranean meal of bread, ham, apples, and wine.

The result of Weege's more scientific investigation was the working out of a new plan. The western half of the complex (Fig. 7.11) proved to be conventional, with the rooms grouped about a peristyle with garden and fountain. Rooms 37 and 43 have alcoves: it is easy to imagine them as the Imperial bedchambers of Nero and his beautiful red-haired wife Poppaea. In Nero's bedchamber were hung the 1808 gold crowns he won in athletic competitions in Greece, if competitions they can be called, when all the prizes were awarded to Nero in advance, and armed guards drove off all would-be rivals.

The eastern wing (Fig. 7.12) is more unorthodox in plan, and more interesting. The main approach opened into Room 60, the Hall of the Gilded Vault, so called from the ornate painted stucco ceiling, divided into round and rectangular fields in gilt, green, red and blue, depicting mythological and erotic scenes, very different in tone from the restraint of the subterranean basilica. Hippolytus, off to the hunt, receives a letter containing incestuous proposals from his stepmother Phaedra. Satyrs rape nymphs, Venus languishes in the arms of Mars, Cupid rides in a chariot drawn by panthers. And yet we are told that the painting in this pleasure dome was done by the solemn dean of Roman artists, Fabullus himself, the John Singer Sargent of his day, who always painted in full dress, wearing his toga.

Room 70 is a vaulted corridor 227 feet long, with sixteen windows opening to the north in the impost of the vault, which is painted sky-blue as a *trompe d'oeil*. Seabeasts, candelabra, and arabesques, sphinxes with shrubs growing out of their backs, griffins, centaurs, acanthus-leaves, Cupids, gorgons' heads, lions' heads with rings in their mouths, dolphins holding horns of plenty, winged horses, eagles, tritons, swags of flowers make up the riotous décor. In re-

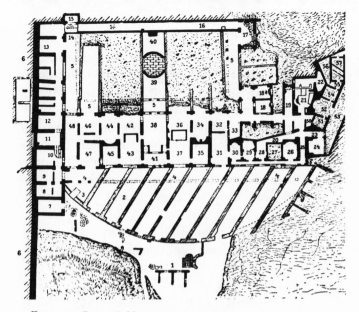

Fig. 7.11   Rome, Golden House, west wing.
(G. Lugli, *Roma antica*, p. 358)

Fig. 7.12   Rome, Golden House, east wing.
(G. Lugli, *op. cit.*, p. 359)

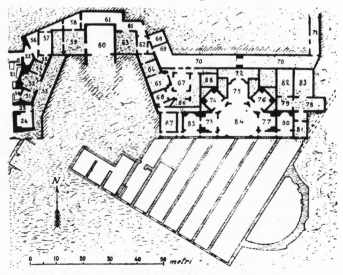

cesses in the walls landscapes and seascapes, impression-istically painted, attempt the illusion of the out-of-doors. Halfway down the corridor the vault is lowered. Here it supported a ramp which led to the gardens above.

Room 84 is octagonal, lighted by a hole in the roof, an-ticipating, as we shall see, Hadrian's Pantheon. Perhaps this was the state dining room, described by ancient sources as hung on an axis and revolving like the world. Its ivory ceilings slid back and dropped flowers and perfumes on Nero's guests.

The most controversial room of all is the apsidal number 80, decorated with scenes from the Trojan war: Hector and Andromache, Paris and Helen, Thetis bringing Achilles his shield. Nero was fascinated by the Trojan War: it was an epic of his own composition on the fall of Troy that he recited as Rome was burning. What was in the apse? Equiv-ocal Renaissance reports place the finding of the Vatican Laocoön somewhere in this area, the apse is of a size to fit the statue, and the subject is appropriate to a room full of Trojan motifs. The statue's baroque quality would have appealed strongly to Nero's taste. This is the circumstantial evidence for room 80 as the findspot of one of the most notorious statues of antiquity. That this survey of the Julio-Claudian age should approach its end, as it began, with mention of the Laocoön, suggests how conventional was the repertory of Roman taste.

But a description of the rooms of the Golden House is not quite the whole story. In 1954 the Dutch archaeologist C. C. Van Essen published the results of careful probing in the whole section of Rome for half a mile around the Coli-seum, where he found traces of Nero's palace in a number of places on the perimeter. For the Golden House was much more than the complex of rooms just described. It was a gi-gantic system (Fig. 7.13) of parks, with lawns, groves, pas-tures, a zoo. Over its central pool later rose the great bulk of the Coliseum. Within these grounds, twice the extent of

FIG. 7.13   Rome, Golden House, reconstruction drawing of whole area. (*Fototeca*)

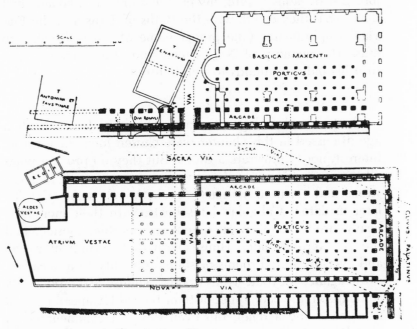

FIG. 7.14   Rome, the Neronian Sacra Via.
(E. B. Van Deman, *Mem. Am. Ac. Rome*, 5 [1925])

Vatican City, was a great Versailles in the midst of the
teeming metropolis. The eighty-odd rooms we have been
describing made up but one of several palaces in the
grounds. And an American, Miss E. B. Van Deman, working
from some very unlikely-looking architectural blocks piled
beside the Temple of Antoninus and Faustina in the old
Forum, was able in 1925 to restore on paper (Fig. 7.14) the
monumental approach, over 350 feet wide, to the palace
grounds from the old Forum and Palatine. It was a mile
long, with arcades of luxury shops, and eight rows of pillars.
Its plan is concealed today under mounds of dumped earth
between the Hall of the Vestals and the Arch of Titus. Beside it rose a colossal statue of Nero, 120 feet tall, now
marked by a pattern in the pavement. When Hadrian desired to remove the statue to make room for his Temple of
Venus and Rome, it took twenty-four elephants to do the
job. But decades before, his predecessors the Flavians had
done what they could, with the Baths of Titus and the Flavian Amphitheater (the proper name of the Coliseum) to
erase the memory of Nero's monstrous extravagance, and
turn his palace grounds to public use.

The four archaeological examples from the Julio-Claudian
age discussed in this chapter were chosen for their intrinsic
interest, not to illustrate a thesis. But they do prove a point
all the same. Tiberius' *al fresco* dining room, with its monstrous and tortured statuary (even though some of it be
later in date); Caligula's houseboats, with their incredibly
heavy profusion of work in colored marble, mosaic, and
bronze; Nero's Golden House, with its labyrinth of gaudy
and over-decorated rooms of state, all testify to a decadent
extravagance beyond Hollywood's wildest aspirations. By
comparison, the cool, quiet taste of the subterranean basilica
is an oasis and a relief, but even this is a commentary on
Claudius' intolerance. And it has about it an air of holier-

than-thou Brahminism, the furthest possible contrast with the warmth, the close contact with common people, which marked the Christianity that was to be preached in Rome not long after the basilica-sect was outlawed. One cannot but marvel at the staying-power of the organism that could survive this prodigality, this cleavage between class and mass, for over three centuries. But as we focus our attention upon the excesses of court and of metropolis, we ought not to forget that in the municipal towns of Italy and the Empire life went on, more modestly, quietly, and decently. Archaeology gives us precious proof of this in a pair of buried cities of the Flavian Age, Pompeii and Herculaneum.

8

The Victims of Vesuvius

One day in 1711 a peasant digging a well on his property in Resina, on the bay five miles southeast of Naples, came upon a level of white and polychrome architectural marbles, obviously ancient. This chance find led to the discovery of what proved to be the buried town of Herculaneum, destroyed in the eruption of Vesuvius of August 24, A.D. 79. Workmen digging in 1748 by the Sarno canal, nine miles farther along the bay, found bronzes and marbles on a site which an inscription, discovered fifteen years later, identified as Herculaneum's more famous sister city, Pompeii. Thus began a saga of excavation which has told the modern world more about ancient life than any other dig in the long history of archaeology, and this in two towns which have left almost no record in literature. In a few hours of a summer afternoon the eruption stopped the life of two flourishing little cities dead in its tracks: dinner on the tables, the wine-shops crowded, sacrifices at the moment of being offered, funerals in progress, prisoners in the stocks, watchdogs on their chains. The townsfolk had not even time to gather their possessions. Ironically, going back for their little hoards of gold and silver spelled death for many of them, under the hail of pumice-stone and ashes (or, at Herculeaneum, the river of lava) which asphyxiated (Fig. 8.1) or engulfed them. At Herculaneum, on the afternoon of the eruption, rain turned the volcanic ash to mud, which solidified, burying the town thirty to forty feet deep. Electric drills and mechanical shovels are needed to dig there, so progress has been slow. Even Pompeii, under its shallower layer of pumice-pebbles and light ash, is still only about three-fifths excavated.

FIG. 8.1   Pompeii, victims of Vesuvius, from House of Cryptoporticus. (V. Spinazzola, *Pompeii: . . . Via dell'Abbondanza*, 1, p. 443)

For a century and a half after their rediscovery the two sites were treated almost entirely as a quarry for works of art, as a plaything for the various dynasties that misruled Naples, and as a romantic stop on the Grand Tour. The discovery of ancient artifacts here revolutionized the taste of Europe: Ludwig of Bavaria built a replica of a Pompeian house at Aschaffenburg; Winckelmann, the great Romantic art historian, conceived here many of his notions of the wonders of Greek art; Casanova's brother copied some of the paintings, and did a brisk business in forgeries. Nelson's mistress, Lady Hamilton, was a frequent visitor: her husband was British ambassador to Naples. Goethe was impressed by Pompeii's smallness; Napoleon's marshal Murat supervised the dig, and Garibaldi made Alexandre Dumas his Director of Antiquities here. A generation of Victorians sobbed over *The Last Days of Pompeii,* and the young Queen herself visited the site in 1838.

But it was not till the era of scientific archaeology—which came to Pompeii and Herculaneum with Fiorelli in 1860 —that the buried cities began to add their never-ceasing stores to the sum of our knowledge of ancient town-planning, public life, private life in town and country houses, trade and tradesmen, religion, and art.

One of the results of scientific excavation at Pompeii was to reveal at last the town plan (Fig. 8.2), after decades spent in sporadic digging for treasure trove, in cutting paintings out of walls, filling in the excavated houses, and moving on without system to a new area. The plan as now revealed (Fig. 8.3) shows the least regular streets in the southwest quadrant of the town around the Forum; this, therefore, should be the oldest part; and in fact architectural terracottas found here, in the so-called *Foro triangolare,* are dated in the sixth century B.C. Elsewhere the pattern of a rectangular grid is clear, making possible the division of the city for purposes of archaeological reference into nine regions. Each region is subdivided into numbered blocks, or *insulae;* each *insula* into numbered houses. The whole 160 acres, big enough for a population of from fifteen to twenty thousand, is surrounded by a wall, in which archaeologists, on the basis of building materials and techniques, have detected four phases. The earliest, with a facing of squared limestone, dates from the fifth century B.C.; the latest, marked by the addition of high towers, from the

FIG. 8.2   Pompeii, air view. (University of Wisconsin Classics Dept. collection)

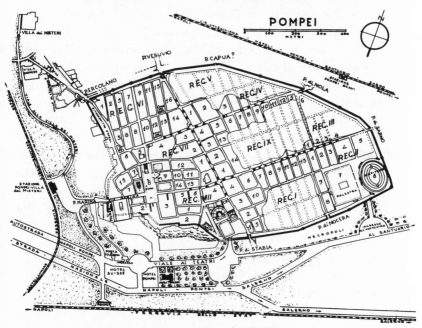

FIG. 8.3   Pompeii, plan. (MPI)

time of Sulla, who settled some of his veterans here in a colony grandiosely named the *Colonia Veneria Cornelia Pompeianorum*. Masons' marks from the third phase (280-180 B.C.) are in Oscan letters, the alphabet of ancient Italy's major language, next after Latin and Greek. Inscriptions (street signs for example) show that Oscan persisted as Pompeii's third language, along with Latin and Greek (for the area around Naples had originally been settled by Greeks, and they kept their culture), down almost to the time of the eruption. The wall shows the marks of the stone catapult-balls of the Sullan siege; some of the balls were found preserved as souvenirs in houses. After the Sullan phase the wall was allowed to fall into disrepair, mute evidence of the security of the Augustan peace.

Whatever curtailment of liberty seemed a price worth paying for security in Rome, Pompeii at least enjoyed an active political life. The evidence is a vast series of election "posters," painted in red and black on house and shop walls. In these, individuals and groups (for example, the fullers or laundrymen, the fruit-vendors, the fishermen, dyers, bakers, goldsmiths, muleteers, and a private club of gay blades who call themselves the *seribibi*, late drinkers) urge their fellow-citizens to vote for candidates for aedile, the highest municipal office. For one block of supporters the candidate's gratitude must have been extremely limited: the notice read: "The sneak-thieves support Vatia for the aedileship." The bases for the invitations to vote for a candidate like "Vote for X: he won't squander public funds," will have a strong appeal for the modern reader.

There was no interference with due process, to judge by the basilica in the Forum, where Pompeii's legal business was transacted: it is Pompeii's largest and most important public building. Tiles found in it stamped in Oscan come from a level which shows that the building dates at least from 120 B.C. Across the Forum from the basilica is the *comitium*, for town meetings and elections: at the south end of the Forum are three buildings, identified as the meeting-place of the town council, with municipal offices on either side.

Pompeii was well-supplied, too, with public amenities. The streets were paved, and supplied at the main intersections with stepping stones, which did not interfere with the passage of high-axled wagons, though some stepping stones were removed in 1815 to allow the Queen of Naples' coach to pass. (Nowadays visitors with a taste for ostentation can be carried through Pompeii in a sedan chair.) Lead water-pipes found everywhere show that all but the very humblest houses were supplied with running water. There were no less than three sets of public baths, of which the largest was under construction when the catastrophe came. The baths had radiant heating and elegant stuccoed vaults. There were separate sets of rooms for men and for women, and an enormous number of lamps found in one establishment shows that it was in use also in the evening hours.

That the intellectual as well as the physical needs of the population were catered to is deduced from the existence of two stone theaters, one open to the sky, with a capacity of 5,000; one roofed, a *théatre intime*, for about 800. Both antedate the earliest stone theater in Rome. But the Pompeians did not push the intellectual life to extremes. The portico behind the large theater was remodelled in Nero's reign to make a barracks for gladiators, complete with armory and lock-up, where three of them were found asphyxiated in the stocks. The amphitheater has seats for 12,000. Legends scrawled on its walls, and on house-walls all over town, testify to the gladiators' popularity with their fans: gladiatorial records are registered (twenty-four fights, twenty-four victories; the losers most often are murdered and forgotten), and one champion is recorded as SVSPIR-IVM PVELLARVM, the one the girls sigh for.

But Pompeii's greatest contribution is to our knowledge, almost indecently intimate, of the private life of its inhabitants. This information comes primarily from the town houses and the suburban and rustic villas. The best guidebooks go into some detail on seventy-eight of these in Pompeii, and thirty-one in Herculaneum; hundreds more go unrecorded. In the face of this *embarras de richesse*, rigorous selection is necessary, and a description of a few houses and villas must suffice. To represent town houses I choose the "House of the Moralist" (*Regio* III, *Insula* iv, House 2-3), on the Via dell' Abbondanza, a shopping street of average houses. (The aristocratic quarter was in *Regio* VI.) Excavations on this street by Vittorio Spinazzola between 1910 and 1923 were carried out according to a method new in Pompeii, which made the dead street come alive with extraordinary vividness. Spinazzola's meticulousness preserved and reconstructed the traces of upper stories, with windows, balconies, and loggias; of gardens, with the discovered roots of their trees and plants replaced by modern ones of the same species. The colorful painted signs and notices on the house and shop fronts, instead of being detached as in the past and transferred to the museum in Naples, were left *in situ*, protected by glass and awnings, and the house interiors, with their furniture and wall-paintings, were kept intact. All this Spinazzola published in 1953 in a colossal book of 1110 folio pages, with over 1000 figures and ninety-six large plates. His account is the more important because the House of the Moralist, having been kept inviolate by volcanic ashes for so many centuries, was badly damaged by Allied bombs in 1943. (There were Germans quartered in the hotels near the excavation entrance.) The ground floor plan (Figs. 8.4 and 8.5) of that house shows two dwellings thrown into one. The smaller, on the left, has typical features: its vestibule leading to an *atrium* or patio off which open a summer and a winter dining room and a light-well planted with flowers and shrubs.

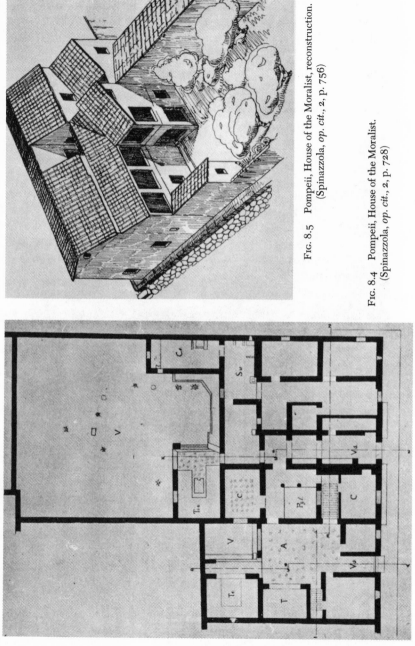

FIG. 8.5   Pompeii, House of the Moralist, reconstruction.
(Spinazzola, *op. cit.*, 2, p. 756)

FIG. 8.4   Pompeii, House of the Moralist.
(Spinazzola, *op. cit.*, 2, p. 728)

The winter dining-room is frescoed in glossy black; it has a vaulted, coffered ceiling, and a high window closed by a shutter planned to slide into the wall. The usual peristyle, or rectangular portico behind the *atrium,* is missing, its function supplied by the loggias on the upper floor and the large sunken garden behind the larger house. The garden was planned as a little grove sacred to Diana. Her

FIG. 8.6   Pompeii, House of the Moralist, triclinium.
(Spinazzola, *op. cit.,* 2, p. 752)

statue was found in the middle of the garden, with a little bronze incense-burner in the shape of a ram still in place on its pedestal, and large trees planted around it. The pleasant summer dining room fills the garden's southwest corner. In it the marble-topped table was found set for a meal or sacrifice (Fig. 8.6). In the corner was a brazier and a pitcher for hot water. Three couplets painted on the wall prescribed etiquette for the diners, and give the house its name: "Don't put your dirty feet on our couch covers; if you bicker at table you'll have to go home; be modest and don't make eyes at another man's wife." There was a dumbwaiter to serve the pleasant loggias on the upper floor overlooking the garden. The pointed jars, amphorae, in the basement, suggest that the Moralist was a wine merchant. A stamp found there gives his name: Gaius Arrius Crescens. Election notices painted on the house front show that he and his family were up to their ears in local politics.

A sumptuous suburban dwelling is the sixty-room Villa of the Mysteries outside Pompeii's Herculaneum gate, the noblest and grandest known of its kind. It was built on a seaward-facing slope, with a terrace and subterranean vaults. A careful analysis by its excavator, Amedeo Maiuri, of its building materials and décor shows six phases, of which the earliest, in squared blocks of local limestone, includes the rectangular block of rooms numbered 2-8 and 11-21 in the plan (Fig. 8.7), and is dated 200-150 B.C. At this stage the villa was surrounded on three sides by a pleasant open portico, and the curved exedra or belvedere (see the plan) did not yet exist. The next stage is marked by the use of handsome light gray tufa instead of limestone, includes the peristyle and small *atrium* (*atriolum* in the plan), and the modest bathing rooms (42-44) beyond. It dates from the time of Sulla. The next two periods are dated from the prevalent styles of wall-painting, to be discussed in the section on art below. They take the villa's building history through the reign of Augustus. In the Julio-Claudian period—the date is again made precise by the style of painting—the villa became useful as well as ornamental: the rustic quarters 52-60 were added, and an upper floor overlooking the vestibule. The latter is more elegant than the rustic quarters, less so than the noble eastern rooms. The inference is that in this period the owner used the villa only occasionally, leaving the management of its business

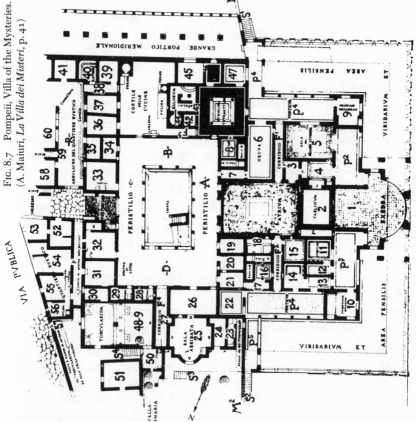

FIG. 8.7 Pompeii, Villa of the Mysteries.
(A. Maiuri, *La Villa dei Misteri*, p. 41)

LEGGENDA

1 - Veranda ed "exedra."
2 - Tablino.
3 - Cubicolo ad un'alcova.
4 - Cubicolo a doppia alcova.
5 - Sala del grande dipinto.
6 - Sala (oecus) con decorazione di II stile.
7 - Corridoio fra la Sala N. 6 e il peristilio.
8 - Cubicolo a doppia alcova.
9-10 - Cubicoli diurni.
11-12 - Grande cubicolo con "procoeton."
13-14 - Grande cubicolo con "procoeton."
15 - Stanza con decorazione di II stile.
16-17 - Cubicolo a doppia alcova con "procoeton."
18 - "Apotheca."
19-21 - Cubicoli con "procoeton" intermedio.
22 - Stanza (disus).
23 - Vano subscalare.
24 - "Apotheca."
25 - Stanza absidata: "Larario" (?).
26 - Ambiente di accesso alla stanza absidata.
27 - Corridoio e avanco ingresso secondario.
28-30 - Cubicoli rustici.
31 - Ambiente rustico.
32 - Ambiente con strumenti agricoli e cucina.
33 - Ambiente rustico con cucina.

34 - Piccolo ambiente rustico.
35 - Stanza con impronta umana.
36-37 - Ambienti del corridoio della cucina.
38 - Corridoio fra il cortile e l'ambulacro del quartiere rustico.
39 - Ambiente rustico.
40 - Latrina.
41 - Ambiente rustico.
42-44 - Bagno.
45 - Ambiente rustico.
46 - Stanza con pavimento "ibthattoton."
47 - Stanza con pavimento "ibthattoton."
48-49 - "Torcularium."
50 - Passaggio alla "Cella Vinaria."
51 - Ambiente rustico.
52-56 - Stanze del quartiere servile.
57 - Ingresso secondario della Villa, per il "torcularium" e la "Cella Vinaria."
58-60 - Ambienti rustici parzialmente scavati.

A-B-C-D: Ambulacri del peristilio.
F¹-F²-F³: Corridoi di uscita dall'atrio.
M¹: Metro di sostegno del portico meridionale.
M²: Muro di recinzione della "Cella Vinaria."
P¹,P²,P³,P⁴: Ale del portico.
S¹,S²,S³,S⁴,S⁵: Scalette di discesa al piano di campagna.

end to a resident factor who lived on the upper floor (see the reconstruction, Fig. 8.8) where he could keep his eye on the bailiff and the slave farm-hands. The portico (P 1-4) was now provided with a windowed wall between its columns, and the sunrooms (9-10) were created, with their splendid view, open to the southern sunshine, ideal for a winter siesta.

When the volcano finally struck, the villa was undergoing extensive remodelling, having apparently not yet recovered from an earlier catastrophe for which there is other evidence, both archaeological and literary: an earthquake in A.D. 62. The master's quarters were found empty of their contents, as though after the earthquake he had moved out altogether, and sold his elegant furniture at auction. A stamp reveals the name of the new owner: Lucius Istacidius Zosimus. Istacidius is a noble Samnite (Oscan) name; Zosimus is Greek. The inference is that the new owner was a freedman of the former master, who bought up the property and turned the entire establishment into a farmhouse. Evidence of the tasteless change from elegance to stark practicality was found everywhere: piles of mortar, columns and architraves taken down and stored, rooms closed off, an ugly new wall run straight across one of the most tasteful rooms in the master's quarters (6), a heap of onions piled on a mosaic floor in an alcoved master bedroom, farm tools in the graceful southwest sunroom (9). The apsidal room (25) was apparently destined to become a shrine to the Emperor. In it the statue of Augustus' consort, the Empress Livia, in painted marble with the head inserted in a second-hand torso (which was found [Fig. 8.9] propped against the peristyle wall) was apparently to be set up.

On the rustic side of the villa, business was going on as usual. The winepress (Fig. 8.10) was ready for use in the coming vintage; rough wine was ready in large amphorae protected by woven straw like a modern *fiascone* of Chianti

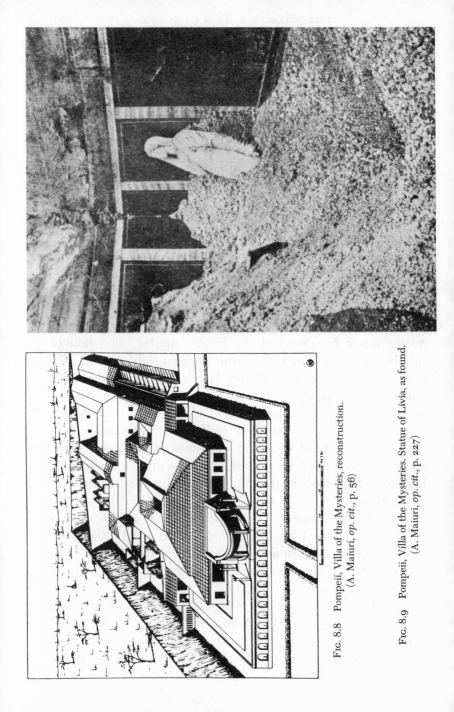

FIG. 8.8   Pompeii, Villa of the Mysteries, reconstruction.
(A. Maiuri, *op. cit.*, p. 56)

FIG. 8.9   Pompeii, Villa of the Mysteries. Statue of Livia, as found.
(A. Maiuri, *op. cit.*, p. 227)

or Vesuvio. Farm tools (picks, hoe, shovel, hammer, pruning hooks) were found hanging in a room (32) beside the vestibule. The porter was on duty. He was found dead in his dark little room (35), on his finger a cheap iron ring set with an engraved carnelian, by his side the five bronze coins which may have been his life savings. He must have heard the dying screams of the adolescent girl whose skeleton was found in the vestibule nearby. Three women were crushed in the rustic quarters (55) when the roof fell in. The excavators found their disordered skeletons, their gold rings and bracelets, a necklace of gold and glass paste beads, and, lying nearby, ten silver coins. In the cryptoporticus were found the bodies of four men, with wine or water jugs by their side. They had hoped the sturdy vaults would hold, and they did, but the mephitic fumes proved deadly. (Altogether, it is calculated that Vesuvius claimed 2,000 victims in Pompeii.) The nine wretched cadavers in the Villa of the Mysteries were the last inhabitants of a mansion which in its day had been one of the most elegant in all Italy.

Though space does not permit a detailed account of the fascinating things Herculaneum has to tell us, the subject of suburban villas cannot be left without mentioning a famous one there, still not fully explored, where in 1752 were found, in a narrow room with cupboards, a vast number of what were at first taken for charred billets of wood. Later, traces of writing were found on them: they turned out to be papyri, a whole library of 1800 rolls. A machine invented to unroll them ruined more scrolls than it unwound, but finally, by 1806, ninety-six were deciphered. They proved to be works of an Epicurean philosopher named Philodemus, to whose patron Lucius Calpurnius Piso (father of Caesar's wife Calpurnia) and his descendants the villa may have belonged. It had a gracious peristyle, gardens, fishponds, and a belvedere overlooking the sea at the end of a long graveled walk. In the garden was

FIG. 8.10   Pompeii, Villa of the Mysteries. Wine-press, reconstructed.
(Maiuri, *op. cit.*, p. 101)

found a whole gallery of sculpture in bronze and marble, now included among the most famous pieces in the National Museum in Naples. Here a cultured Roman patrician could combine in the ideal Epicurean way the calm contemplation of the beauties of nature and of art with the philosophic study of the atomic structure of the universe.

A more rustic villa, between Pompeii and Boscoreale to the north, shows what the establishment of a capital farmer of the first century A.D. was like. The owner's quarters were modest. Business came first: most of the ground floor is taken up with stable, wine and oil presses, threshing floor, and slaves' quarters. Slaves were a problem: one rustic villa has quarters for thirty and stocks for fourteen. The Boscoreale wine store had a 23,000 gallon capacity, and enough stone jars were found to hold 1,300 gallons of olive oil. The proprietor of this villa, however, was not without his fondness for aesthetic ostentation. In a wine vat here was found in 1895 a treasure of 108 embossed silver vessels and 1000 gold coins. They were bought by the banker Count Edward de Rothschild, much to Italian disgust, and presented to the Louvre. One pair of cups represents a series of skeletons, one garlanded, another with a heavy bag of money, a third with a roll of papyrus, a fourth with a lyre; the whole bears the legend, the tragic irony of which the proprietor of the villa was to discover: "Seize hold on life; tomorrow is uncertain." Another treasure in silver, of 118 pieces, all now securely in the Naples museum, was discovered in 1930 in a nail-studded chest in the strong room under a town house (I.x.4) called the "House of the Menander" after a fresco of the dramatist on the walls.

But it is not only the nabobs, their villas, and their treasures which Pompeii reveals to us. Ancient tradesmen, their lives, work, and tastes, about which literature tells us almost nothing, become more real for us here than anywhere else

in the ancient world except Ostia. In the market facing the
Forum the excavators found fruit in glass containers, and
the skeletons of fish and sheep. There are inns for muleteers
and carters by the city gates, and innumerable wine shops,
the bar open to the street, its top pierced to hold cool
amphorae of wine or covered bronze vessels for hot drinks
(Fig. 8.11). Wine prices are scratched on walls, together
with other *graffiti* of more or less extreme indecency, referring usually to the oldest of the professions. One says,
"I am yours—for two *asses*" (the *as* was a small copper coin
worth, at the time this *graffito* was scribbled, about two-
and-a-half cents). Another, in large letters over a bench
at the Porta Marina, advises loungers to READ THIS SIGN
FIRST, and offers the charms of a Greek prostitute named
Attiké at sixteen *asses*. This sort of thing prompted the
more sober-sided Pompeians to write more than once on
the walls (of the large theater, amphitheater, and basilica)
the couplet, one of the most famous of the hundreds found
at Pompeii:

> "*I wonder, wall, that you do not go smash,*
> *Who have to bear the weight of all this trash!*"

Other *graffiti* complain of unrequited love: "I'd like to bash
Venus' ribs in" (from the basilica), or "Here Vibius lay
alone and longed for his beloved" (perhaps from an inn).
Snatches from the love-poets, Ovid and (strangely) the
tortured, neurotic Propertius, are frequent, and tags of
Vergil remembered from schooldays. *Graffiti* keep a running account of daily purchases of cheese, bread, oil, and
wine; or the number of eggs laid daily by the chickens. A
reward is offered for the recovery of a stolen bronze pitcher.
Income property is advertised for rent, or gentlemen's up-
stairs flats (*cenacula equestria*). A metal worker, doing a
brisk business in chamber pots, has scratched on his wall
a memo of the days fairs are held in nearby towns. He made

surveyors' instruments as well: our only example of a surveyor's plane table (*groma*) comes from his shop. In a bronze-bound chest in the house of a rich freedman banker, Lucius Caecilius Jucundus, were found his complete (and involved) accounts, on 153 wax tablets. His bronze bust, with its shrewd, ugly, kindly face, warts and all (Fig. 8.12), was also found in the house. It reveals the very type of the *nouveaux riches,* not in the least ashamed of being "in trade," who came to be the ruling class in the last days of Pompeii.

The wealth of tradesmen can be judged by the quality of the decoration of their houses, in which they often plied their trade, for the ancient world's slave economy did not foster the factory system. Thus in the house of the jeweler Pinarius Cerialis (III,iv,4), his showcase was found containing fine engraved cornelians, agates, and amethysts, some of the work unfinished, and also the tiny, delicate tools of his trade. In the House of the Surgeon (VI.1,9-10) surgical instruments were found, including probes, catheters, gynaecological forceps, pliers for pulling teeth, and little spoons, perhaps for extracting wax from the ears. These provide our best evidence for ancient surgical techniques.

Stephanus' *fullonica* (laundry: I.vi.7) was found with the imprint of the fallen front door left clearly in the ashes. The padlock was on the outside, from which the inference is that this establishment served as laundry only; if it had been a dwelling, the lock would have been on the inside. A skeleton behind the door had with him a bag of 107 gold and silver coins. Since two-thirds of them had been minted years before, under the Republic, one assumes that this was not merely the day's take, but a hoard; all the shop's moveable capital. Built in at the back were the small vats where the dirty clothes were trodden, to get out the dirt and grease, and the larger ones for rinsing. The upper floor and courtyard were used for drying: in the courtyard wall were found the small putholes for the canes over which the wet

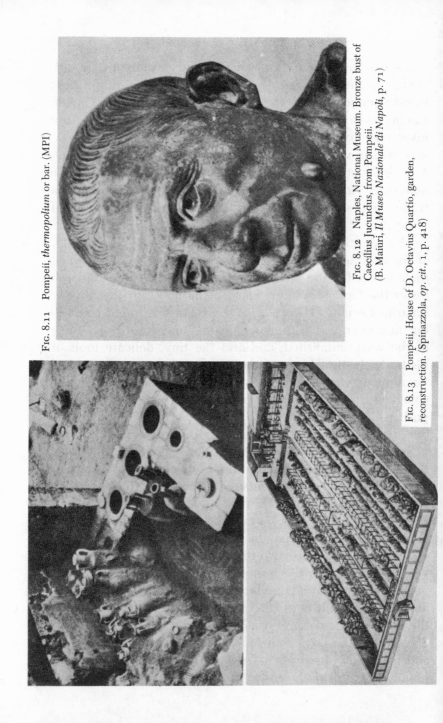

FIG. 8.11 Pompeii, *thermopolium* or bar. (MPI)

FIG. 8.12 Naples, National Museum. Bronze bust of Caecilius Jucundus, from Pompeii. (B. Maiuri, *Il Museo Nazionale di Napoli*, p. 71)

FIG. 8.13 Pompeii, House of D. Octavius Quartio, garden, reconstruction. (Spinazzola, *op. cit.*, 1, p. 418)

clothes were hung. Near the entrance was the clothes press, in which a pressing board was worked down upon the folded clothes by means of a pair of large wooden screws.

Across the street from the laundry a painted shop front shows the operations of a felter's establishment, where wool was matted together with a fixative, under repeated manipulation and pressure, until it acquired a consistent texture, like a piece of cloth. Felt was in demand for caps, cloaks, slippers, and blankets (the latter for both man and horse). The shop sign shows workmen at tables holding the carding comb and knives of their trade. In the middle of the picture other men, naked to the waist, are at work at shallow troughs impregnating the wool with the coagulant (Pliny the Elder says it was vinegar) which is being heated by a stove beneath the troughs. To the right, the proprietor—his name was Verecundus—proudly holds up a red-striped finished sample. To the left, Mercury, the patron of tradesmen, is painted emerging from a Tuscan temple with a money bag in his hand ("Hurrah for profit," says a Pompeian *graffito*). Below is the proprietor's wife at a table, in spirited conversation with a female customer who is trying on slippers. No literary discussion, primary or secondary, can match the vivid concreteness of this archaeological record.

The house (II.v.1-4) of Decimus Octavius Quartio (or Marcus Loreius Tiburtinus—authorities differ about the occupant's name) belonged to a potter, to judge by a small kiln, with the potter's stool and samples of his wares, found in a workroom. This is interesting enough, but more interesting still is this tradesman's taste, as revealed by his house and garden. Hardly a corner of the house is left unfrescoed, and the paintings include two ambitious cycles; nine episodes from the saga of Hercules, and fourteen from the *Iliad*. (The House of the Cryptoporticus [I.vi.2-4] presents twenty-five *Iliad* episodes from an original 86, badly damaged when the last owner, an obvious Babbitt, turned the cryptoporticus into a wine cellar and made over the dining room for public use.) The potter was besides a connoisseur of gardens; his is the most charming that Pompeii can boast. His *impluvium*—for catching rainwater in the *atrium* (courtyard or patio)—is double-walled, for flower-boxes; behind the *atrium* is a formal flower bed, with walks around it on three sides; the chief feature of the sunken back garden (Fig. 8.13), nearly twice the area of the house itself, is a pair of long narrow fish pools, planned perpendicular to each other to form a T, and trellised (Fig. 8.14) so that vines could grow over them. The walls of the pools were painted blue to deepen the color of the water. At one end of the crossbar of the T is the pleasantest *al fresco* dining alcove imaginable. Statuettes embellish the alcove and the sides of the pool. There is a little shrine in the alcove; another, with a fountain, where the two pools meet; still another, with a fountain in front of it, two-thirds of the way along the upright of the T. Putholes in the garden wall show that there were shed roofs there to protect exotic plants and flowers. The plum trees, oaks, shrubs, arbors, and plants with which the garden was filled in orderly rows, with walks between, have been replanted, after identifying them from their roots found in the ashes. Forty-four amphorae were found buried to their necks in a row along one side of the garden. Perhaps they served as flower pots; it is equally possible that they were a wine store, for this potter's house has no wine cellar. In a corner and under the arbors along the walks there were wooden seats and little marble tables, for rustic picnics in the pleached shade. The difference of levels, the fountains, shrines, statues, arbors, trees, and the painted colors, red, gray, green, yellow, and blue, all judiciously restored, make this age-old garden extraordinarily vivacious. Here archaeology has once more given the lie to the hackneyed stereotype of the lifelessness and colorlessness of classical antiquity, and has proved that in landscape-gardening, at any rate, there is something to be said for the *bourgeois* taste of Pompeian tradesmen.

Fig. 8.14 Pompeii, House of D. Octavius Quartio, garden, with trellis and pool. (Spinazzola, *op. cit.*, 1, p. 396)

Some had a taste for music, too, to judge by some frescoes in the small but gracious House of Fabia (I.vi.15). One portrays the mistress of the house with sheet music in her hand. Another shows what appears to be a music lesson, our only example of the lyre being played four hands. Indeed archaeology, by revealing these middlebrows to us in three dimensions, their shops and artifacts, inns and bars, street signs and *graffiti*, loves licit and illicit, tools and equipment, their tastes and pleasures, has given us, especially in Pompeii, a truer picture of the average, ordinary ancient Italian man than Latin literature provides. For Latin literature, with some exceptions like Plautus' plays, tends to be written by highbrows for highbrows. (Yet paradoxically, the best literary picture of an ancient Babbitt, Petronius' Trimalchio, *was* drawn by a highbrow for highbrows.)

Pompeii has enriched, too, our knowledge of the ancient Italian's relation to his gods. The archaeological documents for Pompeian religion include the temples, innumerable household shrines, wayside altars, frescoes, inscriptions, and *graffiti*. Of the ten temples, three, ruined in the earthquake, had not been repaired at the time of the final débacle, seventeen years later. One had reverted to the use of a private association, and two were dedicated to the Imperial cult, to which generally only lip service was paid. One piece of evidence on this is the cynical *graffito* from a farm in nearby Boscotrecase: "Augustus Caesar's mother was only a woman." Of the rest, only the temple of the Egyptian Isis shows real signs of the prosperity that comes from devout support. The truth is that the real god of Pompeii—as of most other cities ancient and modern—was the God of Gain. The state religion, cold and formal, offered little comfort: the warmth and promise came from Oriental religions, of which Isis-worship was one and Christianity another. There is no evidence of Christianity's having penetrated Pompeii by A.D. 79, unless the ominous *graffito*, "SODOMA, GO-

MORA," be taken as a sign. But Pompeii, close to the Italian end of the trade-route from Alexandria, is permeated with things Egyptian, and there is much evidence of enthusiasm for the cult of Isis. The earliest building stones of the temple (VII.vii) belong to the end of the second century B.C., and were thrown down in the earthquake of A.D. 62. But *this* temple was not left derelict: it was immediately reconstructed from the ground up in the name of a six-year-old boy, who was rewarded for his piety by honorary membership in the town council. The cult, with its promise of personal immortality, received rich gifts from its votaries. Its marble lustral basin, for holy water; statues and statuettes, including of course the goddess herself, with her rattle that kept off evil spirits; the striking bronze bust of an actor-donor; lamps; sacrificial knives; the ornamental marble curb of a well; candelabra, and rich frescoes, some with likenesses of white-robed, shaven-headed priests, which decorated the precinct and the walls, are now among the treasures of the National Museum in Naples.

Family cults flourished in Pompeii more than the official religion, to judge by the fact that nearly every house and workshop has its private shrine, usually housing busts of ancestors (for in this the Romans were downright Japanese), and adorned with a picture of a snake, representing the family's Genius, or guardian spirit. Sometimes, as in the House of the Cryptoporticus, there is a handsomely decorated private shrine to one of the Olympian deities, in this case Diana. The trades had their patron saints: Mercury (god also of thieves) for commerce; Minerva, who invented weaving, for the clothmakers; the hearth goddess Vesta for the bakers. The front of the felter's shop described above is emblazoned with a magnificent Venus in a chariot drawn by four elephants. Sex, too, had its enthusiastic worshipers: a dyer's vat (IX.vii.2) bears a relief of an enormous winged phallus, set in a temple whose *acroteria* are also phalluses, of smaller size. But perhaps the perfect symbol of the religion of this tradesmen's town is a fresco in the House of the Cryptoporticus, in which the family of Aeneas (the symbol of Rome) is shown guided to its destiny by Mercury, the god of trade.

Is all this great art? A fair answer to the question should come from an analysis of what is usually regarded as the masterpiece of Pompeian painting, the fresco in Room 5 of the Villa of the Mysteries.

This analysis must be prefaced by a word about the four more or less successive styles into which archaeologists have succeeded in dividing the vast corpus of Pompeian painting. The First (or "incrustation") Style, found in buildings (e.g., at Palestrina) dated by their fabric and technique from 150 to 80 B.C., uses colored stucco to imitate marble dadoes, rusticated blocks, and revetments. The Second (or "architectural") Style (80 B.C.-A.D. 14) imitates architectural forms, uses perspective, and throws the field to be painted open to mythical or religious subjects. The Third (or "Egyptianizing") Style (A.D. 14-62) flattens out painted architectural detail into painted "surrounds" or frames for panels which look like hanging tapestries, worked out with fine detail in a miniaturist's technique. The Fourth (or "ornamental") Style (A.D. 62-79) features infinite vistas, with figures moving amid fantastic architecture. Examples of the last three styles are frequent in the Villa of the Mysteries, but the great sequence from which the Villa takes its name is of the Second Style and Augustus' reign.

In this sequence, against a background of brilliant Pompeian red, are painted, almost life-size, a series of twenty-nine figures subdivided into ten groups. At the left of the door in the northwest corner (as one enters from Room 4) a boy reads what is apparently a ritual from a papyrus roll; a woman, perhaps his mother, points to the words with a stylus. Next is a scene of ritual washing of a myrtle branch;

FIG. 8.15   Pompeii, Villa of the Mysteries, fresco: woman being scourged. (MPI)

one of the servers, in deep décolleté, and with pointed ears, carries the papyrus ritual roll at her waist in a fold of her *stola*. In the next group a fat, blonde-bearded, naked old Silenus plays a lyre, a faun plays his pipe, and his consort gives suck to a goat. Then comes the figure of a woman in motion so violent that her drapery swirls about her as she raises a hand in horror at one of the scenes that follows. But between her and the scene that repels her are three other groups. First, another trio, of a Silenus and two fauns. The Silenus is giving one of the fauns a drink out of a silver bowl; the other faun frightens the drinker with a Silenus mask held so as to be reflected in the surface of the wine. Second, the central scene, in the center of the east wall: a naked god, identified as Bacchus by the thyrsus (the staff tipped with a pine cone) which lies athwart his body, and by the vine leaves in his hair, leans back in the lap of a figure who must be his bride, Ariadne. Third, a kneeling woman unveils an erect purple-draped object, surely the Mystery of Mysteries, a phallus. Beyond her is the scene of horror (Fig. 8.15): a half-naked female figure with huge black wings raises a whip to scourge a woman, surely the candidate for initiation, who cowers, her back bare, her face buried, in the lap of a seated woman who strokes the victim's dishevelled hair to comfort her. Beyond her a naked Bacchante whirls in an orgiastic dance, clicking castanets high in the air above her head. In the last two scenes a woman in bridal yellow, on an elegant ivory stool, does her hair while a Cupid holds a mirror. Another Cupid, with his bow, looks on. And finally, a matron, with her mantle draped over her head like a priestess, sits, leaning on a cushion of purple and gold, on a chair with a footstool, and watches gravely.

This fresco, which clearly portrays a Dionysiac ritual, and connects it with marriage and fertility, has undeniable power. It packs into a confined space—it is less than sixty feet long, on three sides of a room measuring only 16 x 23 feet—movement, rest, fear, horror, magic, abandon, and orgy. It illustrates better than anything else from Pompeii how the Augustan age assimilated Hellenistic Greek art into an Italian idiom. Yet somehow the final impression, here and in lesser examples of Pompeian painting, is that the artist is working from a memory of great paintings seen in collections or museums, from a repertory, or from sketch books of famous works of art. His work is well above the inn-sign or wallpaper level, he is competent and sophisticated; no hack, but no genius either. And so, with all respect for the natural enthusiasm of the excavator, the question with which this section began must be answered in the negative. This is not great art, but it is the next thing to it, and no modern *bourgeoisie* since the sixteenth-century Dutch has had the taste to fill its houses with such able work. But we must conclude that the great value of Pompeian art is in documentation, of the practical taste of ordinary people.

Maximilian, later to be Emperor of Mexico, when he visited Pompeii in 1851, found it terrible, its rooms like painted corpses. Since then, modern archaeological methods (scientific, not miraculous) have brought the corpses to life. What archaeology has presented to us here, as at its best it always does, is not things but people, at work and play, in house and workshop, worshiping and blaspheming, and after their fashion patronizing the arts. So vividly does archaeology reveal them that we are moved to say with Francis Bacon, "*These* are the ancient times, when the world is ancient, and not those which we account ancient, by a computation backwards from ourselves."

As the rain of ashes was covering Pompeii, and the river of lava engulfing Herculaneum, life in Rome, that Eternal City, went on. It was the age of the Flavians. Vespasian, the *bourgeois* founder of the dynasty, died just a month before Pompeii was buried. He and his sons, the good Titus and the wicked Domitian, enriched Rome with splendid art and architecture.

9

Flavian Rome

Two *fora*, an amphitheater, an arch, a sculptured relief,
a palace, a stadium: these may stand as typical of archaeology's contributions to our knowledge of the Flavian age. As
in the Julio-Claudian dynasty, the buildings and the sculpture epitomize the atmosphere of the time, the last three
decades of the first century A.D. After the excesses of Nero
and the bloodbath of A.D. 69—a year of civil war which saw
three Emperors in succession, Galba, Otho, and Vitellius,
raised to the purple and then murdered—the Roman people
wanted "normalcy." Under Vespasian and Titus they got
it; under Domitian the pendulum swung again—and so did
the headsman's ax.

Flavian architecture and art sum up, too, the personalities
of the Emperors. The bluff, no-nonsense Vespasian, the
Emperor of reconstruction, symbolized, in his majestic Forum
of Peace, what one of his staff called the "immense majesty"
of the peace he had brought to a war-torn world, and
Vespasian gave credit, in the frieze of the *Forum Transitorium*, to the artisan class which was his ardent supporter.
Again, true to his *bourgeois* origins, he built for the people,
over the pool of Nero's Golden House, the great amphitheater which posterity was to call the Coliseum. Titus

summed up the great moment of his short life when he immortalized his capture of Jerusalem on his arch at the top of the old Forum. Domitian, would-be *triumphator*, would-be rival of his great predecessors, exalted, in the reliefs recently found under the Cancelleria palace in Rome, the military prowess of the dynasty which in his view culminated in himself. He took over Vespasian's *Forum Transitorium*, to thrust himself into a class with Augustus and his own

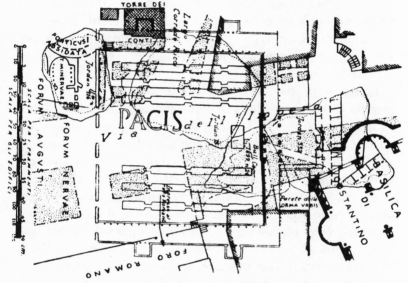

FIG. 9.1 Rome, Forum of Peace, Colini and Gatti reconstruction from *Forma Urbis*. (G. Lugli, *Roma antica*, Pl. 6)

father; reared on the Palatine a palace to outdo the Golden House; and, with philhellenism genuine or affected, built in the Campus Martius a stadium for footraces in the Greek fashion.

Since very little of Vespasian's Forum of Peace remains above ground, recourse for information about it must be had in the first instance to literature. Pliny the Elder, who was on Vespasian's staff, described it as one of the most beautiful squares in the world, embellished as it was with trophies of war, including the famous seven-branched gold candle-stick from the temple in Jerusalem, carved in relief on the Arch of Titus.

A fragment of the previously mentioned Marble Plan of Rome, the *Forma Urbis*, inscribed with the letters CIS (Fig. 9.1), is easily restored to something like [Forum Pa] CIS, Forum of Peace. It shows a portico, on one side walled, on the other colonnaded, the colonnade approached by steps. An open space is incised with a series of three long indented strips, apparently representing formal garden-plots. The fragment also shows one right angle of a structure which should be an altar.

Faced with the thousand pieces of the Marble Plan, archaeologists play the fascinating game of making joins, as in a jigsaw puzzle. In 1899 Lanciani announced the dis-covery of a new fragment which joined with the piece of the Marble Plan already mentioned. It filled out the rec-tangular shape of the altar, added two more rows of garden-plots, and supplied another side to the portico, at right angles to the other. This side had two rows of columns, four of which were represented as of larger dimensions than the others, and as standing on plinths or square bases. These two fragments made possible restoration, on paper, of a considerable part of the Forum's plan. Given the Roman architectural principle of axial symmetry, Lanciani could be sure that the altar belonged in the middle of one side of the portico-surrounded space, towards the back. He could restore two more column-bases; and, knowing that there must have been three rows of garden-plots on either side of the altar, and that the scale of the Marble Plan was 1:200, he could arrive at the original length of one inner side of the portico—about 325 feet. But there paper hypothesis had to rest, awaiting excavation.

The opportunity did not arise until 1934, in connection with systematizing and beautifying with lawns the borders

Fig. 9.2   Rome, *Forum Transitorium, Colonnacce* before excavation.   Fig. 9.3   Rome, *Forum Transitorium, Colonnacce* after excavation. (M. Scherer, *Marvels of Ancient Rome*, Pls. 162 and 165)

of Mussolini's grandiose new Via dell' Impero, already men-
tioned as having been cut through slums from the Coliseum
to the Piazza Venezia. The two projecting columns of the
Forum Transitorium ("Forum of Nerva"), southeast of the
Forum of Augustus, were cleared, under the direction of
A. M. Colini, of medieval and modern detritus down to their
plinths (Figs. 9.2 and 9.3); the podium of the Temple of
Minerva, at the end of this Forum, uncovered; and the

FIG. 9.4 Rome, Imperial Fora, model. (F. Castagnoli, *Roma antica*, Pl. 4)

peperino wall behind the projecting columns isolated. Close
in back of this wall, on the Forum of Peace side, Colini found
large columns in African marble, which, he inferred, marked
the missing northwest side of that Forum. Its general location had been known since 1818, but only now was there a
precise point in modern Rome's subsoil from which, with
the help of the Marble Plan, the true dimensions of Vespasian's portico could be measured. Also, another fragment
of the Marble Plan, not joining the two previously mentioned, showed the very stretch of wall and the columns

which Colini had been excavating, as well as the plan of
Minerva's temple, whose podium he had uncovered.

Now that the plan of Vespasian's Forum could be precisely fitted into the plan of modern Rome, it became clear
that some fragments of large fluted white marble columns,
found in the southeastern part of this area as long ago as
1875, belonged to the part of the portico where the larger
columns shown on the Marble Plan would fall. Colini now
made another join on the Marble Plan, adding to Lanciani's
fragment another piece, previously known but not connected,
which showed the Temple of Peace at the back of the portico.
It was an apsidal building, wider than it was deep, with
a pedestal for the cult statue indicated in the apse. If it
survived today it would come within a few feet of touching
the north corner of the Basilica of Maxentius. The south
side of the rectangular hall to the right of it coincides with
the actual wall of the church of Sts. Cosmas and Damian,
which was the findspot—in 1562—of the fragments of the
Marble Plan itself. This square hall was one of the libraries
of Vespasian's Forum. Since the principle of axial symmetry
nearly always operates, justifying the hypothesis that what
appears on one side of the axis of a Roman plan will have a
twin on the other; and since the Romans usually built their
libraries in pairs (one Latin, one Greek), Colini quite
reasonably restored on paper another rectangular hall to
the left of the apsidal temple. A section of the polychrome
marble pavement, excavated by Colini east of the church
wall, was less than an inch thick, too thin to be exposed to
the weather. Colini inferred that it must have been part
of the flooring of the library in which the Marble Plan was
displayed.

An ingenious combination—"joins" recognized on the
Marble Plan, actual excavation, and inference—had now
made the Forum's general outline clear, but Colini was not
yet done. Overlying the Forum's outer (northeast) perimeter wall, as he had plotted it, rose the medieval Torre dei

Conti, built by the brother of Pope Innocent III. Re-examining beneath this tower the ancient remains, in squared travertine, ordinary tufa, and *peperino*, Colini was able to establish that they formed part of Vespasian's Forum, a great ornamental rectangular niche on its northeast side, with two columns of African marble in front of it. Symmetry would dictate another matching niche further to the southeast in the same wall, and a pair on the opposite side to correspond. Pink granite columns found in the excavations belonged to the portico; marble gutters proved that it had a pitched roof. Finally, in 1938, the plan was complete enough for a model of the Forum to be made (Fig. 9.4) for Mussolini's Mostra Augustea della Romanità, a great exhibition of models and photographs of Roman architecture and engineering, casts of inscriptions, and replicas of artifacts.

But Vespasian's Forum, famous as it was, and valuable as its restored plan is to illustrate archaeological inference at work, is overshadowed by his mightiest monument, which has survived to become the very symbol of pagan Rome to modern times: the Flavian Amphitheater or Coliseum. More perhaps than any other classical monument, its stones are steeped in blood and memories; in the blood of gladiators and wild beasts, and perhaps of Christian martyrs, in memories of medieval battles, Renaissance plundering of stone (much of the travertine in St. Peter's came from it), and Victorian moonlight visits. Having resisted earthquakes, fire, and demolition, it is now menaced by the vibrations of modern traffic. Work on strengthening its walls against this new threat has been going on since 1956.

For sheer mass the Coliseum deserves its name. It is a third of a mile around, and the Italian engineer G. Cozzo has calculated that 45,000 cubic meters of travertine went into its outside wall, over twice as much into the whole structure. But the achievement here is not mere massiveness, but precise engineering, careful calculations of stresses and strains, avoidance of crowding at entrances and exits, perfect visibility, ingenuity in the arrangements for getting the wild beasts into the arena. (Perhaps this is the place to recall that it was upon the Coliseum that Charles Follen McKim based his design for the Harvard Stadium.) The site chosen, the bed of the pool of Nero's Golden House, was good propaganda and good engineering. Propaganda-wise, it made for good public relations to turn a detested Emperor's pleasure grounds into a place for public enjoyment. (Neither Vespasian nor the Roman mob would have thought of the slaughter of men and beasts as anything but enjoyable; their attitude at best was that of Hemingway to a bullfight.) From the engineering point of view, it saved much costly excavation to pump out the pool and use it for the substructure of the arena, and in the low, soft ground, footings could go deep: eight feet of concrete under the *cavea*. Besides, the huge mass of debris from the demolished Golden House could be cannily reused in the new fabric. The first step was to erect a skeleton of travertine piers, a double row, built of squared blocks held together not with mortar but with metal clamps. The holes where these clamps were wrenched out, 300 metric tons of them, in the metal-starved Middle Ages, are visible today throughout the fabric. Differences in construction suggest that the huge project was divided into four quadrants, each assigned to a different contractor. Most of the work is honest, so that, for example, one cannot get the proverbial penknife blade into the joints between the blocks of the piers, but in the northwest quadrant the work is shoddy. This is precisely the section that has given the most trouble under the strain of the traffic vibrations of modern times.

Inside the second concentric ellipse of piers begins a set of radial walls which supported the seats. The slope of the seats was perfectly calculated for perfect visibility. The vaults of the lower levels were left open until the upper level piers were finished. This made possible the use of derricks to lift heavy blocks to the upper levels. The third-story piers have one course of blocks projecting, to provide a step to support the scaffolding required for building the wall on the fourth level. This wall is built of smaller blocks than those used on the lower levels, to facilitate lifting, and it is full of second-hand materials; column drums, for example, which may have come from the Golden House. The outer face of the fourth-level wall is equipped with 240 consoles, projecting brackets jutting out from the wall to support masts. Corresponding to each in the cornice above is a hole for the mast. The mast, Cozzo argues persuasively, was fitted with rope and pulley. The rope descended obliquely and was fastened to another below which ran elliptically at a convenient height above the podium of the arena. Awnings, fixed to these ropes, could be rolled up or down in strips as the sun's position dictated. Awnings being made of canvas, this duty was assigned to detachments of sailors —the logical Roman administrative mind at work.

When the skeleton was finished, the space between the piers in the radial walls was filled in, on the ground level with tufa, on the second level with lighter materials, brick and cement. Only then were the vaults completed. The stairs were ingeniously planned to give access from the ground direct to each level separately. This both emphasized distinctions (VIPs in the lowest tier, women at the top; compare the separate second-balcony stairs in modern theaters) and facilitated entrance and exit. Each outside entrance—there were originally eighty—bears a Roman numeral. This corresponded to a number on the admission ticket, and divided the 45,000 or 50,000 spectators into manageable groups.

The arena proper was surrounded by a wall, high enough to protect the spectators from the beasts (VIPs not being regarded as expendable), but not so high as to block the view of the arena from the seats behind. Slots in the top of this wall are the postholes for a dismountable fence which supplied additional protection. Literary sources say it was of gilt metal surmounted by elephants' tusks. In front of the fence ran a catwalk where archers were stationed to shoot beasts which got out of hand.

The arena was originally floored with wooden planking, removable for the mock naval battles which were staged here in the early years of the amphitheater's existence. Since this had been the site of Nero's artificial pool, flooding must have been comparatively easy. But though slaves fought and killed each other in these naval battles, they were less sanguinary, and therefore less popular, than gladiatorial contests or beast fights, and changing back and forth from murder on water to murder on land was a nuisance, so the naval battles were transferred elsewhere. The area below the arena floor was then filled in with complicated substructures, which finally revealed their secret to Cozzo in 1928.

The area under the catwalk in each quadrant contains eight cell-like rooms (A in Fig. 9.5), each big enough to hold a man, and approached by a short corridor. Opening out of each corridor, forward and to the left of a man sitting in the cell, are three adjoining shafts, a small square one (a), a large rectangular one (b), and another square one (c) of medium size. How are these to be explained? Cozzo reasoned that a beast was released from his cage near the center of the substructure, into the corridor (1) shown in Fig. 9.6, with a portcullis (a) at the end of it. The portcullis was raised, and the beast charged into the transverse corridor (2). This was too narrow for him to turn back; he was therefore forced to go forward into the open elevator-cage (3). The attendant in the cell (A in the previous figure) then released a counterweight, whose rope ran in shaft (a) of Fig. 9.5, while the weight itself rose and fell in shaft (c); the elevator-shaft is (b). The

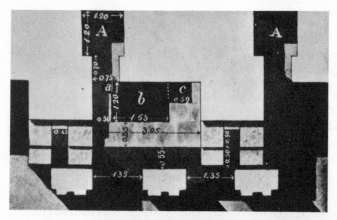

Fig. 9.6
Rome, Coliseum,
beast elevator,
elevation.
(Cozzo, *op. cit.*, Fig. 175)

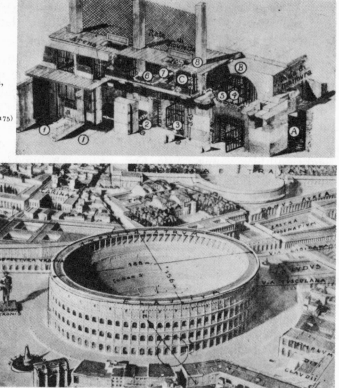

FIG. 9.7   Rome, Coliseum, model, showing colossal statue of Nero (left center),
Arch of Constantine (bottom left), and gladiators' barracks (right center).
(P. Bigot, *Rome Antique*, fac. p. 44)

elevator door then closed; the elevator rose, activated by the counterweight, to position (4) in Fig. 9.6. The beast emerged into the narrow upper-level corridor (5-6), raced up the ramp (7), and emerged, slavering for fresh meat, through the trapdoor (8) into the arena.

This is not the only ingenious device in the Coliseum. The substructure piers along the arena's long axis are cut obliquely. Why? Cozzo reasoned that on them rested, at an angle below the horizontal, hinged sections of the area flooring, on which stage sets could be placed, and the whole section of flooring raised by counterweights to the arena level, to provide appropriate backdrops or scenery for the fights. Against such backdrops, scenes from myth or history were acted out, the protagonists tortured to death before delighted spectators. We hear of 11,000 beasts, and 5,000 pairs of gladiators, fighting to the death in one session in the arena. In 1937, demolition of houses east of the Coliseum revealed the ground plan of part of the gladiators' barracks, with armory, infirmary, baths, and, for training bouts, a miniature amphitheater, with seats for rabid fans (Fig. 9.7). To celebrate the millennium of Rome, in A.D. 248, elephants, elk, tigers, lions, leopards, hyenas, hippopotamuses, a rhinoceros, zebras, giraffes, wild asses, and wild horses (captured in Africa; see Fig. 13.5) were slaughtered in the Coliseum. This market of flesh did not cease till the sixth Christian century.

Vespasian did not live to see the Coliseum completed. It was dedicated, still unfinished, under Titus in A.D. 80. The chief surviving monument of Titus' reign is his arch, commemorating his conquest of the Jews in A.D. 70, but, since the inscription upon it refers to him as deified, it is clear that the arch was not finished until after his death. Built of valuable Pentelic marble, it would never have been preserved if it had not been incorporated, in the Middle Ages, into a fortress of the powerful family of the Frangipani. The last vestiges of the Frangipani tower were not removed from the arch until 1821. It was then reinforced and its missing portions restored in travertine. It is chiefly famous for the relief on its inner jamb showing (Fig. 9.8) Titus' army carrying in triumph the spoils of Jerusalem, including the table of the shewbread, the seven-branched candlestick, and the silver trumpets. In the relief opposite, Titus stands in a four-horse chariot, with the goddess Roma leading the horses, and Victory crowning him with a laurel wreath. The frieze under the cornice, not unrelated to the small inner altar frieze of the Altar of Peace, portrays a procession of priests, sacrificial animals, and troops carrying on their shoulders small platforms bearing representations of cities and places conquered by Roman arms, including a personification of the River Jordan. The motif in the highest part of the inner vault, showing Titus—who was a burly man—carried off to heaven by an eagle, is as conventional as the Ganymede in the vault of the underground basilica at the Porta Maggiore. In the years since Augustus, Roman official art had become conventional without ceasing to be historical.

To the good Titus succeeded the wicked, psychopathic, tyrannical Domitian, the greatest builder-Emperor since Augustus, and one under whom the Empire took a long stride on the road to absolutism. One evidence of Domitian's self-aggrandizement turned up unexpectedly in 1937, under the Palazzo della Cancelleria in the Campus Martius, seat of the papal chancellery, and an enclave of Vatican City. Curiously, the palace already had an intimate connection with the Flavians: many of the stones in its fabric were robbed in the late fifteenth and early sixteenth century from the Coliseum. In connection with extensive repairs to the building, deep excavations beneath it revealed the tomb

FIG. 9.8 Rome, Arch of Titus, showing relief with spoils of Temple at Jerusalem. (Fototeca)

FIG. 9.9 (*top and bottom*)   Vatican City. Cancelleria reliefs. (Musei Vatican)

of the consul Aulus Hirtius, a lieutenant of Julius Caesar's, who died in office, and in battle against Mark Antony, in 43 B.C. Leaning face inwards against this tomb were five slabs which proved to be part of a marble historical relief. A sixth slab was found later nearby, still within papal jurisdiction; a seventh, found under the sidewalk, technically outside the Pope's control, was first claimed by the Roman civil authorities, but a trade was made for the slab of the Altar of Peace then in Vatican hands, and all the slabs are now reunited in a courtyard of the Vatican Museum.

The seven slabs combine into two sections of some sixteen figures each, almost complete (Fig. 9.9). The more fragmentary of the two contains near its right end an instantly identifiable figure, with the characteristic beaked profile of Vespasian (Fig. 9.10). He is greeting a young man, surely one of his sons. Comparison with known portraits of Titus and Domitian leads to the conclusion that it is the latter who is represented here. The greeting is taking place in the presence of lictors, Vestals (identified from their characteristic headdress), *apparitores* or beadles (at either end), a helmeted female figure (the goddess Roma or, according

FIG. 9.10   Vatican City. Cancelleria reliefs. Detail of head of Vespasian. (Musei Vaticani)

to others, the war-goddess Bellona, or the personification of martial courage), and two male figures, one bearded (the Genius of the Senate), and one beardless, with a cornucopia (the Genius of the Roman People). The other section is at once more complete, more difficult to interpret, and more interesting. Several of the conventional figures recur: the lictors, Roma, the two *Genii*. There are also six soldiers (in the uniform and with the arms of the praetorian guard); the wing of a Victory; a helmeted female wearing the *aegis*, the characteristic breastplate of Minerva; the helmeted, bearded male figure beside her must be another divinity, Mars. The remaining figure, the first on the second slab from the left (see Fig. 9.11), is rendered in profile, and is clearly intended as a portrait, but close examination, by Dr. F.

FIG. 9.11   Vatican City. Cancelleria reliefs. Detail showing how head of Domitian was transformed into that of Nerva. (Musei Vaticani)

Magi, Director of the Vatican Museums, shows that it was reworked in antiquity.

Here archaeological ingenuity again goes to work. The two sections of the total relief obviously (from the similar technique and the recurrence of conventional figures in both) belong together. The presence of Vespasian places both sections in the Flavian age. Of the three Flavians, only Domitian was sufficiently hated to have had *damnatio memoriae* practiced upon him, to alter his portrait into another's. And the most conspicuous alteration of the head consists in hacking off a fringe of curls on the forehead; such a fringe was Domitian's characteristic hair-style. It remains to inquire whose the new profile is. In the context, it must be an Emperor. The most likely candidate is Domitian's successor, Nerva, the first of the "five good Emperors." The new profile, with its irregular nose, lined forehead, and sunken cheeks, suits the known iconography of that tired old man. Left with the question why, then, the portrait of Domitian on the other section of the relief was left undamaged, Magi argued that the Senate, on second thought, had considered the alteration into Nerva not enough: the relief was dismantled altogether, and its slabs carefully stacked against Hirtius' tomb for the future use of one of the stonecutters whose yards are known to have been numerous in the area.

Two questions remain: the occasion for carving the relief in the first place, and the building that housed it. The occasion for greeting Vespasian must be the most memorable one of his reign: his triumphant return from Jerusalem in A.D. 70. The occasion for greeting Domitian must be an equally memorable one, almost certainly his setting out on a campaign, or his return from a military victory (because of the prominence of the winged figure and the Mars on the relief). Domitian's military successes were not many; the likeliest is his campaign of A.D. 83 against a German tribe, the Chatti. If carving the monument would take a year, as competent sculptors report, the earliest possible date for the finished relief would be A.D. 84; on grounds of style one authority, Miss Jocelyn M. Toynbee, would date it eight or nine years later. To celebrate the same victory, Domitian built the Temple of Fortuna Redux (Good Luck and Safe Return), and this temple, Magi thinks, is a reasonable place to suppose the reliefs to have been displayed. In them the whole Roman state is portrayed as asking of the founder of the Flavian dynasty and of his son the peace and prosperity which the Julio-Claudians had failed to give. Like the fresco of the Villa of the Mysteries at Pompeii, the relief is not great art but a great document, a measure of the distance Roman sculpture had travelled in the scant century since the Altar of Peace. It is a courtier's exaltation of a monarch; a solemn, highly rhetorical affirmation of Imperial sovereignty and pride in Rome's dominion. And perhaps there is a moral in it, too: it summarizes the history of the dynasty, from the triumphant reception of the first Flavian to the explosion of hate which damned the memory, by altering the face, of the last. And these slabs, the expression of a despot's pride, end leaning against the simple tomb of a lieutenant of Julius Caesar who died fighting, he would have said, to save for his fatherland its free institutions.

In A.D. 86 Domitian set about continuing the work begun by Vespasian on the narrow Forum between the Forum of Peace and that of Augustus, which we have had occasion to mention earlier. (The final dedication was not to occur until Nerva's reign.) In effect this Forum was an ingenious device to monumentalize the street which led from the old Republican Forum to the unsavory Subura district and workers' quarter to the north. Caesar's Forum was Venus' precinct; Augustus' belonged to Mars. A convention had been established, a canonical way of doing things: hence

Vespasian dedicated his larger Forum to Peace, the *Forum Transitorium* to Minerva. Domitian, his devotion to Minerva already established by his having given her prominence on the Cancelleria relief, now remodelled Vespasian's temple to her, raising it on a high podium. The podium alone remains, with its relieving arch marking where the Cloaca Maxima or great sewer passed below. But the original monumentalizing of the street by Vespasian had involved building a colonnade, of a type common in the frescoes of the Pompeian Third and Fourth Styles. Along its architrave, which was richly decorated on its under side, ran a continuous frieze whose technique resembles that of the Cancelleria relief on a small scale, for the art of the Flavian reigns is recognizably related. The dentils in the cornice show between them the characteristic "spectacles-signature" of the architect Rabirius, who may have worked for Vespasian as well as for Domitian.

The surviving section of the frieze portrays Minerva among the nine Muses, and the punishment of Arachne, who for presuming to rival Minerva's skill at weaving was turned into a spider. The sculptor took the occasion to carve artisans (the figure of a fuller survives) and household scenes, of spinning, weaving, and dyeing, all under Minerva's special patronage. One sees the wool basket, the upright loom, the scales for weighing the day's stint, the proud display of a finished roll of cloth. In the attic above the surviving section of the frieze stands the goddess in relief, wearing the characteristic cloak of a Roman general!

Recent excavation has added little to earlier knowledge of this Forum, but it is of absorbing interest for what it adds to our portrait of the Flavians. Domitian takes over his father's plan, and pushingly insinuates himself, as it were, between his father and the Empire's founder, both of whom he envied and tried to emulate. But it was beyond even his effrontery to associate himself with the Minerva who was patroness of artisans; nothing could be more incongruous than his connecting his elegant dilettantism with the homely arts of the household. The frieze is probably a part of Vespasian's plan: its theme suits his plain personality, and the references to handicrafts suit its location on a street leading to a worker's quarter. The support of the workers (and of their wives, whose influence was all the more important to win because it was indirect) was worth having, and meanwhile Minerva's connection with the Muses (the creative arts and literature) could be turned by Domitian to his purpose: he desired to be known as a patron of the arts.

The showiest surviving result of Domitian's patronage of the art of architecture is his palace on the Palatine, planned by the famous Rabirius, and finished perhaps in A.D. 92. Here is a return, after the comparative austerity of his father's and brother's reigns, to the baroque extravagance of Nero. Since no final publication of this important complex has ever appeared, the best archaeology can do is to comment on the palace as reflecting Domitian's personality, as indebted to earlier, and seminal of later Roman architecture. Its throne room (21B on the plan, Fig. 9.12), with its colossal niches for statues, was built for an Emperor with delusions of divinity. The dining room (H) had a dais to elevate the god-Emperor above his guests, but the peristyle (D), originally faced with marbles polished like mirrors (to reflect possible assassins), was planned by a terrified mortal who feared stabs in the back. (Blocks from the peristyle cornice show, as in the *Forum Transitorium*, Rabirius' "spectacles-signature.") The restless inward and outward curves of the rooms at 21E in the west block (the public part) of the palace, and at 23C and D in the eastern private quarters, were made possible by the flexibility of poured concrete, which, as we saw in Chapter V, makes it possible to enclose space in any shape (see reconstruction, Fig. 9.13).

Fig. 9.12   Rome, Palatine, Palace of Domitian, plan. (G. Lugli, *Roma antica*, Pl. 8

Fig. 9.13   Rome, Palatine, Palace of Domitian, reconstruction. →
(F. Castagnoli, *Roma antica*, Pl. 44.1)

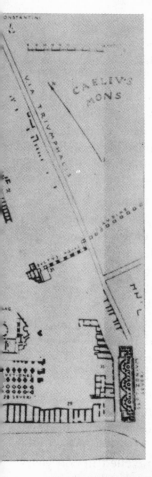

This fluidity appealed to Hadrian, the most gifted amateur architect among the Emperors, and he imitated it, as we shall see, in his Villa near Tivoli.

The *impluvium* (pool for rain-water) in the peristyle (23B) of the private quarters contained a fountain, and is curiously treated with cut-out segments of circles, with cuttings in its top face for setting statues. This combination of plays of water and works of art is in the taste of the Sperlonga villa of Tiberius: ancient sources find a parallel between that monarch's suspicious, tyrannical nature and Domitian's. The small temple in the upper peristyle (24E), connected with the "mainland" by a curious seven-arched bridge, was built, to judge by its materials and technique, two centuries later than Domitian. But his is the "stadium" (26). Its portico makes it unlikely that it was ever a track for running races in the Greek style; he was to build such a stadium full-scale in the Campus Martius in A.D. 93. The Palatine stadium, in spite of its apsidal Imperial spectator's box (the model for Bramante's Vatican Belvedere), was probably a garden for shady strolling. Perhaps Hadrian had this plan in mind when he built the so-called "Painted Porch" or "Poecile" of his villa, to which we shall return. It is hard to realize that all this splendor lies only 100 yards from the site of "Romulus'" straw hut. The difference measures the distance Roman culture had travelled in 800 years.

Nowadays, one can sit under the umbrella pines of a summer evening and hear symphony concerts played in Domitian's stadium-garden. On such occasions it may seem less of a pity that the Palatine is incompletely excavated. Here, on this hill of dreams, as Miss Scherer calls it, one can imagine Domitian's palace rich with many-colored marbles, bright with paintings and gold. One can wander in the dappled light among oleander and orange-trees, golden broom and scarlet poppies, and admire how the mellow brick glows rose-colored in the afternoon sunlight. One can appreciate the mood of the Romantics for whom, a century and a half ago, all Rome had this dream-like quality. One can argue that their attitude may not have been scientific, but it produced the classical revival in architecture. Here is the old dilemma, but its horns are properly labelled not art and science, but sentiment and intelligence. If we want truly to understand ancient Rome, the choice is clear. Sentiment is not a Roman quality; intelligence is. The atmosphere of Domitian's reign was not dream but nightmare. The natural beauty of the Palatine is attractive but adventitious; the essence of the place is of another kind, starker, grander, more disciplined, than a nineteenth-century water color, and behind it looms always the shadow of violence.

Not violence but intelligence, and the affectation of Hellenism, lies behind Domitian's stadium (for Greek games) and odeum, or music hall (for literary and musical competitions) in the Campus Martius. The shape of the stadium has been preserved almost intact in the loveliest of Rome's squares, the Piazza Navona (Fig. 9.14). In 1936 the driving of a great new street, the Corso del Rinascimento, north and south through the Campus Martius, as a part of Mussolini's ambitious new city plan, gave an opportunity for definitive examination of the stadium's remains, preserved in the cellars of shops and the crypts of churches. This Colini undertook, and emerged from his mole-like labors with a plan (Fig. 9.15) and a model (Fig. 9.16) of the stadium, a prime example of what archaeology can do with bits and pieces. Nowadays remains of the hemicycle are visible under an insurance building outside the north end of the *piazza*, and one travertine pier is to be seen under the arcade of the Corsia Agonale, in the middle of the stadium's east side. Beneath this area are traces of the footings, of cement poured in caissons, thicker and stronger the farther east they go, to support the increasing weight of the rising tiers of seats above. Brick stamps found here date the building to A.D. 93 or a little after, with evidence of major repairs under Hadrian—another Greek lover—and Caracalla—another violent despot.

Colini found that Domitian's architect, to compensate for

FIG. 9.14   Rome, Piazza Navona, air view.
(A. M. Colini, *Stadium Domitiani*, frontispiece)

providing here only one *ambulacrum* or vaulted corridor for sauntering, where the Coliseum had two, widened his corridor at regular intervals between the stairs to provide halls where spectators—the stadium had seats for 30,000— might congregate between footraces. The stadium was built in a repeated sequence: stair, entrance, hall, entrance, stair,

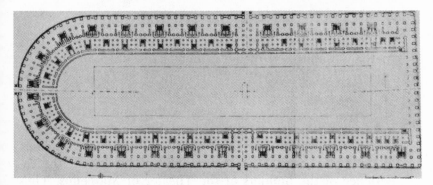

FIG. 9.15   Rome, Stadium of Domitian. (Colini, *op. cit.*, Suppl. Pl. B)

FIG. 9.16   Rome, Stadium of Domitian, Gismondi model.   (Colini, *op. cit.*, Pl. 16)

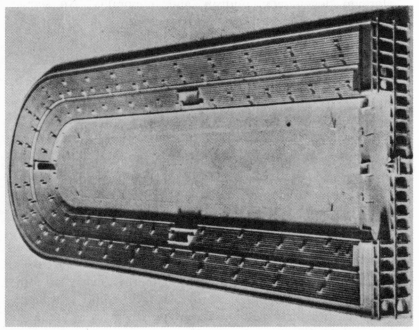

which gives classical orderliness and efficiency to the plan
(perhaps Rabirius'). In the center of the west side was the
Imperial box: the crypt of the church of Sant' Agnese marks
its substructure. Here, according to legend, the good saint
suffered martyrdom, condemned by the Emperor Diocletian
to the brothels that flourished in the stadium arcades. The
whole building profited by the experience of the builders
of the Coliseum, as they in turn had profited from the experience of the builders of the Theater of Marcellus. Thus
its exterior was adorned with engaged columns, Doric on the
first level, Corinthian on the second. But the total effect
was deliberately different, graceful where the Coliseum was
massive, dedicated to Greek footraces instead of Roman
blood-sports. The only thing of its kind outside the Greek
world, the stadium was a deliberate flouting of Roman tradition. This was in Domitian's manner. The Roman people
rejected it, in theirs. To them, Greek footraces represented
foreign degeneracy, nudism, and immorality. No sooner
was the tyrant murdered (in a courtier's plot sparked by
his wife) than they went back to their simple pleasures of
watching the murder of gladiators and wild beasts. Domitian's odeum, traces of which were found south of the stadium in 1936-37, did not suffer the same fate, for it could
be used for pantomime (see Fig. 13.1) and other degraded
forms of dramatic art.

Here then, is a part, a small part, of what archaeology
can tell us of the prodigious Flavian activity in architecture
and in art. It will be noticed that, not for the first or the
last time in Roman history, the greatest tyrant is also the
greatest builder. (He is also Rome's last great Emperor who
did not come from the provinces.) Absolutism was the price
Rome paid for its grandeur. But, in the century after Domitian's murder, absolutism marked time. Nerva's successor,
the Spaniard Trajan, is the second of the "five good Emperors," under whom the metropolis and its port prospered,
and the provinces lived content.

10

Trajan: Port, Forum, Market, Column

Archaeologically speaking, the most important sites in Italy to illustrate Roman events and the Roman way of life in the happy reign (A.D. 98-117) of Trajan—called *Optimus Princeps*, "best of princes"—are the port of Ostia, which in his time reached its apogee, and his Forum, the last and grandest of the Imperial Fora.

Our present knowledge of Ostia, extending far beyond the early *castrum* discussed in Chapter IV, is due in large part to the devoted skill of Guido Calza. Under some pressure from Mussolini, who wanted the dig finished for an exposition scheduled for 1942 (but never inaugurated), he supervised the removal in four years of over 600,000 cubic yards of earth, recovering some seventy of the 170 acres enclosed within Ostia's Sullan wall. What he uncovered he rejuvenated but did not falsify: his method was much the same as Spinazzola's in Pompeii. This was his principle: "Better to brace than repair, better repair than restore, better restore than embellish; never add or subtract." His aim was not to suppress inconvenient ugliness, but to remove impediments to study and understanding. He restored mosaics, making a clear distinction between the old *tesserae* and the new; re-erected columns, put balconies back in place, rebuilt wooden ceilings to protect houses from the weather. He detached wall-paintings, reinforced them with cement and wire mesh, and replaced them, covered with glass, and protected against mold by the insertion of lead plates into the wall below the painting, to retard the spread, by capillary action, of dampness. He sealed the tops of walls, freed flights of stairs from rubble, opened out windows which had been bricked up in late antiquity. He planted trees, and set a privet hedge to mark the line of the city wall. He restored the ancient drainage-system. The result of all this careful work was to present to the modern world a picture of Roman life under the Empire only a shade less vivid than Pompeii. And the picture is not of a provincial town, but of the very vestibule of Rome itself, in fact a Rome in miniature, for Ostia gives an excellent notion of what life in the metropolis was like at the height of the Empire. And thanks to the careful work on the brick stamps by Professor Herbert Bloch of Harvard, most of the buildings excavated can be dated with a very fair degree of precision, so that Ostia's development can be accurately traced from end to end.

We know from an inscription that Trajan's artificial harbor, whose completion marked the beginning of Ostia's peak of prosperity, was built in A.D. 104. Ostia proper was at the very mouth of the Tiber, but silting, which today has put the beach of modern Ostia (Ostia Lido) three miles beyond the seawall of the ancient town, early made the city docks impracticable for any but the smallest vessels, so that Trajan built his harbor beside (indeed over the necropolis of) Claudius', two-and-a-half miles northwest of the town. The traffic in grain and luxury goods to feed and pander to the more or less refined tastes of the largest and richest city in the world made Ostia vastly prosperous. The evidence is building activity, dated by brick stamps, impressed on building tiles, and bearing the names of consuls, tile manufacturers, or both. There was a slight time-lag, while prosperity built up. Only twelve per cent of the datable buildings in Ostia belong to Trajan's reign; forty-three per cent were built or restored under Hadrian. Then activity tapers off again: seventeen per cent of the buildings are of Antonine date (A.D. 138-192), while only twelve per cent belong to the age of the Severi (A.D. 193-235). Thereafter Ostia, whose fortunes rose with Rome's, declines with her also.

The most illuminating way to describe what archaeology has to tell us about Ostia is to follow the plan used for Pompeii, treating in order the town and its population, municipal life and public amenities, housing arrangements, trade and industry, and the evidence for Ostia's religious life. Art in Ostia hardly deserves separate treatment: it is, naturally, less well-preserved than at Pompeii, and what there is seldom rises above the level of pure documentation.

The plan of Ostia (Figs. 10.1 and 10.2) is regular but not regimented. It has unity in variety; it combines utility, a monumental quality, and the scenic. Its backbone is the major east-west street, the *decumanus,* nearly a mile long, and once colonnaded, which runs from the Porta Romana straight to the Forum. Beyond the line of the west *castrum* wall it forks sharply to the left, ending at the Porta Marina, which once fronted directly on the sea. The main north-south street, the *cardo,* began at the Porta Laurentina on the south—Ostia's triplicity of gates is an Etruscan heritage —and ran, shaded and porticoed, northwestward to the dazzling whiteness of the colonnaded, marble-enriched Forum. Then it split in two on either side of Hadrian's Capitolium and passed north between balconied houses to the river. Sixteen per cent of Ostia's total area, exactly the same proportion as a modern city such as Madison, Wisconsin, was devoted to streets. Twelve per cent of Ostia was taken up by baths, fifteen per cent by warehouses (for Ostia was first and foremost a commercial town), and fifty-seven per cent by houses, most of which are middle-class apartment

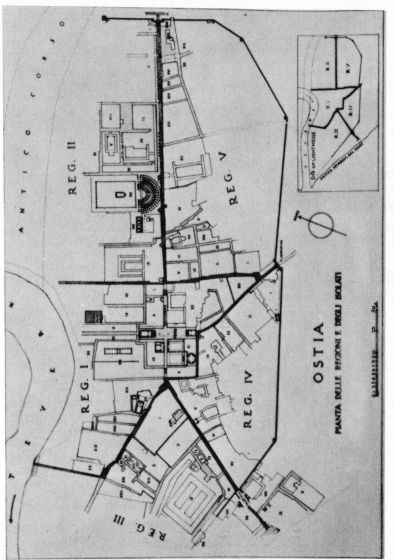

Fig. 10.1 Ostia. (G. Calza, *Scavi di Ostia*, 1)

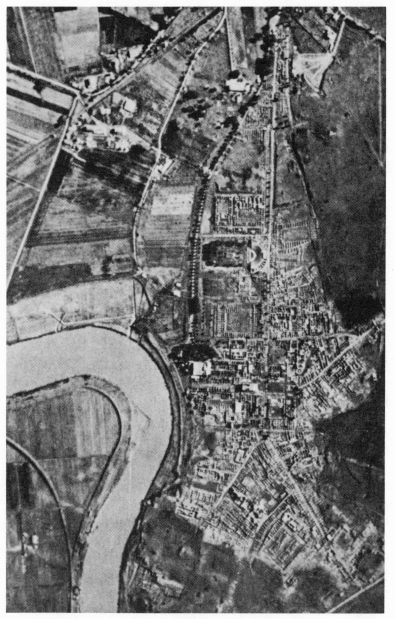

FIG. 10.2   Ostia, air view. (H. Kähler, *Rom und seine Welt*, Pl. 199)

blocks. Knowing the total housing area available, and calculating twenty-six square meters of space for each person, Calza reckoned the maximum population at 35,000 to 40,000.

The evidence for Ostia's municipal life comes mostly from inscriptions, over 6000 of them, many unpublished. They show that Ostia, like most Italian towns, imitated Rome: since Rome had a pair of chief municipal officers, the consuls, Ostia had a pair also, the *duoviri*. There was a town council of 110 members, which met in a marble-floored council house facing the Forum. Legal activity went on across the street in the basilica, also paved with marble, and with a pleasant portico facing the Forum. It had a charming frieze of Cupids carrying garlands. Both buildings are of Trajanic date; the prevalence of marble in them can be explained by the ease with which the stone could be brought by ships in ballast. There was a municipal plutocracy, whose names occur and recur on honorific decrees (praising them for benefactions), and on tombs near the Porta Romana and Porta Marina. The names are those of businessmen and freedmen, not of the old Roman aristocratic families. And as the years wear on men seldom hold office more than once, for it grew to be an expensive honor. If taxes assessed by the Imperial treasury were not collected in full, town officers had to make up the deficit out of their own pockets.

Public amenities included a theater, baths, and a fire department. The theater, built in Augustus' reign (about 12 B.C.), and often restored and enlarged, seats 2700, and is used nowadays for outdoor performances of Greek and Roman plays. Behind it is a portico where theater patrons might saunter, with a temple in its midst built by Domitian. In a combination of business with pleasure typical of Ostia, seventy offices face the four sides of the portico. These offices, to be discussed in more detail below, were maintained by local branches of firms from all over the Empire.

Ostia was well equipped with public baths. The three most interesting belong to the middle years of the second century A.D. The Baths of Neptune, near the theater (*Regio* II, *Insula* iv), have a large entrance hall paved with a spirited mosaic showing Neptune driving four sea-horses, surrounded by Tritons, Nereids, dolphins ridden by Cupids, fabulous sea monsters of every kind, and two young men swimming. The Baths of the Seven Sages (*Reg.* III,x) are named from a painting in their dressing room which depicts the seven wise men of Greece, each labelled with an off-color couplet describing in some detail the intimate connection between constipation and the intellectual life. The most interesting of all are the Forum Baths (*Reg.* I,xii). A recent study by an American heating engineer, E. D. Thatcher, underlines how well the Romans understood the principles of radiant heating (of floors, walls, bathing pools, and even vaults), and orientation of bathing rooms to catch the maximum amount of sunlight, and to provide a wind-break, so that, although the large windows were not glazed, the rooms were usable on most days of the year, even in winter, with additional provision, proved by put-holes, of a rigging of canvas for the coldest days. If the windows had been glazed, bathers could not have acquired a tan, whose therapeutic and fashionable implications were the same for an Ostian as for us. Thatcher calculates that an unglazed room in the Forum Baths was usable ninety-eight per cent of the time: hence glazing was not worth while. The Romans knew, as the Forum Baths show, that the flow of heat is always from a hotter body to a colder one, and that air temperature alone is no criterion of comfort. In fact one may be comfortable in a much lower air temperature than that found in most American houses and public buildings, provided one does not lose more heat than one is generating at the time. The floor and wall surfaces of the Forum Baths radiated enough warmth to keep bathers comfortable in relatively cool air with unglazed windows.

The courtyard of the baths was paved with white mosaic to reflect light and heat. A room which commanded a maximum of sunlight has radiant heat in the floor only, not in the walls. The various rooms of the baths were heated to different temperatures; Romans achieved with differently heated areas what we achieve with thermostats. The whole complex of the Forum Baths, Thatcher concludes, shows a sophistication in the use of radiant heating well beyond what modern engineers have achieved.

Though brick construction made Ostia more nearly fireproof than a modern city of frame dwellings, the grain for the dole stored in the city's numerous warehouses was too valuable a commodity to risk, so a cohort of firemen detached from the main corps in Rome was kept at the ready in barracks behind the Baths of Neptune (*Reg.* II,v). The barracks, built under Hadrian, surround an arcaded courtyard with rooms opening off. A latrine with a shrine in it thriftily combines cleanliness with godliness. At the end of the courtyard opposite the entrance is a platform which still bears the bases of statues of Emperors worshiped by the firemen as a part of the Imperial cult.

As at Pompeii, so at Ostia, the houses are the most interesting part of the city, not least because Ostian houses differ completely in plan from Pompeian ones. The great majority are apartment houses, tall, many-windowed brick blocks, with or without shops on the ground floor. They were designed to be rented out in flats, with separate access to the upper stories from the street. Some have balconies, opening both on the street and on garden courtyards where many families shared the pergolas, fountains, trees, shrubs, pools, and statue-studded lawns, as they shared also the large common latrines. The Casa dei Dipinti (*Reg.* III,iv; see Fig. 10.3) is such a block, built in Hadrian's reign. The ground-floor flats have mosaic floors and paintings of mythological scenes, figures of poets and dancers, landscapes, and fantastic motifs. At the end of the garden is yet another

FIG. 10.3   Ostia, Casa dei Dipinti, Gismondi's reconstruction. (Alinari)

of Ostia's combinations of the useful with the ornamental: a number of large *dolia,* terracotta jars sunk in the ground for storing oil or grain. Despite the panegyrics of the excavators, there is a certain deadly sameness about these flats where the lower middle class lived their lives of quiet desperation, as they do in the unfashionable quarters of Rome today.

The occupants of Ostia's flats were largely tradesmen or minor civil servants. Their livelihood came from Ostia's two artificial harbors (Fig. 10.4). The earlier, begun under Claudius in A.D. 42, is now the site of a military airport, whose engineers have preserved the traces (Fig. 10.5) of the two curving moles which enclosed a basin over 850,000 square yards in area. Ancient sources say there was an artificial island between the arms of the moles, with a lighthouse on it which became the symbol of Ostia: it is often figured in mosaics. A canal, now the Fiumicino branch of the Tiber, connected the harbor with the main stream.

Grandiose as it was, the harbor was ill-protected from prevailing winds: a storm in A.D. 62 wrecked 200 ships anchored or berthed in it. Trajan therefore built a smaller but more efficient basin (Fig. 10.6), hexagonal in shape and with numbered berths where ships might tie up to discharge their cargoes directly into warehouses on all six sides. A complicated entrance with a right-angled turn protected it completely from the hazards which had plagued Claudius' harbor; it also was connected with the Claudian canal. Nowadays it forms a pool on the Torlonia estate, and access to it is almost invariably refused.

The ships that unloaded at the quays of Claudius' or Trajan's harbor came from all over the Mediterranean. Their agents had their in-town offices in the portico behind the Augustan theater, called by the Italians the *Piazzale delle Corporazioni.* Each office had an emblem in mosaic before its door, indicating the commodity it imported or the service it rendered. These mosaics, plus inscriptions, document the

FIG. 10.5 Ostia, harbors of Claudius (traces of the mole show in a different color in the air photograph), and of Trajan (the hexagon). (Italian Ministry of Aeronautics)

FIG. 10.4 Ostia, harbors. (Calza, *op. cit.*)

FIG. 10.6 Ostia, harbor of Trajan, model. (Mostra Augustea della Romanità, *Catalogo*, Fig. 104)

greatest variety of goods and services, giving a clear idea
how busy the port of Rome was in the high Empire. The
commodities included furs, wood, grain, beans, melons, oil,
fish, wine, drugs, mirrors, flowers, ivory, gold, and silk.
Among the service personnel were the caulkers, cord-
wainers, grain-measurers, maintenance-men for the docks,
warehouses, and embankments, shipwrights, bargemen, car-
penters, masons, muleteers, carters, stevedores, and divers
for sunken cargoes. The home offices, often recorded in
the mosaics, include ports famous or forgotten in North
Africa, Sardinia, Gaul, and Spain. Ostia proper, as well as
the ports, was full of warehouses where these multifarious
goods were stored. Their plan, multistoried around a courtyard, was to influence the luxurious *palazzi* of the Renaissance. (When McKim, Mead, and White built the Boston
Public Library, for example, their ultimate model was an
Ostia warehouse.) The headquarters of the various guilds
grew, in the second and third centuries, very luxurious, with
airy courtyards and temples in imported marble, testifying
to the power and prosperity of these ancient labor unions.
Perhaps, then as now, the labor leaders were more prosperous than the rank and file, for in Ostia as in Pompeii,
the multitude of small shops, of fishmongers, fullers, and
millers, and the omnipresent *thermopolia* or bars, are humble enough, often with dark, cramped living quarters behind or on a mezzanine.

Ostia's world-wide trade made her a melting-pot, and
her temples reinforce the point. Besides the temples of the
Imperial cults and the official religion, like the Temple
of Rome and Augustus, Hadrian's lofty Capitolium, and
the half-scale Pantheon, all in the Forum, there is, near
the Porta Laurentina (*Reg.* IV,i) the temple of the Phrygian
Great Mother, where her emasculated priests once clashed
their cymbals. Near the Porta Marina (*Reg.* III,xvii) is the
temple of the Egyptian Serapis, conveniently located for
sailors just in from the Levant. Everywhere there were

shrines of the Persian Mithras: eighteen of them have been found, ranging in date from A.D. 160 to 250. They always occupy a retired, obscure corner of a pre-existent building; they are apparently intended to symbolize the cave where Mithras was born to his life of struggle with the powers of darkness for the immortal souls of men. They are usually oblong with shallow benches along the sides, with an altar or cult statue at the end. The favorite cult statue is of Mithras slaying the bull; being washed in the blood of a freshly slaughtered bull brought redemption into immortality to Mithras' votaries. One Ostian Mithraeum, that of Felicissimus (*Reg.* V,ix; see Fig. 10.7) has a mosaic pavement representing the seven stages of initiation, somewhat like the degrees of freemasonry. Each has its appropriate symbol: the Crow, the Bridegroom, the Soldier, the Lion, the Persian (with a scimitar), the Sun-runner, and the Father, or Worshipful Master. The cult was for men only: it appealed to merchants, freedmen and soldiers.

In the fourth century in Ostia some of these were won away by another Oriental religion, Christianity. A house (*Reg.* IV, iii) with a mosaic of the communion chalice, set with the Christian symbol of the fish (the initial letters of the word for "fish" in Greek stand for "Jesus Christ, Son of God, Saviour") may have been the residence of the bishop. A remodeled bath (*Reg.* III,i) made over into a humble Christian basilica, may be the place where Augustine worshiped in A.D. 387, as recorded in his *Confessions.* Part of the tombstone of his mother Monica, who died in Ostia, was found a few years ago in the neighboring modern village of Ostia Antica. The altar of the Mithraeum next to the basilica was found smashed by Christian wrath into a thousand pieces.

When Saint Augustine worshiped in Ostia, the city was already in full decline. The Emperor Constantine had revoked its municipal status, and assigned it to the village called Portus which had grown up around Trajan's harbor.

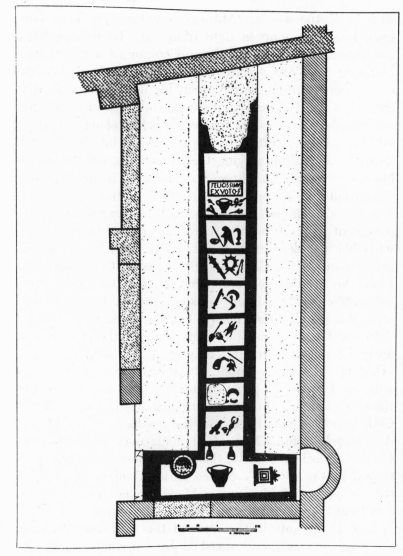

FIG. 10.7   Ostia, Mithraeum of Felicissimus.
(G. Becatti, *Scavi di Ostia*, 2, p. 107)

The cemetery of Portus, on Isola Sacra, the island between the Fiumicino and the principal mouth of the Tiber, contains a few Christian burials. It is chiefly noteworthy for the class distinctions it reveals between the wealthy in their fine vaulted brick tombs, embellished with paintings and mosaics (very like those found in the cemetery under St. Peter's), and the poor, whose ashes rest in the miserable amphorae stuck in the low-lying ground. By the end of the fourth century, burials in this cemetery ceased, mute and pathetic evidence of the decline of Portus itself. Ostia proper agonized on to its end. The flat slabs of inscriptions are re-used as shop-counters, or to mend pavements. Architectural marbles are sawed up into latrine-seats. Statues are reduced to lime or used, whole or decapitated, to repair breaches in the city wall. The water-pipes break and are not repaired, fallen house-walls are left lying, rubble piles up forty feet deep. Sacked by the barbarian, decimated by malaria, Ostia by the fifth century was desolate, and the road to Rome overgrown with trees. Only a Christian chapel by the theater, marking the spot where a Christian was martyred, was left to mark the spot.

Besides embellishing the Forum at Ostia with its basilica and council-house, Trajan, through his architect, the Syrian Apollodorus of Damascus, adorned Rome with the last, largest, and finest of the Imperial Fora (see Figs. 5.13 and 9.4). We know from an inscribed record, the *Fasti Ostienses,* found in re-use to repair a floor in an ancient private house in Ostia, that its dedication day was May 18, A.D. 113. Its general plan has been known since the French excavations of 1812. Its inspiration is the porticoes of Caesar's Forum and the apses and the Hall of Fame of Augustus'. In conception it is axially symmetric and tripartite: the Forum proper, the basilica, and the famous Column behind, flanked by a pair of libraries. Hadrian added the Temple of the

Deified Trajan, now destroyed, which closed the vista to the west.

The Forum proper lay at right angles to the Forum of Augustus, its facade bowed slightly out, like the *Forum Transitorium*. Its entrance was through a triumphal arch, added in A.D. 117, after Trajan's death. In the middle of the great porticoed square, over 620 feet wide, with apses on either side, was placed a great equestrian statue of Trajan; the Romans used to say that never did a horse have such a stable.

At the back of the open square which forms the Forum proper lay the basilica, its two short sides curved, like the sides of the Forum, into apses. The basilica presents its long side to the Forum as Italian basilicas regularly did, but was much grander than the basilicas of Alba, Cosa, or even the Basilica Julia in the old Forum. The basilica had two double rows of columns, in gray granite and polychrome marble: the yellow *giallo antico*, from Numidia; the striated green *cipollino*, "onion-stone"; the purple-streaked *pavonazzetto*, "peacock-stone"—Italian masons have over 500 different names for marble. The architraves were marble, crystalline white from Mt. Pentelicus in Attica. The walls were veneered with marble, from Carrara. The roof was plated with gilt bronze. It was this magnificence which the Christians sought to imitate in their great early basilica churches in Rome, where the high altar stood in the place of the judges' tribunal: Old St. Peter's, Santa Sabina, St. John Lateran, St.-Paul's-Without-the-Walls, San Lorenzo. Trajan's goodness as *optimus princeps* was legendary to early Christians; Trajan's basilica supplied a noble model for early Christian churches; Pope Sixtus V did Trajan a grave injustice when he replaced his statue at the top of the Column with one of St. Peter.

Behind the basilica a pair of small libraries, one Greek and one Latin, faced the tiny square in the midst of which rose Trajan's 100-foot column. Its shaft, of Parian marble, was wound about with 155 scenes on the twenty-three spirals of the great scroll, whose bands grow wider the higher they go, so that they were "readable" to a great height, especially from the library balconies. Unrolled, the scroll would be 650 feet long. It described in 2500 figures the events of Trajan's two campaigns, of A.D. 101-102 and 105-106, against the Dacians, ancestors of the modern Rumanians. It is because of Trajan's conquests, imposing Roman culture, that Rumanians speak a Romance language, derived from Latin, today.

To what that great scroll has to tell us about the Roman attitude—and the sculptor's—to the art of war we shall return. For the moment another matter is of interest: the inscription on the column-base. It states that the column marks the height of earth that was removed to make room for it. For centuries it was inferred that Trajan's engineers had cut away a whole saddle connecting the Esquiline with the Capitoline Hill. But in 1907 Boni published the results of excavations around the base of the column, which revealed a street, a wall, and houses, dated by their pottery—Arretine and earlier—to the late Republic. Hence there probably never was a saddle of hill here. What then does the inscription mean? Boni fixed his eye on the terraced slope of the Quirinal to the north of the Forum, and concluded—rightly, as later excavation proved—that what Trajan was referring to was the cutting down and terracing of this slope for some purpose to be connected with the Forum. What that purpose was did not transpire until 1928, when Corrado Ricci cleared the area of medieval and later accretions and discovered the six levels of Trajan's Market (Fig. 10.8).

The terrace treatment clearly goes back for inspiration to the Sanctuary of Fortune at Praeneste. Brick stamps show that the Market was built before the Forum: the shape in which the hill was dug out left space for the Forum apse when it came to be built. Form follows function: the hemicycle shows the classical virtues of symmetry, regularity, and creative exploitation of tradition, but the shape is practical, too: it allows space for nearly twice as many rooms as would have been possible with a rectilinear front. The shop fronts are good-looking as well as utilitarian. The ground floor rooms are handsomely framed in travertine; the second level windows are arched, and framed with pilasters, much as at Praeneste, with pediments alternately

FIG. 10.8   Rome, Trajan's Market. (Fototeca)

curved and triangular; the triangular pediments are sometimes deliberately broken, never coming to an apex, a trick of style imitated with success by eighteenth century English furniture designers like Chippendale. But this is an old thing in a new way, for here the material is not stone but brick, the beautifully-proportioned rose-red Roman kind, used unashamedly without veneer of stucco or marble, like the rose-red arcades of Renaissance Bologna.

Some of the rooms have drains in the floor for carrying off spilled liquid; the inference is that these were wine or oil shops; those without such provision would be for dry commodities like grain. There are 150 of these shops altogether, all more or less identical. The whole complex has the air not of private enterprise but of a government project, and it seems a reasonable guess that here we have the headquarters of the *annona,* the government dole of wine, oil, and grain, the cargoes of the ships that docked in Trajan's port of Ostia.

Access to the second level is by stairs at either end of the hemicycle, not in the middle. The split approach is borrowed from the exedra of Terrace VII at Praeneste. (It was brick stamps in these stairs that enabled Bloch to date this complex in the first decade of the second century A.D.). The second-floor shops open onto a semicircular vaulted corridor with windows opening on the Forum. On the third level variety within unity, plus ease of access for wagons, is achieved by a semicircular street on which the third level shops face. A straight stretch of paving running north and south, called the Via Biberatica—Pepper or Spice Street— and concealed by the façade, contains shops with balconies, as at Ostia. Stairs ascend from this level to a great rectangular cross-vaulted basilical hall, with shops opening off it at two levels. Some archaeologists think this was the place where the dole was distributed; others see in it ancient Rome's wholesale grain, oil, and wine market, like the Pit in Chicago where bidding fixes the day's commodity prices. The interconnecting suites of rooms on the fifth and sixth levels are clearly not shops, but offices for administrative personnel. One large centrally-located room, with a view over the whole complex, would be a good place for the office of the superintendent of the entire affair, the *praefectus annonae.*

Trajan's Market did not let his people forget his generosity. Trajan's Column did not let them forget his prowess in war.

Though casts have often been made of the reliefs on the column—the earliest to the order of Francis I of France, in 1541—the best photographs were not taken until 1942, when a scaffolding erected around the column to protect it from air attack made close-ups possible. The *optimus princeps* appears more than fifty times, larger than life. He dominates the sea voyages (he handles the tiller personally), the marches, the river-crossings, the councils of war, the reviews, the encounters in the open field, the sieges, the sacrifices, the submissions of enemy chiefs.

Because of the fascinating detail of the reliefs, Trajan's Column tells us as much about the Roman army and navy as Pompeii and Ostia do about civilian life. Nor is this all: we learn a great deal, too, about provincial and native customs and culture. Most important, the unknown sculptor has impressed his personality and his feelings upon what he carved. There is an occasional touch of rough humor—a slave falling off a mule, a Dacian ducked in the Danube—and a scene or two in which Trajan, deprecating the humility of submissive native chiefs, seems to be following Vergil's advice to spare the meek. But the dominant note is Vergil's, too: the horror of war. Some of the detail is worth recording.

The army and navy first. The transports, with cars in two banks, and auxiliary sail, have ramming-beaks, adorned with an enormous eye, for luck, or with a sea monster. The soldiers are jacks-of-all-trades: we see them woodcutting and reaping, but most often at the interminable work of building palisaded camps, with tents of skins, a new camp every night when they were on the march. They built their permanent camps of squared stones: the sculptor shows the soldiers carrying them in slings on their shoulders, or in baskets. The walls had towers, with balconies, from which flaming torches gave signals by night. Catapults were mounted on the battlements; other catapults are horse or mule drawn, or mounted on improvised wooden bases like stacked railroad ties. We see the standards of the legions—

the famed Eagles—and the standard-bearers, wearing animal heads for helmets, like Hercules. On the march the men carry their gear in bundles on the ends of their pikes, like tramps with their worldly goods done up in a bandanna.

We see something of provincial towns and their citizens. The army embarked from an Adriatic port, Ancona or Brindisi, and sailed across to Illyricum. Here the cities ape Rome, with arches, columned temples, theaters, and amphitheaters. The citizens turn out in a body, leading their children by the hand, to greet their Emperor with upraised right arms, as in a Fascist salute, and to offer sacrifice. The Danube is crossed on a great bridge, the work of Apollodorus, with masonry piers and wooden super-structure. Then one is in wild country, with exotic flora and fauna, including an especially bloodthirsty wild boar. The natives live in straw huts, and wear trousers: this last, to a Roman, sure proof of barbarism. In battle they use short hooked swords, and carry sinister dragon-head standards. Their cavalry, horses and all, are protected from head to foot with scaly armor.

It is exciting, but it is terrible. Dacian women burn Romans alive; Romans impale the severed heads of Dacians before the walls of their camp (Fig. 10.9), or present them, dripping with gore, to the Emperor. A Dacian is assassinated with a sword thrust as he pleads for mercy. Bodies are trampled underfoot in battle, prisoners are dragged along by the hair. The Dacian king commits suicide rather than fall into Roman hands; his subjects burn their capital to the ground to deny it to the Romans. The story of the first campaigns is separated from the second by a Victory writing on a shield; immediately thereafter the deadly, monotonous round begins again. The pathos of some of the scenes heightens the horror, as when two comrades carry tenderly from the field the limp body of a mortally wounded Dacian youth, or a whole tribe, with babies in arms, or children carried on their fathers' shoulders, comes to make the act of submission. At the end looting, with the Dacian treasure loaded on the backs of mules. These scenes, with their implied criticism of warfare, are the closest the Romans ever came to pacifism.

FIG. 10.9   Rome, Trajan's Column, detail.
(P. Romanelli, *La colonna traiana,* Fig. 60)

The province won with so much blood, sweat, and tears by Trajan was consolidated by his successor Hadrian (who had fought in the campaigns) and taught the arts of peace. Hadrian, that restless traveler, spent little of his reign in Rome, but he adorned the city with some of its grandest buildings, for which he himself probably drew the plans, and he built near suburban Tivoli a villa greater than Versailles.

11

An Emperor-Architect: Hadrian

About Trajan's successor Hadrian (A.D. 117-138) archaeology and literature, interlocking, tell us so much that we can write his biography from his buildings, with an occasional assist from written sources. The buildings of his reign are numerous and brilliantly designed. We shall take as examples three from Rome and three from the unique complex of his Villa near Tivoli: the Temple of Venus and Rome, the Pantheon, and his mausoleum; the *Teatro Marittimo*, the *Piazza d'Oro*, and the Canopus. All can be dated with more precision than usual, because in Hadrian's time the practice became general of stamping bricks with the names of the consuls of the year they were made. Professor Bloch's accurate study of, and sound inference from, over 4600 stamps, most of them from Hadrian's reign, have put all students of Roman archaeology deeply in his debt.

An attempt to understand Hadrian through his buildings rests upon the hypothesis that he was himself his own architect, inspired by the ferment of building activity in Rome in Domitian's and Trajan's reigns, when he was growing up. The hypothesis is perhaps justified by an inference from an anecdote recorded by Dio Cassius, a Roman senator and consul from Bithynia in northwest Asia Minor, who wrote in Greek a history of Rome from the beginning to A.D. 229. Dio's story is that once when Trajan was in conference with his architect, Apollodorus of Damascus, Hadrian interrupted, and Apollodorus, angered, said, "Oh, go and design your pumpkins!" We infer that Apollodorus' reference to "pumpkins" was intended to pour scorn on certain of Hadrian's designs for vaults, involving pumpkin-like concave segments with re-entrant groins between, such as are still to be seen in Hadrian's Villa, in the vestibule of the Piazza d'Oro, and in the Serapeum at the end of the Canopus (Fig. 11.1). The same anecdote records that Apollonius so piqued Hadrian, later, by his criticisms of the design of the Emperor's Temple of Venus and Rome, that Hadrian had him first exiled and then put to death. This is how Hadrian is established as an architect, and a vindictive one at that.

Hadrian's most baroque flights of architectural fancy are to be seen at his villa near Tivoli, where the various complexes of buildings are scattered over an area 1000 yards one way by 500 yards the other. The buildings, which far outdid Nero's Golden House in extent and grandeur, include palaces, large and small, for manic and for depressive moods (plan [Fig. 11.2] A,G,R,S,T,U,V,W), guest-quarters (B), a pavilion (C), dining rooms (D,E,K), baths (F,O,P), a library (the apsed building to the right of G), porticoes (H,J), pools (between H and J, and northwest of X), slave quarters (J,N), a stadium (L), many cryptoporticoes (for example, M), firemen's barracks (between A and M), a palaestra or wrestling ground (Q), and a vaulted temple of Serapis (X). Excavation, and the carrying off of statues, with which Roman museums are crammed, began as early as 1535, and continues to the present. It has been followed by reconstruction (Fig. 11.3) and general tidying up: the Italian authorities report the clearing away of 13,200 pounds of briers!

The setting of Hadrian's villa near Tivoli takes full ad-

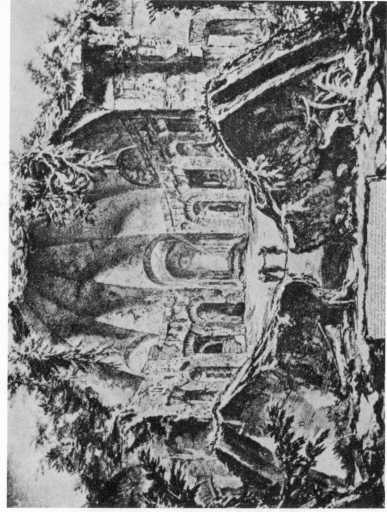

FIG. 11.1 Tivoli, Hadrian's Villa. Serapeum at Canopus, showing "pumpkin" vaults. (Piranesi)

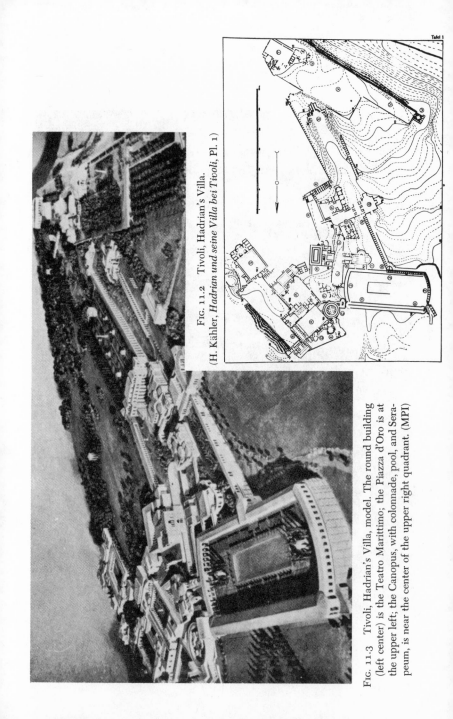

FIG. 11.2 Tivoli, Hadrian's Villa.
(H. Kähler, *Hadrian und seine Villa bei Tivoli*, Pl. 1)

Tafel 1

FIG. 11.3 Tivoli, Hadrian's Villa, model. The round building (left center) is the Teatro Marittimo; the Piazza d'Oro is at the upper left; the Canopus, with colonnade, pool, and Serapeum, is near the center of the upper right quadrant. (MPI)

vantage of landscape: the view embraces mountains in one direction, distant Rome and the sea in the other. There is the color of pines, olives, ripe grain, pasture, and vineyard, the sound of cicadas by day and nightingales at twilight. And when the villa was new, everywhere was the sound of water and the color of marble. For this enormous Folly, this Roman Versailles, the immensity of all this space devoted to the whims of one man, untrammelled by any limitations of technique or money, is the perfected product of 200 years of Roman experience in elegant country living. Its builder occupied it but little. Eleven of the twenty-one restless years of his reign were spent in foreign travel. He named parts of his villa for famous buildings and places he had seen in the Greek East: the Academy and the Painted Porch (*Stoa Poecile*) in Athens, the Canopus near Alexandria. He even created a mile of cryptoporticoes which he called a "Hell" (*Inferi*, the Lower Regions): in his tortured life he had been there, too, as we shall see. But the buildings are idiosyncratic, not imitative, except in the creative Roman way. Hadrian, the Spaniard, was quick to learn. He always spoke Latin with an accent (his Greek was better), but his architecture was pure Graeco-Roman, using the architectural vocabulary of the past to create a new architectural language of his own.

His earliest architectural essay at the villa, to judge from the brick stamps, is the so-called *"Teatro Marittimo"* (the round complex at G; see also Fig. 11.4). Its earliest bricks date from the first year of his reign. (Of course the bricks need not have been used in the year they were made, and indeed will often have been put aside for several years to season.) Some bricks in the fabric of the *Teatro Marittimo* are dated A.D. 123, an *annus mirabilis* in Roman brick production, to meet the vast requirements of Hadrian's many projects, some ready to build, some still on the drawing-board. These bricks point to later restorations of the original plan, but the point here is that the fundamental design, very characteristic of Hadrian, must have been laid down early. Much light on this complex, and on the villa as a whole, has been cast by the sensitive, perceptive work of the German Heinz Kähler, who, undaunted by the burning of all his carefully drawn plans in World War II, redid and published them in 1950, illuminating as never before our picture of Hadrian as man and architect.

The entrance to the *Teatro Marittimo* was through a portico to the north (at the bottom of the air photograph)

FIG. 11.4   Tivoli, Hadrian's Villa, Teatro Marittimo, air view.
(H. Kähler, *Rom und seine Welt*, Pl. 188)

which approached a door in a high circular brick wall, insuring complete privacy from the rest of the villa. Inside the wall was a circular portico, concentric with the portico a moat. The *Teatro Marittimo* is now restored (through the philanthropy of an Italian tire manufacturer, impressed by the likeness of its plan to his product), and the moat is filled with water. When it was dry, its floor showed a pair of grooves in an arc, one on either side of the main axis. The grooves were made by the rollers of a drawbridge worked from a small room on the edge of the inner circle. On the site of one of the drawbridges there is now a permanent foot-bridge, visible in the air photograph. On the circular island, the columned arc between the drawbridges is a vestibule where the Emperor might receive his friends. Beyond it is a diamond-shaped peristyle, originally with a fountain in the middle: its sides are segments of circles which if projected would be tangent to the outer wall of the moat. Beyond the peristyle is an apsidal room; the apse has the same arc as the vestibule. This would be a pleasant place for intimate dinner parties. The rooms on either side might be bedrooms. A broad window opens from the dining room onto the moat, with a view directly on an alcove let into the circular wall on the axis of the far side. From the alcove the view leads through eleven differently shaped and differently lighted spaces back to the entrance portico and a far-distant fountain to the north.

It remains to describe the rooms east and west of the peristyle. The central apsidal room of the three on the west (to the right of the peristyle in the air photograph) is a deep bath with a window over the moat. Steps lead up to the low sill: Hadrian could choose between tub and moat for bathing. To the south is the dressing room, to the north the steam bath and furnace room. East of the peristyle is a circular room whose interior cross-walls form a double T, creating two alcoves for reading. Each would be appropriate to its season: the eastern for winter mornings and summer afternoons, the western for summer mornings and winter afternoons. The two adjoining rooms would be just right for a small library, of some 1500 rolls, half Greek and half Latin; the main library lay conveniently to the southwest (right center in the air photograph). It is tempting to see in this suite of rooms the study where the Emperor wrote his resigned, sentimental, mannered little poem to his soul (or is it to the soul of his beloved Antinous?):

> *"Little soul, gentle and drifting,*
> *Guest and companion of my body,*
> *Now you will dwell below in pallid places,*
> *Stark and bare;*
> *There you will abandon your play of yore."*

The remaining odd corners would house latrines, little conservatories, cupboards, and pantries.

This earliest Hadrianic building perfectly expresses one aspect of the man: his genius, his moodiness, his striving for form, his restlessness. With its wall, its moat, and its drawbridge, it is all designed for privacy and quiet. From any room one gets a view of variously lighted sections of space: *chiaroscuro* to match moods grave and gay. In the midst of axial symmetry, unrest is everywhere: in the curved forms, in the abrupt switches from light to dark, from roofed to open spaces, from horizontal architraves to the vertical play of the central fountain. The unrest is central: the midpoint is water and inaccessible. Tension and split are expressed in the divided bridge approach. All is indirection, schizophrenia, avoidance of forthrightness. As an architectural exercise, it is uniquely abstract, a proposition of Euclid in brick and marble, at one moment seeming to involve nothing but circles, at another, nothing but squares. It is probably no accident that its total diameter is almost exactly the same as the Pantheon's. It would have suited the complexity of Hadrian's mind to design a grandiose habitation for all the gods to the self-same dimensions as this splendid toy, the habitation of a restless, schizophrenic man whom his subjects worshipped as a god. The gods had made Hadrian in their own image; seconded by flattering courtiers, he was returning the compliment.

The next building in Hadrian's architectural biography is his Temple of Venus and Rome, built facing the Coliseum to rival the most splendid buildings of Athens and the Greek East. Literary sources give its foundation date as Rome's birthday, April 21, A.D. 121; the brick-stamps, of 123, 134, and the fourth century, tell the story of long years of building and late restoration. The restoration probably followed Hadrianic lines; at any rate the proportion of straight to curved profiles in the apses—exactly half and half—is Hadrianic language, repeated in the Pantheon. The essence of the plan is two apses back to back, one for Venus and one for the goddess Roma. They may be interpreted as a colossal architectural pun. Venus is a goddess of love, Love is AMOR, and AMOR is ROMA spelled backward. The symbolism does not stop here. Hadrian is Caesar: his is the heritage, if not the blood, of the Julian line, and the temple is a reminder of the greatness of Rome, firmly established by Augustus, and smiled upon by Augustus' ancestress, Venus. The plan (Fig. 11.5 and 11.6) was ingenious and devious, in Hadrian's manner. The exterior is foursquare and conventional: the interior, with its vaults and apses, was novel and emphasized curves: compare the interplay of the square and the round in the *Teatro Marittimo*. Daring as it was, the design was the butt of the criticisms which cost Apollodorus his life. He had said that the temple should have been set on a high podium, which could have housed various paraphernalia useful in the Coliseum opposite, and that the vaulted apses had been designed too low for the statues in them: "If the goddesses wish to get up and go out, they will be unable to do so." The first half of Apollodorus' criticism is unjustified: Hadrian was designing a Greek temple, not an Italic one. About the second half we cannot judge, for certain, for brick stamps show the apses to belong to the fourth century reconstruction, but the proportions, as we saw, are Hadrianic (Fig. 11.7). The temple was set in the midst of a forest of sixty-six columns of grey granite. When it was re-excavated in 1932, some of the columns were re-erected; the positions of others were ingeniously marked by clumps of shrubbery trimmed to the proper shape. The excavators found under the pavement an octagonal room

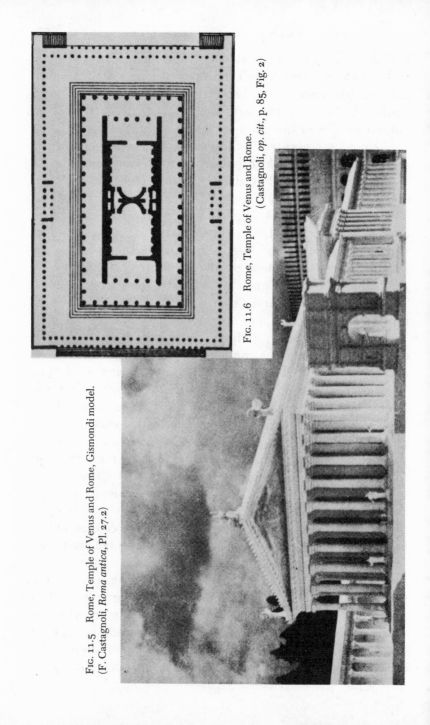

FIG. 11.5 Rome, Temple of Venus and Rome, Gismondi model.
(F. Castagnoli, *Roma antica*, Pl. 27.2)

FIG. 11.6 Rome, Temple of Venus and Rome.
(Castagnoli, *op. cit.*, p. 85, Fig. 2)

interesting in itself, and significant for its place in Roman architecture. The level at which it was found is lower than that of Nero's Golden House. (Hadrian's temple was built in the grounds of what had once been the Golden House; the reader will recall the twenty-four elephants needed to move the colossal statue of Nero and make room for the temple.) The octagonal shape appears in the dining room of the Golden House itself, in Domitian's palace on the Palatine, and in a room in the Small Baths at Hadrian's villa (O on the plan, Fig. 11.2). The cupola of Nero's octagonal dining room, together with its lighting through a hole in the roof, reappears on a grand scale in the Pantheon. This is what we mean by saying that Hadrian adapted to his own new architectural language the vocabulary of pre-Neronian, Neronian, and Domitianic buildings. Here once again modern archaeology illuminates the development of Roman architecture by demonstrating and dating the classical use of new things in old ways, and old things in new.

Shortly after the consecration of the Temple of Venus and Rome, Hadrian set out on the first of his great tours of his Empire. He visited the western provinces, making arrangements, among other things, for the building of the great wall bearing his name that runs from Tyne to Solway in the north of England. He visited the provinces of Africa, Cyrene and Crete. Finally, in A.D. 123, he reached Bithynia, and there met Antinous (Fig. 11.8), the sulky, langorous, adolescent boy who, for the remaining seven years of his short life, and even more after his tragic death by drowning—perhaps suicide—in the suburb of Alexandria called Canopus, was to dominate Hadrian's existence and inspire his whole creative activity. It is not surprising that the Emperor, childless and unhappily married, should find deep satisfaction in the company of this boy. The psychological aspects of the affair, and the possible effect of Hadrian's infatuation upon his architecture have been treated with delicacy and understanding by Marguerite Yourcenar and Eleanor Clark.

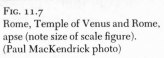

FIG. 11.7
Rome, Temple of Venus and Rome,
apse (note size of scale figure).
(Paul MacKendrick photo)

FIG. 11.8   Antinous. (Alinari)

The first Hadrianic building that could have been designed after the meeting with Antinous is the Pantheon (Fig. 11.9), "the oldest important roofed building in the world that still stands intact." On the evidence of the brick-stamps, its framework was complete by A.D. 125, and the whole building perhaps finished by 128. Until 1892 the building passed as the work of Augustus' lieutenant Agrippa, because the inscription that runs across the architrave of the

FIG. 11.9 Rome, Pantheon. (Fototeca)

rectangular porch in front of the drum, "Marcus Agrippa built this when he was consul for the third time" (27 B.C.), was taken at its face value. But in 1892 the entire fabric was found to be full of stamped bricks of Hadrianic date, and the building therefore Hadrianic throughout (with Severan restorations, also recorded in an inscription). The Agrippa inscription partly follows the Roman practice of repeating the original dedication in a restored structure,

partly reflects the Emperor's mock modesty. His involuted
nature found satisfaction in seldom inscribing his own name
on the buildings he designed. His contemporaries knew well
enough who the architect was. And the elaborate mystifi-
cation served also to point up his identifying himself with
Augustus, which we saw first in the Temple of Venus and
Rome. Whether Hadrian thought of himself as a new Augustus or not, certainly Augustan domed buildings at the sea-
side resort of Baiae, on the Bay of Naples, influenced his
architecture. Hadrian played the game out in the way he
handled the transition between the circular and the rectangular parts of his plan (Fig. 11.10). On either side of the
entrance to the drum, behind the porch, he designed rectangular projections with huge half-vaulted apses cut out
of the front: one of these apses would have contained a
statue of Agrippa, the other of Augustus. And Romans passing between them (through the great bronze entrance doors
that still survive) would marvel at how self-effacing was
their Emperor-architect.

The interior (Fig. 11.11) carries forward that liberation
of religious architecture from the Greek tyranny of the rectangular box, which can only come about through the use
of poured concrete, and which we saw first in the Sanctuary
of Fortune at Praeneste. Here Hadrian plays with geometrical abstractions, as in the Teatro Marittimo. The game is to
describe a sphere in a cylinder: if the curve of the dome
were projected beyond the point where it meets the vertical
walls of the drum, the bottom of the curve would be just
tangent with the floor. The very pavement, with its alternation of squares and circles, plays up the geometrical *jeu
d'esprit*. (Beneath this pavement lies the simple rectangular
plan of Agrippa's temple.) Furthermore, both the plan and
the interior view show that the walls of the drum are not
solid, and that they continue the architect's vast toying with
geometrical concepts. The walls are lightened with niches
(for statues; one, of Venus, wore Cleopatra's pearls in her

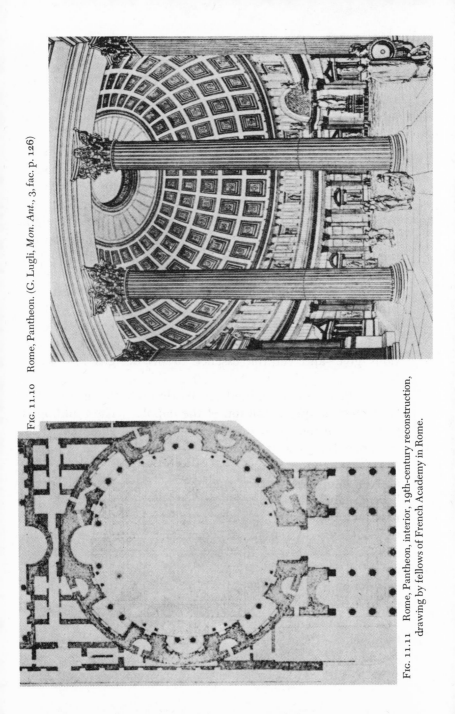

FIG. 11.10   Rome, Pantheon. (G. Lugli, *Mon. Ant.*, 3. fac. p. 126)

FIG. 11.11   Rome, Pantheon, interior, 19th-century reconstruction, drawing by fellows of French Academy in Rome.

ears). The niches are alternately rectangular and curved; the result is that the hemispherical cupola is supported not on a solid wall but on eight huge piers. In order to reduce the bearing weight of the superstructure upon the niches, into the concrete fabric above the apertures were built, concealed by polychrome marble revetment, elaborate brick relieving arches, which run as barrel vaults right through the walls. The cupola itself is designed with sunken stepped coffers, to lighten it, and to exaggerate the perspective, and to play yet again with the alternation of curve and straight line. The concrete of the cupola, which is thinner toward the top, is made with pumice, the lightest material available. But in spite of the pains taken to lighten the enormous mass, the piers gave under the weight of the cupola, and external buttresses proved necessary (see plan, Fig. 11.10), which spoiled the exterior effect. Hadrian is an amateur to the end; his vaults do not hold, his cupolas need bracing, his foundations give—and yet the essence of his designs has lasted forever.

The Pantheon is lighted solely through the great hole, thirty feet across, at the top of the cupola. (The building is so large that the inconvenience from rain is negligible.) The best possible idea of the perfection of this great building is to be gained by looking down into the interior from high above, from the edge of the hole in the roof. This dizzy height, at which one may glory or despair according to the measure of one's acrophobia, is reached by a stair behind the left apse in the porch. The stair gives access to the cornice at the top of the drum; one then walks half-way round the cornice, which is wide but unrailed, to the back of the drum, where a flight of steps, only half-railed, leads up over the lead plates (the original gilt bronze was sent to Constantinople in the seventh century), to the aperture, from which those with a head for heights can gauge the aesthetic satisfaction of realizing that the interior is exactly as high as it is wide. The total effect, massive, daring, playing with space, yet not entirely successful technically, reflects the man.

One wonders what Hadrian's tortured and cynical spirit would make of the vicissitudes his building has suffered. A Barberini pope in the seventeenth century used the bronze of the porch roof to make the canopy over the high altar of St. Peter's, and guns for the papal fortress, Castel Sant' Angelo (which had once been Hadrian's mausoleum); of this vandalism the wags of 1625 made the famous epigram, *"Quod non fecerunt barbari fecerunt Barberini,"* which might be paraphrased, "The Barberini rush in where barbarians fear to tread." At the same time Bernini added a pair of ridiculous bell towers—called "the ass's ears"—which were not taken down until the nineteenth century. Perhaps Hadrian would be better pleased to know that men like himself were buried in his building: a great creative artist—Raphael—and two Italian kings.

While the Pantheon was being built, an activity unexampled in the history of Roman architecture was going on at the villa. To the fruitful years after 125 belongs the uniquely inspired plan (Fig. 11.12) of the most important palace in the villa complex, called the *Piazza d'Oro*, the Golden Square. Its "pumpkin" vestibule (K in the plan) has already been mentioned. In many of its features, including the hole in the roof, the eight supporting piers, and the alternation of curved and rectilinear niches, it is a quarter-scale Pantheon, but there is greater frankness in the display of the structure, both internally, in the groined vault, and externally, where the octagonal plan is left clearly visible, instead of being concealed by the skin of the drum, as in the Pantheon. Except perhaps for the cross-vaulted passages N,N, the portico is conventional; excavation in the summer of 1958 revealed footings for formal flower beds, as in the portico of Pompey's theater, and in Vespasian's Forum of Peace.

The part of the complex which shows Hadrian's full

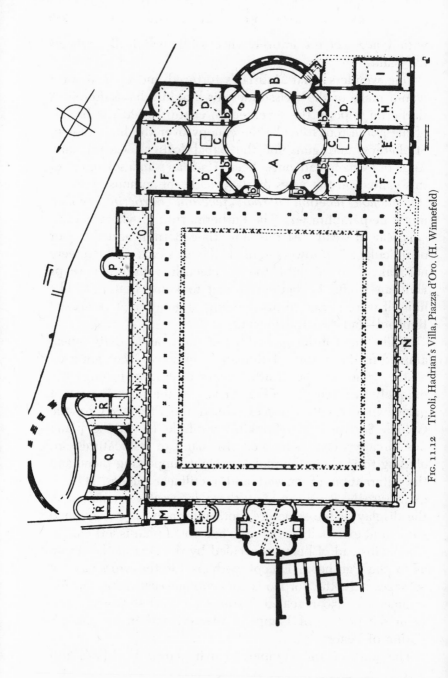

Fig. 11.12 Tivoli, Hadrian's Villa, Piazza d'Oro. (H. Winnefeld)

genius is the palace-block, south of the portico (plan A-I).
Here the vastness, sweep, and richness of the *Piazza d'Oro*
comes to its climax in a design which has been called lyrical,
feminine, and even Mozartian. Here, if anywhere, can be
detected the influence of Antinous. The frieze-motif, for
example, is Cupids (riding sea-monsters), but since this
theme is borrowed from the *Teatro Marittimo*, which, at
least in its earliest phase, antedates Antinous, too much
should not be made of it. The center of the composition is
the four-leaf-clover room at A, with a fountain in the middle.
Its walls sweep in and out, with a sinuous, wave-like movement, as though the room were alive, and breathing. The
outswinging arcs open into light-wells (C,C; B is a curved
nymphaeum, with statue-niches alternately curved and reti-
linear, from beneath which the water flowed down steps
into a reflecting pool; the fourth side is the entrance). The
inswinging arcs open into bell-shaped rooms (a,a,a,a). These
serve to counter the thrust of the centrally-pierced cupola
(see the reconstruction, Fig. 11.13), which may have suc-
cessfully solved the problem of transition from octagonal
ground-plan to circular dome. The cupola was supported
(none too well, for it has fallen and left no trace) on eight
delicate piers, in what we now see to be Hadrian's standard
but ever-varied manner. The six tiny apsidal rooms (b) are
latrines; their water-supply came from fountains at the back
of the bell-shaped diagonal rooms, yet another example of
the Roman combination of the useful with the ornamental.

Off the central clover-leaf open on each side five rectangular rooms (I is a late addition), all but one barrel-
vaulted; the exception (G) had a cross-vault. Each set opens
onto a light well. At the back of the central room (E) in
each set is a statue-niche. The view from the back of these
rooms runs, as in the *Teatro Marittimo*, through variegated
light and shade. E was diagonally lit from the light-well;
the light-well itself, a variant on the conventional atrium,
had probably a square *compluvium*, or open skylight; the

central room was lit by the round cupola-aperture, and so
on. The whole design, with its indirect lighting, plays of
water, and works of art, is light and gay, reflecting the
Emperor's brief years of pleasure with his *inamorato;* what
the Empress Sabina thought is not recorded. But here again
is the tension that comes from an inaccessible midpoint.
And whose statues were in the niches? Whatever may have
been the case in Antinous' lifetime, after his death Hadrian
deified him, identifying him with Apollo, Dionysus, Hermes,
Silvanus, Osiris, and other gods, and surrounded himself
with reminders of him in marble. Of the statues of Antinous
in Roman museums, a number variously estimated at from
sixteen to thirty comes from the villa.

Hadrian's happiness was short-lived. In A.D. 128 he set
out again on his travels, accompanied by Antinous. They
wintered at Athens, which Hadrian enriched with monuments, passed over into Asia Minor, and down through Syria
into Egypt. Here, in 130, Antinous died, probably a suicide,
to please his master or to avoid his passion. Hadrian's grief
was more baroque than any of his buildings. From this point
his life becomes one long death-wish. The most massive symbol of this is his mausoleum, whose great concrete drum,
approached by Hadrian's bridge, the *Pons Aelius* (nowadays the Ponte Sant' Angelo) still dominates the right bank
of the Tiber near St. Peter's. The latest Hadrianic bricks in
it are dated A.D. 134; it must have become an important part
of the Emperor's plans when he returned to Rome, mourning Antinous, in 132 or 133. Its plan goes back to Etruscan
tumuli, via the Mausoleum of Augustus—creative imitation
again. The square block on which the drum rests has almost exactly the dimensions of the Augustan monument's
diameter. A spiral ramp leads up to the tomb chamber in
the very center of the drum. The top was spread with earth
and planted with cypresses, the trees of death (Fig. 11.14),
and the whole surmounted by a colossal group in bronze,
perhaps of Hadrian in a four-horse chariot, now replaced by

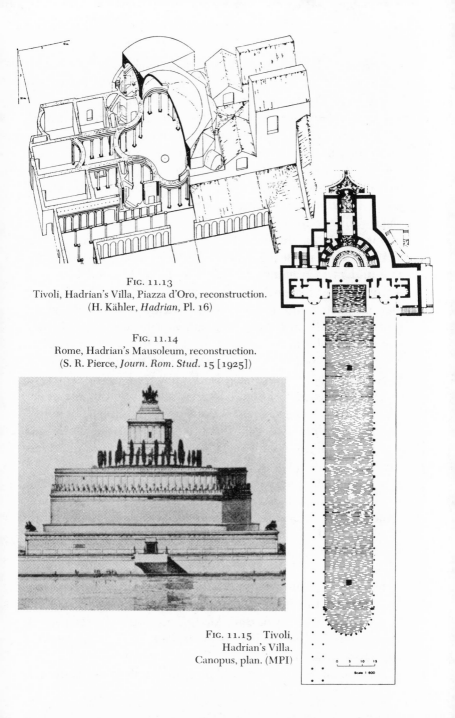

FIG. 11.13
Tivoli, Hadrian's Villa, Piazza d'Oro, reconstruction.
(H. Kähler, *Hadrian*, Pl. 16)

FIG. 11.14
Rome, Hadrian's Mausoleum, reconstruction.
(S. R. Pierce, *Journ. Rom. Stud.* 15 [1925])

FIG. 11.15   Tivoli,
Hadrian's Villa,
Canopus, plan. (MPI)

the archangel Michael, who gives the mausoleum its present name, Castel Sant' Angelo. When the death he longed for agonizingly came, from dropsy, in A.D. 138, Hadrian's ashes were laid beside those of the wife he had never loved, in the core of the monument which symbolized his despair at the death of the only creature to whom this strange man had ever given his affection. The great pile has been successively fortress, prison (immuring, among others, the great Renaissance scientist Giordano Bruno), and, since 1934, military museum.

But before his death Hadrian dedicated one more section of the villa to mourning his loss. This is the Canopus (Figs. 11.1 and 11.15), named for the suburb of Alexandria where Antinous met his untimely and unhappy end. The original plan may have antedated Antinous' death—the latest stamps reported by Bloch are dated A.D. 126—but after the disaster Hadrian, deliberately turning the knife in the wound, must have made this complex a memorial of the place where it happened. For the approach is along a pool (excavated and restored 1954-1957) intended to be reminiscent of the canal which gave access to the Canopus at Alexandria. The latest finds make it possible to restore the pool with its south end fitted with dining couches. The north end is apsidal, edged with a curious colonnade whose architrave is flat over one pair of columns and arched over the next pair. Along the sides were found perfect (and entirely unimaginative) copies of the Caryatids, the maidens who upheld the south porch of the Erechtheum; these would be memories of past happiness in Athens. Flanking the maidens were Sileni. Other marbles, adorning the apsidal north end of the colonnade, included, in order, an Amazon, a Hermes, a river god representing the Tiber, another representing the Nile, an Ares, and another Amazon. All this uninspired archaism is depressing; in the ageing, heartbroken Hadrian taste and inspiration alike are dead.

The colonnade led to the terminal half-dome (another

"pumpkin," it will be recalled) and secondary structures, the whole long known as the Serapeum (there was such a temple in the Alexandrian Canopus). It is complex in plan, at once *nymphaeum* and temple, with its hemicycle deepened at the back into a long narrow apsidal gallery in which some commentators have seen a deep sexual significance. Here Hadrian has turned, to catalyze his flagging inspiration, to older civilizations, dead or dying like himself. Once again, for the last time, and feebly, he has made of what they have to offer something uniquely his own. In the Canopus, as in the Teatro Marittimo and the Piazza d'Oro, there is no single satisfactory viewpoint: the result is an effect of motion, in curved space, in varied light and shade, involved with water, the whole a polyphonic counterpart to Hadrian's own restlessness.

The buildings we have studied present a partial portrait of the man. Hadrian the hunter, the soldier, the statesman comes out clearly in reliefs, coins, and inscriptions we have not room to treat. But the buildings reflect the dilettante Hadrian, uneasy, moody, whimsical, formal, distant, unapproachable, tense, self-conscious, cold. They show many facets of his character: in the Teatro Marittimo, his love of privacy, and his restlessness; in the Temple of Venus and Rome, the neat, abstract quality of his mind, his sense of humor, his self-conscious pairing of himself with Augustus; in the Pantheon, abstraction and Augustus again, plus an awareness of his own grandeur; in the Piazzo d'Oro, complication, involution, febrile gaiety. In the mausoleum, the obsession with his own grandeur and with the memory of Augustus recur, and something new has been added: deathwish and posturing with grief. These last two attitudes are to be read again in the fabric of the Canopus, together with a failure of creativity which marks the beginning of the end.

Hadrian is not the only Emperor whose personality may be read in the artifacts of his reign, but he is unique in being himself his own architect. This in turn creates a problem. How much in his work is genuine self-expression, how much mere playing with form? But the very putting of the question gives insight into Hadrian's character. The key is schizophrenia: unrest and self-consciousness where there might have been the easy confidence born of unchallenged Empire; loneliness in the midst of a crowded court; genius that failed; a love that killed. These are the contradictions that have caused Hadrian to be saluted—a dubious compliment—as "the first modern man." In his architecture, perhaps more eloquently and poignantly than in any other Roman work, the mute stones speak.

With Hadrian an era ends. Juvenal, who wrote during his reign, is the last secular classical Latin poet of importance. Hadrian's successor, Antoninus Pius (A.D. 138-161) was modest and plain-living where Hadrian had been flamboyant and extravagant. The autobiography (written in Greek) of *his* successor, Marcus Aurelius (161-180), is throughout a tacit criticism of Hadrian: his boy-love, his architecture, his dilettantism. Marcus Aurelius' son and successor, Commodus (180-192), was a monstrous megalomaniac beside whose excesses those of Caligula, Nero, or Domitian pale into insignificance. The next dynasty, the Severi (193-235), founded a military absolutism which degenerated into anarchy (235-284). Under Diocletian (284-305) absolutism is intensified and grows more rigid. Under Constantine (306-337) the Empire's creative center shifts to Constantinople (old Byzantium made new, in the Greek east), a new religion triumphs, and the story of Christian archaeology begins. True, the two centuries from Hadrian through Constantine are represented by some of Rome's most impressive surviving monuments: the Temple of Antoninus and Faustina, the Column of Marcus Aurelius, the Arches of Septimius Severus and of Constantine, the Baths of Caracalla and Diocletian, Aurelian's Wall, and the Basilica of Maxentius. But, artistically, many of these are derivative; *e.g.*, Marcus Aurelius' Column imitates Trajan's; Constantine's arch incorporates reliefs from earlier, more creative reigns. Yet while the artistic impulse flickers and dies, Roman skill in military and civil engineering, as exemplified in baths and aqueducts, roads and walls, continues unabated.

12

Roman Engineering

In this chapter strict chronology must be violated, and steps retraced, to discuss in specific detail something of what archaeology has to tell us about the most practical aspect of the Romans' genius: their talent for engineering. This is best exemplified in roads, baths, aqueducts, and for-tification-walls.

We have reached in our historical survey the end of Hadrian's reign, A.D. 138. By this date the main lines of the great consular roads leading from Rome had all been laid down, and later Emperors faced only the problems of maintenance, till the barbarians cut Rome's lines of com-munication, and the moving of the administrative center to Milan, Ravenna, and Constantinople reduced their im-portance. The most recent archaeological investigation of Roman roads in Italy has concentrated on tracing the lines of major and minor Roman highways and the native tracks that preceded them, a work of great urgency, in view of the modernization which is rapidly changing the face of Italy, especially in the vicinity of Rome.

If we turn to Roman baths, like those of Caracalla in Rome, begun in A.D. 211, we are back on the chronological track again, but we find that the last major archaeological work upon them was done at the end of the last century, and that their chief interest today lies in the inspiration they have offered to modern architects.

As for aqueducts, the last important ancient one was built under the Emperor Alexander Severus, in A.D. 226, but working back from that date we can profitably review the difficult and absorbing topographical work done in tracing the courses of the major aqueducts by a devoted Englishman and an American woman.

Finally we shall review the work of another Englishman in tracing the chronology and building techniques of ancient Rome's last great fortification, Aurelian's Wall, begun in A.D. 271 and still in large part standing. Its alterations and repairs have been traced down to the middle of the sixth century of our era. The examples chosen should justify the Romans' high reputation for engineering skill, and illuminate Roman history, at the same time underlining on the one hand our debt, for the facts we know and the inferences we draw, to the careful work of modern archaeologists, and on the other the catalytic effect, in the case of the baths, of Roman work upon our own architecture of the day before yesterday.

Roman roads (see Fig. 4.1) echoing to the measured tread of marching legions, had made a large contribution to unifying Italy by the time the last great consular highway, the Via Aemilia, opened up the Po valley from Ariminum to Placentia in 187 B.C., but their work of carrying commerce and ideas was unceasing. Of course there were roads in Italy before the Romans: the name and route of the Via Salaria, from the salt-pans at the Tiber's mouth up the valley into the Apennines, suggest that it must have been in use since prehistoric times. The Via Latina, named not for a Roman consul but for a people potent in central Italy until the Romans broke their league in 338 B.C., must count as a pre-Roman road, and its winding course along the foothills must antedate the draining of the Pomptine marshes and the laying down of the straight course across them from Rome to Tarracina and thence to Capua of the *regina viarum*, the queen of roads, the Via Appia. It bears the name of a Roman censor of 312 B.C. This is the first of the great highways, and it deserves its fame for its bold conquest of natural obstacles, its arrow-straight course across the marshes, but its gravel surface was not replaced by stone pavement until 293 B.C., and then only as far as the suburb of Bovillae. And its course, like that of many

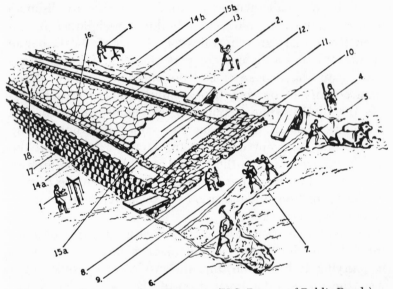

Fig. 12.1   Roman road construction. (U.S. Bureau of Public Roads)

another Roman road, was not always so arrow-straight. In the hills behind Tarracina it followed the contours; it was not until Trajan's time that another bold stroke of engineering cut through the high, rocky Pesco Montano to let the road pass by the more direct coastal route. (Some authorities hold that the Romans preferred straight roads because the front axles of their vehicles were rigid.) Trajan's engineers showed their pride in their work by incising monumental Roman numerals, still visible, to mark the depth of the cut every ten feet from the top down, until the road level was triumphantly reached at ⌈CXX⌉.

Along the Appia, and the other consular roads radiating from Rome, traces of the ancient stone paving are occasionally preserved. The paving blocks are usually *selce* (flint), polygonal in shape and closely fitted without mortar. While most Roman roads prove on archaeological examination to consist of paving blocks laid in a trench and packed with earth and *selce* chips, it will be worthwhile to record the ideal method of laying a pavement—strictly speaking a mosaic pavement—as recommended by the architect Vitruvius, a contemporary of Augustus. The method illustrates the Roman engineer's infinite capacity for taking pains.

After the field engineer (1 in the reconstruction, Fig. 12.1), assisted by the stake man (2), had aligned the road with his *groma*, he ran levels with the *chorobates* (3) with the roadman's help (4). A plow (5) was used to loosen earth and mark road margins; then workmen dug marginal trenches (6) to the depth desired for the solid foundations. Laborers (7) shoveled loose earth and carried it away in baskets. The next step was to consolidate the roadbed with a tamper (8). Now the roadbed was ready for its foundation, the *pavimentum* (9), lime mortar or sand laid to form a level base. Next came the *statumen*, or first course (10), fist-size stones, cemented together with mortar or clay, the thickness varying from ten inches to two feet. Over this was laid the *rudus* or second course (11), nine to twelve inches of lime concrete, grouted with broken stone and pottery fragments. Next the *nucleus*, or third course (12), concrete made of gravel or coarse sand mixed with hot lime, placed in layers and compacted with a roller. Its thickness was one foot at the sides, eighteen inches at the crown of the road. Finally, the *summum dorsum* or top course (13), polygonal blocks of *selce* six inches or more thick, carefully fitted and set in the *nucleus* while the concrete was still soft. Sometimes, when archaeologists have taken up a stretch of Roman road, they have found the *selce* blocks rutted on the under side: the economical contractors, happily untroubled by high-priced labor, had repaired their road by turning the worn blocks upside down. Standard curbs (14a and b) were two feet wide and eighteen inches high; paved footpaths (15a and b) often ran outside them. Conduits (16) under the curb, with arched outlets (17) opening beside the right of way, took care of draining surface water. Milestones (18) marked the distance from Rome and the name of the Emperor responsible for repairs. From the names of successive Emperors on milestones of the same road, archaeologists have calculated that the average life of a highway was thirty to forty years.

Two points should be emphasized: first, this represents an ideal method of construction, not often exemplified in practice; second, to a modern engineer a road like this would seem insufficiently elastic, a five-foot wall in the flat, too rigid for the stresses and strains to which it was subjected. Hence perhaps the frequent need for repairs, but Roman traffic was lighter than ours, and the very fact that we can write about the roads at all is a tribute to their durability. Upon roads like these, under the Empire, travelled the Imperial posting service, with relays of messengers, and post-houses where horses and carriages could be changed. Under exceptional conditions the Emperor Tiberius, using this service, once travelled 180 miles in a day, a rate of speed not equalled on European roads until the nineteenth century.

The next major road laid out after the Appia must have been the Valeria, which was needed for eastward communication via Tivoli with the new colony of Alba Fucens, founded, as we saw, in 303 B.C. Archaeology has shown that in general the foundation of a colony precedes the laying down of the metalled military road. This is true of Cosa (foundation date of the colony, 273 B.C.; probable date of the Via Aurelia which served it, about 241); of Ariminum (founded 268 B.C.; reached by the Via Flaminia in 220), and of the Roman colonies in the Po valley; e.g., Bononia (Bologna: founded 189 B.C.; reached by the Via Aemilia after 187). The full extension of the Via Valeria beyond Alba to the Adriatic had to await the pacification of the Samnite tribes of central Italy and the granting of citizenship to Italians after the "Social" War, in 89 B.C. Milestones on this last stretch belong to Claudius' reign (A.D. 41-54).

A recent (1957) survey of the central section of the Valeria by the Dutch scholar C. C. Van Essen illustrates the methods and results of archaeologists working in the field with topographical problems. Faced with the palimpsest of more than two millennia overlying the road he wanted to trace, Van Essen paid particular attention to such roadmarks as Roman milestones; ancient tombs (which regularly lined Roman roads in the vicinity of towns); supporting walls, in Roman headers-and-stretchers; rock-hewn causeways; bridges, where Roman materials and workmanship can be distinguished from modern (as has been recently done for the bridges of the Via Flaminia by Michael Ballance of the British School at Rome; there the striking thing is the predominance and good quality of the work done under Augustus, who had a vested interest in assuring efficient communications with his veterans dispersed in colonies in north Italy). Stretches of ancient pavement are rare on the Valeria, having been destroyed by medieval and modern resurfacing, by the plow, and by torrents and earthquakes, but the trench in which it was bedded can often be distinguished on air photographs. What struck Van Essen chiefly was the frequency with which the ancient Via Valeria would run straight on, with steep gradients, where the modern road resorts to sweeping curves or hairpin bends. Ancient vehicles, the heaviest of which were perhaps only a quarter the weight of a modern light European car (Roman wagon, perhaps 440 pounds; Volkswagen, 1650), and scarcely ever carried loads of over 1100 pounds, would be less troubled by steep gradients than a modern heavy truck. Even so, at Tagliacozzo, about six miles on the Rome side of Alba Fucens, the grade is so steep that Van Essen supposes the ancient inhabitants hired out oxen to help the straining horses on the upslope. Van Essen noted that the telegraph lines, following the comparatively straight course of the ancient road, often gave a clue to its presence. The ancient sixty-eighth milestone of the Valeria, found, as we saw, within the walls of Alba Fucens, provides a good comparison of the respective lengths of the ancient and the modern roads. Since the Roman mile (4861 English feet) was slightly shorter than the English, sixty-eight Roman miles corresponds to slightly over sixty-two English miles, whereas the modern Via Valeria covers about 113 kilometers, or approximately seventy miles, to reach Alba.

Archaeologists have not confined their interests to the great consular roads. Minor highways in areas away from the main stream of traffic are often more rewarding, since they tend to be better preserved, and offer some chance to trace the pre-Roman systems that underlie or intersect them. The district just north of Rome has been surveyed in this way by members of the British School at Rome since 1954, only just in time, for there prevails in this region a situation analogous to the rapid disappearance of Indian remains in the American West with the building of the great hydroelectric dams. In the country north of Rome, since World War II, there has been an extensive program of land expropriation, reclamation, and resettlement of small farmers, an excellent thing for rehabilitating the Italian peasantry, but fatal for archaeological remains, since the plan involves the use of the deep plow, an ideal instrument for obliterating traces of ancient roadways. Thus it is that members and friends of the British School, spurred on by the Direc-

tor, John Ward Perkins, a worthy successor of the inde-
fatigable Thomas Ashby, are to be seen braving wind and
weather as they scour the countryside for Roman and pre-
Roman roads from Veii to beyond Città Castellana, armed
with large-scale maps, air photographs, and brown paper
bags for collecting the potsherds which are the evidence of
ancient roadside habitation.

The British School's most significant recent work has
been carried on from Nepi, a Roman colony allegedly of
383 B.C., twenty-eight miles north-northwest of Rome, and
Falerii Novi, about four miles farther north. Falerii Novi
was built by the Romans from the ground up in 241 B.C.
to house the inhabitants of Falerii Veteres (Città Castellana) a hostile native Faliscan center, which the Romans
completely destroyed. But the old city must have been
resettled, for ruts in the third century B.C. road connecting
the new city with the old are not of standard Roman width,
and were probably made by Faliscan wagons. The *cardo*
of the new settlement is formed by a new road connection
with the south, the Via Amerina (Fig. 12.2); in the course
of exploring this the British archaeologists found traces from
which the older road system (Fig. 12.3) which it partially
supplanted, may be inferred. At Torre dell' Isola, just north
of Nepi, for example, they found, by the wall of a medieval
castle, sherds with the cord-impressed chevrons characteristic of Villanovan ware, and part of one of the portable
hearths which we met first in the primitive hut on the
Palatine in Rome. These sherds provide evidence for habitation here at least as early as on the Palatine. The discovery of similar sherds within the walls of Etruscan Veii
suggests a people inferior culturally to the Etruscans, and
probably living in subjection to them.

These people were the Faliscans. Their settlements must
have required road connections, especially between their
chief city, old Falerii, and Veii, with which it was allied.
These roads the British archaeologists have identified in

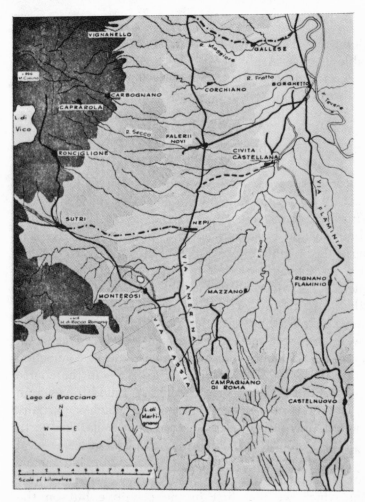

Fig. 12.2   Roman roads of the *ager Faliscus*.
(*Papers Brit. Sch. at Rome* 12 [1957], p. 68)

deep cuttings, identified as pre-Roman by inscriptions in
Etruscan characters. (Faliscan was a dialect of Latin, but
Etruscan inscriptions occur.) These earliest cuttings, sometimes nearly fifty feet deep, are driven impressively through
cliffs, cut downward from the surface in a succession of
working levels to match the slope of the finished road, with
careful attention paid to drainage. Pre-Roman stone piers

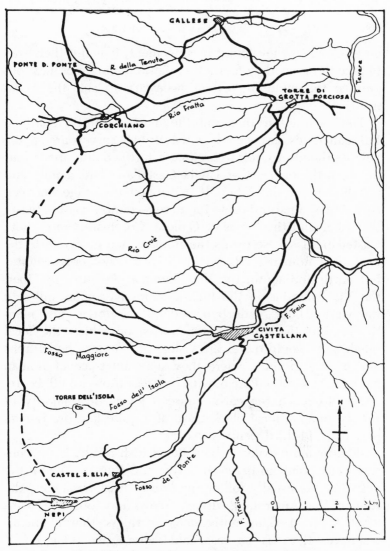

FIG. 12.3   Faliscan roads of the *ager Faliscus*.
(*PBSR, loc. cit.*, p. 105)

probably carried timber bridges, but most of the roads are mere ridgeway tracks, not unlike the medieval and modern farm tracks still to be found in the district. The Faliscans were apparently capable of ambitious engineering, but were driven by poverty to avoid it. The Romans used Faliscan cuttings when they found it convenient, it being their way to take things as they found them, introducing modifications only to the minimum extent necessary to suit their own needs.

The most interesting and the most certainly identified Faliscan roads discovered in the British survey are in the neighborhood of Grotta Porciosa, a fortified site about four miles north-northeast of Città Castellana and a mile and a half west of the Tiber. It controlled the ridge between two gorges, a natural route for a cross-country road between the Tiber and the towns of Gallese, Corchiano, and Città Castellana. In these towns the Romans had no interest: the two main Roman roads in this area run not cross-country but north and south, the Via Flaminia close to the Tiber, the Via Amerina on the high ground five or six miles to the west. These roads bypassed all the towns just mentioned. But the cross-country tracks, on which the local inhabitants would travel, are visible both in air-photographs and on the ground, where they show no trace of Roman paving. At Grotta Porciosa itself, excavation would be required to reach the early Faliscan level; the majority of sherds found is local black glaze of a quite late pre-Roman period (mid-third century B.C.).

What is most striking about the British results is the contrast they point up between native and Roman. Where the native tracks usually follow the line of least resistance, the Roman Via Amerina is driven across any obstacle, with what Ward Perkins aptly calls "ruthless thoroughness," whenever there is no reasonable alternative. One might almost think that the new road was built deliberately to impress; in any case the massive viaducts and lofty bridges served to symbolize to the Faliscan peasantry the Roman conqueror's energy and resources, by which it was hopelessly outclassed. With the same ruthlessness with which they imposed their roads upon the landscape, the Romans imposed law and order upon the countryside. The archaeological evidence is the way in which the peasants shifted from their old anarchical life in small strongholds of armed retainers, which is what Grotta Porciosa must have been, down into settled life in Roman cities, or in the open country beside the Roman roads. The great primeval Ciminian Forest, northwest of Nepi, once the fearsome haunt of brigands, was cleared under the Romans and turned into farms. When after eight centuries Roman power waned, the countryside reverted to pre-Roman conditions; the country-folk crept back into the cliff-top villages, there to remain until quite recent times.

These, the results of careful and enjoyable outdoor work in the Italian countryside by a United Nations of archaeologists, enable us to appreciate how the competence of the Roman road-builders made possible both the cold-bloodedness of the Roman conquest and the security of the Roman peace.

That security brought in its train prosperity, and even luxury, of which the symbol is the grandiose Roman public baths. Though Agrippa, Nero, Titus, and Trajan all built baths whose sites and plans are known, the most grandiose, and the clearest in plan, are the Baths of Caracalla, begun in A.D. 211. The Baths of Diocletian, built a century later, are equally vast, but their plan has been obscured by the incorporation into their fabric of the church of S. Maria degli Angeli and the Terme Museum. The Baths of Caracalla, known to thousands of visitors as the summer setting for Rome's outdoor opera, were built on a vast platform, twenty feet high, with an area of 270,000 square feet, greater than that of London's Houses of Parliament. Excavations in 1938, when the Baths were being prepared for their metamorphosis into an outdoor opera house, revealed in the substructure vaulted service corridors, wide enough for vehicles, widening out at intersections into regular underground public squares, with provisions for rotary traffic. Access to the lower reaches was by stairs let into the central piers of the main building. The principal entrance to the baths was to the north (over the edge of the platform at the top center of the air-photograph, Fig. 12.4). It was flanked by numerous small rooms which in the difficult post-war years housed teeming families of Italy's homeless. (Their unique opportunity of a summer evening to admire the sleek prosperity of the operagoers recreated the gulf that yawned between haves and have nots in Imperial Rome, and contributed not a little to Italy's unrest.)

The main bath building was set in the northern half of the great open space provided by the platform, and was surrounded with gardens. Facing these on the perimeter was a variety of halls, for lectures, reading, and exercise. Those on the east and west were contained in curved projections (exedras). A part of the western exedra appears in the lower left corner of the air-photograph. Beneath it in a subterranean vault was discovered in 1911 what was at that time the largest Mithraeum (shrine of the Persian god Mithras) in Rome.° To the south (lower right on the photograph) was a stadium whose seats were built against the reservoir which supplied the baths: this was fed by a branch from one of the great aqueducts, the Aqua Marcia.

The main block of the baths is distinguished for its axial symmetry. The most prominent room was the circular *caldarium,* or hot bath (just to the right of center in the photograph). It is between its main piers that the opera stage is set. Behind it the vast rectangular open space (82 x 170 feet) is most logically interpreted as a grand concourse whence the patrons of the baths (as many as 1600 in peak hours) could move unimpeded to the bathing rooms of their choice. This central room was groin-vaulted in coffered concrete, in three great bays supported by eight piers

° In 1958 Dutch archaeologists excavated a larger one under the church of S. Prisca on the Aventine Hill.

FIG. 12.4   Rome, Baths of Caracalla, air view. Castagnoli, *Roma antica*, Pl. 35)

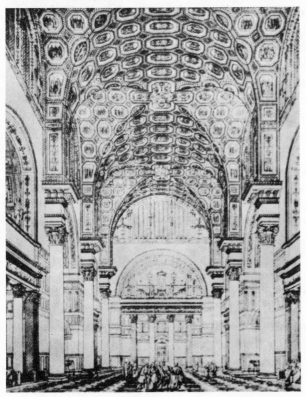

FIG. 12.5   Rome, baths of Caracalla, great hall, nineteenth century reconstruction.

(Fig. 12.5). The rooms around the central rectangle, with their enormously thick walls, were ingeniously arranged as buttresses to resist the thrust of the colossal vaults.

The large open spaces at the east and west ends of the main block were exercise-grounds. The exedras adjacent to their inner sides were decorated in the early fourth century with the splendidly satiric mosaics of athletes now in the Lateran Museum. With their broken noses, low foreheads, and cauliflower ears, they are the very type of overspecialized brutal brawn which intellectuals in all ages have delighted to ridicule.

The large rectangular area at the rear center was the cold swimming pool, or *frigidarium;* perhaps the rooms on either side were dressing rooms. Below the pavement of the baths the excavators discovered tons of L- or T-shaped iron bolted together in the form of a St. Andrew's cross. The possible inference is that some part of the baths was roofed with iron girders, designed to support bronze plates ingeniously contrived to reflect sunlight onto the bathers below. (The evidence for the bronze plates and the sun-room is not archaeological but literary, and, chiefly because the literary source had little or no idea what he was talking about, has raised apparently insoluble controversy.)

Excavations were going on in the Baths on a langorous summer afternoon in late June of 1901 which the American architect Charles Follen McKim spent there. That afternoon bore fruit soon after, when he was asked to design for the Pennsylvania Railroad a great terminal station in New York. McKim, lover of Rome and founder of the American Academy there, belonged to the school of architects for whom the grand manner, as found in Roman baths, the Pantheon, and the Coliseum, formed the basis of design for works of the first rank. He desired to symbolize in Pennsylvania Station the monumental gateway to a great city, which should at the same time perform efficiently its function of handling large crowds. To a man of his training and prejudices, the Baths of Caracalla seemed to fill the bill. He is reported to have assembled on one occasion a huge band of workmen in the Baths in Rome, simply to test the aesthetic effect of huge scale upon crowds passing under the arches. (Crowds there must always have been, in the heyday of the baths, motley, colorful crowds, speaking many tongues; there is easily room for 2500 patrons at a time. We may imagine them bathing, sauntering, making assignations; conversing idly or upon philosophical subjects; thronging the lecture rooms, the library, the picture-gallery; running, jumping, racing, ball-playing, or watching spectator-sports in the stadium at the back.)

The station plan (Fig. 12.6) shows how creatively Mc-Kim imitated Roman architecture. The succession of portico, vestibule, arcade, vestibule, staircase, which leads to what before remodelling of 1958 was the climax in the great central concourse, is noble architectural language, beautiful ordering of space, which Hadrian would have understood, and so is the balance in the façade, the alternating rhythms throughout the building of open and closed, big and little, wide and narrow. In the arcade, the repeated rhythms (now spoiled by advertising) emphasize the traditional, and the movement which is the essence of transportation. The great central hall, once a pool of open space, is even larger (340 x 210 feet, and 100 feet high) than the one that inspired it in the Baths; it is longer than the nave of St. Peter's. In it McKim contrived to preserve simplicity, dignity, and monumentality in spite of mechanical distractions, as when he used the protruding tops of ventilator shafts as pedestals for lamp-standards. The other refinements, too, are in the Roman manner and material. The rich golden stone facing of the great room is travertine imported from Tivoli, here used for the first time in America (and now badly in need of cleaning). The structural steel and glass in the concourse leading to the trains may have been inspired by the girders in the Baths of Caracalla. The statistics that record 1140 carloads of pink granite brought from New England to build the half-mile of exterior walls are in the Roman tradition, and so is the vast extent of the eight-acre structure, and the six years it took to build. The efficiency is Roman, too: access on all four sides, carriage drives twice as wide as the normal New York street of 1910—when the building was opened—a traffic-flow plan that separated incoming and outgoing passengers.

Pennsylvania Station belongs to a vanished era, an era of princely magnificence, of willingness to spend on purely aesthetic pleasure. The young architectural fellows of McKim's Academy in Rome are impatient with what it stands for, but perhaps they are letting their understandable and proper scorn of soulless copying—of which there is far too much in American monumental architecture—stand in the way of their appreciation of a building which has worn well, and earned accolades—especially by contrast with recent tawdry and misguided additions in plastic—from such emancipated critics, friendly to modern trends in architecture, as Talbot Hamlin and Lewis Mumford. In a day of what a less temperate critic than these has called "the monstrous repetition of cellular façades cloaked with vitreous indifference" by "sedulous apes to the latest expressions of technological baboonery," it may be salutary to look with understanding at how successful a modern architect of genius can be with a Roman model.

Roman baths needed oceans of water. It was supplied by another triumph of Roman engineering, the system of aqueducts. The eleventh and last of the ancient aqueducts was built by the Emperor Alexander Severus in A.D. 226; the earliest, the Aqua Appia, dates back to the same builder and the same year—312 B.C.—as the *regina viarum*. The network (Fig. 12.8) supplied Rome with over 250,000,000 gallons of water every twenty-four hours. When New York

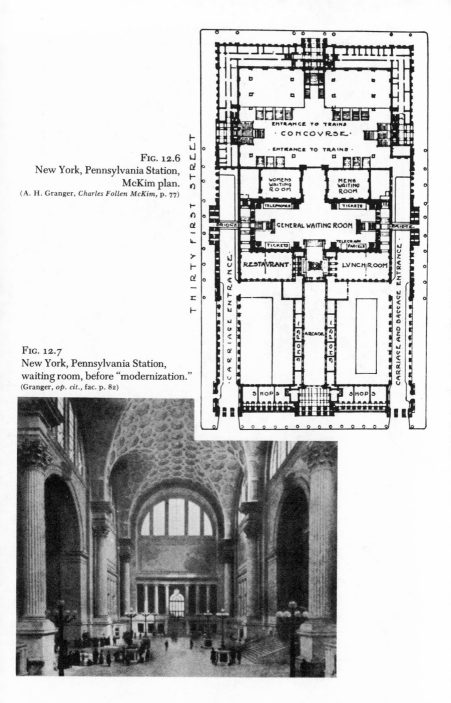

Fig. 12.6
New York, Pennsylvania Station,
McKim plan.
(A. H. Granger, *Charles Follen McKim*, p. 77)

Fig. 12.7
New York, Pennsylvania Station,
waiting room, before "modernization."
(Granger, *op. cit.*, fac. p. 82)

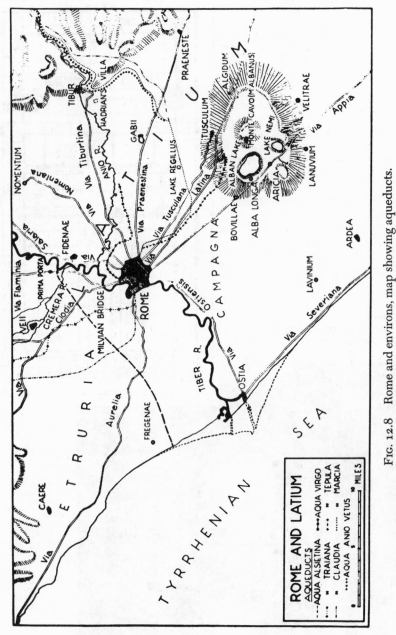

FIG. 12.8   Rome and environs, map showing aqueducts.
(V. Scramuzza and P. MacKendrick, *The Ancient World*, Fig. 33a)

was thrice the size of Severan Rome, its aqueducts supplied only 425,000,000 gallons daily.

We owe our knowledge of Rome's aqueducts to three people, one ancient and two modern: Sextus Julius Frontinus, water commissioner under Trajan, whose book on aqueducts survives, Dr. Thomas Ashby, former Director of the British School at Rome, and Miss Esther B. Van Deman of the American Academy. For over thirty years, before modernity removed the traces, this devoted pair tramped the rough country between Tivoli and Rome, plotting the courses of the major aqueducts. Their definitive work is well-nigh as monumental as the aqueducts themselves. Together they explored the mazy course of the aqueduct channels, above ground and below, along crumbling cliffs and the edge of deep gorges, over walls, through briers, across turnip fields, in the cellars of farm-houses and wine-shops. They climbed and waded; Ashby explored down-shafts "with the aid of several companions and a climber's rope," and when they were through, the courses and the building history especially of Rome's four major aqueducts, the Anio Vetus (272-269 B.C.), the Marcia (144 B.C.), the Claudia (A.D. 47), and the Anio Novus (A.D. 52)—all repeatedly repaired—were better known than they had been since Frontinus' day, and fellow archaeologists were in a position to draw from their detailed pioneer work important conclusions about Roman hydraulic engineering and about Roman culture.

Following Frontinus' indications, Ashby and Miss Van Deman found the sources of the four great aqueducts at over 1000 feet above sea level, in springs or lakes in the upper reaches of the Anio valley, near Subiaco, Mandela, and Vicovaro. The airline distance of the sources from Rome varies from twenty-four to twenty-seven miles, but to follow the contours the aqueducts took a circuitous course, so that their actual length is from forty-three to sixty-two miles. Though the modern reader associates Roman

aqueducts with the magnificent lines of arches (Fig. 12.9)
stretching across a once-empty Campagna near Rome, the
fact is that well under a third of a Roman aqueduct's course
was normally carried on arches: the rest was tunnel or side-
hill channel. The reason for this was in part économy, in
part strategic considerations: an aqueduct below ground is
harder for an enemy to find and cut. When the Goths finally
did cut the aqueducts in the sixth century A.D., the seven

FIG. 12.9   Aqueducts near Capannelle, reconstruction (painting).
(Deutsches Museum, Munich)

hills of Rome became, and remained for centuries, unfit
for civilized habitation.

The four aqueducts, Ashby and Miss Van Deman found,
followed the course of the Anio fairly closely from their
source to just below Tivoli, where, having lost half their
altitude, they turned south along the shoulder of the hills
to Gallicano. In this stretch, at Ponte Lupo, the Aqua
Marcia crosses a gorge on a bridge that would test the
mettle of the most seasoned archaeologist, for it epitomizes
Roman constructional history in stone and concrete for

almost nine centuries. After Gallicano the intrepid pair traced the aqueducts' course westward, where, by a system of tunnels, inverted siphons (the Romans knew that water would rise to its own level), and side-hill channels they cross the broken gorges of the Campagna to a point south of Capannelle racetrack, six miles from Rome, whence they proceed on the famous arches to the Porta Maggiore. From reservoirs in the city the water was distributed in lead pipes (one, of Hadrianic date, has walls three inches thick, and weighs eighty-eight pounds per running foot), with a strict priority, first to public basins and fountains (the Aqua Julia alone supplied 1200 of these), next to baths (extensions of the Marcia supplied those of both Caracalla and Diocletian), then to private houses. Surplus was used for flushing the sewers. Attempts were made to control the priorities by running the pipes for private use only from the highest levels of the reservoirs, but Frontinus complains bitterly of illegal tapping.

In the Gallicano-Capannelle stretch special archaeological ingenuity is required, first to find the channels, and then to decide which belongs to which aqueduct. Where the channels have entirely disappeared, through the disintegrating action of floods, earthquake, tree roots, or plowing, the course can be defined by plotting the occurrence of heaps of calcium carbonate on the ground. This is the aqueduct deposit. Roman water is extremely hard, and the heaps mark where once there were downshafts (*putei*) for inspection and cleaning the channels, which without such maintenance would soon have become completely blocked with deposit. Frontinus says the downshafts occurred regularly every 240 feet, and Dr. Ashby found many at just this interval.

For distinguishing one aqueduct from another there are many criteria. The first is construction materials. The earliest aqueducts are built of cut stone, the latest of brick. Miss Van Deman was famous for her precise dating of building materials; she was the only archaeologist in Rome who could date a brick by the *taste* of the mortar. A second criterion is quality of workmanship. The Claudia, for example, is notoriously jerry-built: where abutments are found which should be solid, but are instead one block thick, filled in with earth behind, that channel belongs to the Aqua Claudia. A third criterion is mineral deposits. Thus the Marcia was famous for its purity; the crystalline lime deposits were quarried in the Middle Ages, polished, and used to decorate altars. The Anio Novus, on the other hand, is distinguished by a singularly foul deposit. A fourth criterion is directness of course: the older the aqueduct the more sinuously it runs; a channel found meandering by itself along the contours is likely to be that of the Anio Vetus.

The total impression the aqueducts give is one of efficiency, organization, and heedlessness of expense, under the Republic as well as under the Empire. They were built with the spoils of wars or the tribute of provinces. The Marcia, built with the proceeds of the loot of Carthage and Corinth, cost 180,000,000 sesterces, or $9,000,000 uninflated. The Tepula, of 125 B.C., was perhaps built with the profits from the organization of the new province of Asia. From Agrippa's time onward, and especially in Frontinus' administration, the aqueduct service employed a large bureaucracy; overseers, reservoir-superintendents, inspectors, stonemasons, plasterers (the stone-built channels were lined with two or three coats of hydraulic cement), and unskilled laborers. Maintenance was a constant problem. Arches needed propping, filling in, or brick facing; piers needed to be buttressed or brick-encased. There was no attempt to produce high pressure: lead pipes would not have stood it, and for public use it was not necessary. There was no attempt to make the aqueducts financially self-supporting: their original building was one of the benefactions expected of successful commanders. Since these nabobs expected a *quid pro quo* in the gift of power, the aqueducts are a symbol, under the Republic of irresponsible oligarchy, and under the Empire of increasingly irresponsible autocracy, though "good" Emperors like Augustus, Claudius, Trajan, and Hadrian had a hand in them. In Augustus' reign were built the Julia, the Virgo, and the Alsietina. Trajan built a northern line from Lago di Bracciano to Rome's Trastevere quarter on the right bank of the Tiber: part of its course runs under the courtyard of the American Academy. Hadrian executed major repairs, datable by the omnipresent brick stamps. But even good Emperors knew no way of financing such public works except bleeding the taxpayer. In municipalities, private capital was absorbed in such public enterprise, with no return in income or local employment commensurate with the capital involved. So one major conclusion from Ashby's and Miss Van Deman's work is that the Romans were better engineers than they were economists. Let the last word on aqueducts be Pliny the Elder's: "If one takes careful account of the abundant supply of water for public purposes, for baths, pools, channels, houses, gardens, suburban villas; the length of the aqueducts' courses—arches reared, mountains tunnelled, valleys crossed on the level—he will confess that there has never been a greater marvel in the whole world."

One of the latest pieces of Roman engineering, to a knowledge of which archaeology has recently contributed, is Aurelian's Wall. It has been meticulously studied by a pupil of Ashby's, I. A. Richmond, now Professor of Archaeology of the Roman Empire at Oxford. Two-thirds of it is still standing (Fig. 12.10), to the disgust of those interested in the unimpeded flow of Rome's traffic, to the delight of those in love with Rome's past. It was twelve miles long, twelve feet thick, sixty feet high; it had 381 towers, each with a latrine, and eighteen portcullised gates, nine of which survive (Fig. 12.11). Though the Renaissance humanist

Poggio Bracciolini had examined the wall as early as 1431, and the Frenchman Nicholas Audebert had studied it scientifically in 1574, Richmond was still able to make important contributions. He emphasizes, for example, that one-sixth of the wall incorporated buildings: tombs, houses, park walls, aqueducts, cisterns, porticoes, an amphitheater, a fortress. The inference is that the wall had to be built with speed and economy, in the face of the threat of barbarians in north Italy and a depleted treasury. Strategic

Fig. 12.10   Rome, Aurelian's Wall, from south, near Porta Appia.
(H. Kähler, *Rom und seine Welt*, Pl. 252)

reasons, of course, dictated the protection of the aqueducts. The use of tombstones as latrine covers shows, says Richmond, that the wall builders "had their religious scruples under excellent control." It was a sense of urgency and not solicitude for works of art that prompted them, when they built a garden wall at Porta San Lorenzo into the circuit, to leave the statues in their niches and pack them round with clay.

Richmond also found that in the phase of the wall identified as Aurelian's by building materials and brick stamps,

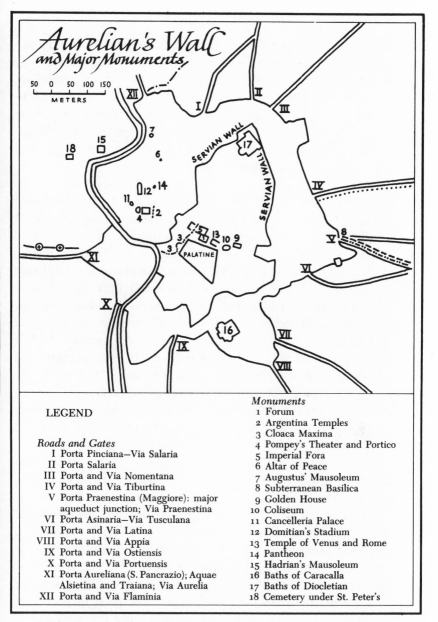

LEGEND

Roads and Gates
 I Porta Pinciana—Via Salaria
 II Porta Salaria
 III Porta and Via Nomentana
 IV Porta and Via Tiburtina
 V Porta Praenestina (Maggiore): major
    aqueduct junction; Via Praenestina
 VI Porta Asinaria—Via Tusculana
 VII Porta and Via Latina
 VIII Porta and Via Appia
 IX Porta and Via Ostiensis
 X Porta and Via Portuensis
 XI Porta Aureliana (S. Pancrazio); Aquae
    Alsietina and Traiana; Via Aurelia
 XII Porta and Via Flaminia

Monuments
 1 Forum
 2 Argentina Temples
 3 Cloaca Maxima
 4 Pompey's Theater and Portico
 5 Imperial Fora
 6 Altar of Peace
 7 Augustus' Mausoleum
 8 Subterranean Basilica
 9 Golden House
 10 Coliseum
 11 Cancelleria Palace
 12 Domitian's Stadium
 13 Temple of Venus and Rome
 14 Pantheon
 15 Hadrian's Mausoleum
 16 Baths of Caracalla
 17 Baths of Diocletian
 18 Cemetery under St. Peter's

FIG. 12.11   Rome, Aurelian's Wall, plan, with major Imperial monuments.

the workmanship differed sharply from one curtain to another. The inference from this was that various stretches were assigned to various gangs of workmen—mostly civilian, since the legions were needed in the North, and for Aurelian's campaign against the Parthians in the East. These workmen belonged to the various city guilds, or *collegia,* some experienced in construction, some not, but all pressed into service in the emergency.

Richmond distinguished the bottom twenty-four feet of the wall as the original phase. It was built of brick-faced concrete—that its bricks were often second-hand is inferred from the many Hadrianic stamps—surmounted by a gallery with loopholes outside and an open, bayed arcade inside, with a crenellated wall-walk above. Access to the wall was by the towers only; Richmond inferred that the planner aimed to keep excited and irresponsible civilians from interfering with defense, and the wall-detail from pilfering or philandering in the adjoining houses and gardens. In this phase the wall was plain, efficient, functional, simple, and uniform, built to a standard size and pattern. Its many gates show that there was no very formidable danger: the intent was to provide a barrier to shut chance bodies of undesirables out of the city as on far-flung frontiers structures like Hadrian's Wall shut them out of the Empire.

In its second phase another thirty-six feet of wall was fitted on to the base provided by Aurelian's. In some places the addition was only six feet thick, the other half of the original width being left as a passage for the circulation of materials and messages. A wall sixty feet high reduced the required number of defenders, since it had nothing to fear from an enemy equipped with scaling ladders. In this phase machines did the work of men: if there were two *ballistae* to a tower, the expensive and impressive total of pieces of artillery would have been 762. Heightening the wall meant heightening the tower, sometimes to five stories. A start was made toward monumentalizing the gateways, but it petered out, though the effect can be admired in the Porta Asinaria near the Lateran, which was restored in 1957-58. For the workmanship of this phase is identical with and therefore of the same date as the Basilica and Circus of Maxentius (who reigned A.D. 306-312); when he was defeated by Constantine at the battle of the Milvian Bridge, and the capital moved to Constantinople, neither the money nor the motive for monumentality any longer existed.

The next major alteration is dated by inscriptions to A.D. 401-403, the reign of Honorius. It was prompted by the threat that the city might be sacked by Alaric the Visigoth. It involved second-hand stone facing for the curtains of the wall, and square bases for the towers. The photograph (Fig. 12.10) shows this Honorian phase at the Porta Appia. The upper stories of the round towers belong to Maxentius' addition, while halfway up the face of the curtain between the rectangular towers to the left of the gate can be seen the patching required to add Maxentius' brickwork to the battlements of Aurelian's original wall. (To distinguish the building phases of the Porta Appia, Richmond had to crawl into the base of a tower through a very small hole, while a small uninvited audience bet on his chances of sticking.) The new battlements were built in a way that shows that in this phase Rome could no longer afford artillery: archers replaced *ballistae*. By now the Empire is Christian, and crosses begin to appear on the keystones of the gate arches, as prophylaxis against the devil. Later, in what Richmond describes as "an age of vanishing standards of faith and hygiene," an indulgence of 100 days was granted for kissing one of these crosses. They were no help: the wall was assaulted by earthquakes (A.D. 442), and by Goths (A.D. 536 and 546), and repeatedly repaired. Belisarius in 547 restored it all, with the help of palisades, in twenty days, and equipped it with spring-guns the force of whose projectiles could impale five men, and with mantraps or deadfalls, harrow-like devices which could be pushed over on assailants. But the repairs are botched work, appropriate to what Rome had become: no longer an Imperial capital, but a minor metropolis of an outlying Byzantine province. All the same, the wall was never really breached till the advent of heavy artillery, when Garibaldi's men attacked the Porta San Pancrazio in 1849.

What Richmond's work has done is to epitomize, in the history of a work of Roman engineering, Rome's decline and fall. This is the latest point in ancient history to which our survey will take us. In the 1300 years since the Palatine huts we have, with archaeology's help, traced Rome's rise to grandeur and her agonizing decline. Spiritually, Rome never fell. The Papacy in a sense is the ghost of the Roman Empire sitting crowned upon its grave: the symbol is the Popes' palace-fortress installed in Hadrian's mausoleum, or St. Peter's basilica overlying what is in part a pagan cemetery. It will be appropriate in the final chapter to confront Caesar with Christ, by describing a late Imperial hunting lodge in Sicily, and a tomb beneath the high altar of St. Peter's, which by the fourth century A.D. was believed to be the last resting place of the apostle who was a fisher of men.

13

Caesar and Christ

In the official Italian archaeological journal *Notizie degli Scavi* for 1951 were reported recent excavations of a grandiose villa near Piazza Armerina, in central Sicily, which had already received some notoriety in the press, for depicting "Bikini girls" in very brief bathing suits (Fig. 13.1). Of this villa traces had always existed above ground, and as early as 1754 the discovery had been reported there of a "temple" (probably the basilica numbered 30 in the plan, Fig. 13.2), with a mosaic floor. In 1881 the trilobate complex (46) was excavated, and in 1929 the great Sicilian archaeologist Paolo Orsi, the expert on prehistoric remains on the island, dug there. Major funds—500,000 lire—made possible large-scale excavation between 1937 and 1943, as a part of *Il Duce's* plans for a major celebration of the bimillennary of Augustus' birth. After the war, government support to the tune of 5,000,000 lire (which inflation reduced in value to $8,000, only a tenth as much as the earlier grant) made it possible to finish excavating the villa and to take steps to preserve *in situ* the mosaics which are its chief glory. This is one of the few excavations on Italian soil whose chief avowed intent was to encourage tourism, and it has succeeded. Piazza Armerina is a boom town, boasting

Fig. 13.1   Piazza Armerina, Imperial Villa, "Bikini girls" mosaic.
(B. Pace, *I Mosaici di Piazza Armerina*, Pl. 15)

a new hotel, and its narrow streets are choked with sight-seeing busses.

Both the mosaics and the villa's ambitious plan make it a sight worth seeing. There are forty-two polychrome pavements, involving the setting by the ancient workmen of 30,000,000 individual mosaic rectangles, or *tesserae*, over an area of more than 3500 square yards, a complex unique in extent in the Roman world. The plan, too, is one of the most ambitious known to archaeology, rivalling that of Nero's Golden House, Hadrian's villa, or Diocletian's palace at Spalato on the Dalmatian cost. The villa lies three-and-a-half miles southwest of Piazza Armerina, nearly 2,000 feet above sea level, on the west slope of Monte Mangone, in the midst of green orchards and pleasant groves of nut trees. Its altitude assured its being cool in summer; its setting under the lee of the hill protected it from winter winds. But the slope required terracing, and so the villa was laid out on four levels centering on three peristyles and a portico (plan 2,15,41,26). The parts are connected by irregular rooms (13,14,40). The technique of the masonry shows that the whole complex is of one build, characterized by asymmetrical symmetry, strange, twisted ground-plans, a fondness for curves, and off-center axes, all of which shows a definite break with conventional classicism. The structure is light and elastic: the dome over the three-lobed state dining room (46), nowadays replaced by an unnecessarily ugly modern roof to protect the mosaics, was built of pumice concrete, lightened still further by setting in it lengths of clay pipe and amphorae, to reduce the weight of the superstructure on the bearing walls.

From a strange polygonal porticoed atrium (2) steps lead down to a porticoed horseshoe-shaped latrine (6) and to the baths (7-12), where spatial architecture runs riot, with single and double apses, a clover-leaf, and an octagonal *frigidarium* or room for taking a cold plunge (9). The middle terrace, east of the baths, centers on a huge trap-

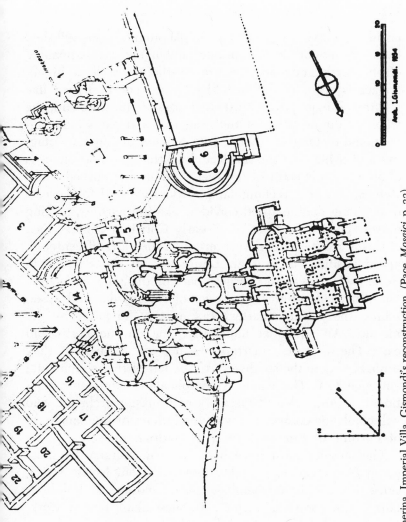

FIG. 13.2 Piazza Armerina, Imperial Villa, Gismondi's reconstruction. (Pace, *Mosaici*, p. 33)

ezoidal peristyle (15), with a complex fountain, embellished by a fish mosaic, in the middle, and living rooms opening off to north and south. South of the peristyle a higher terrace is occupied by an odd elliptical court, shaped like a flattened egg, with a buttressed apse at the west end, the trilobate dining room at the east, and a triple set of conventional rectangular rooms, with mosaics of Cupids vintaging and fishing, to the north and south. The total effect is of an agreeable contrast between straight and curved walls. Returning to the rectangular peristyle, we find to the east of it a long double-apsed corridor, like the *narthex,* or long narrow portico, in front of an early Christian church. East of this is a suite of rooms centering on the vast, off-centered, apsed basilica—larger than Domitian's on the Palatine in Rome—which was the earliest part of the villa excavated. On either side of this is a series of rectangular and apsed rooms, the private quarters and nursery, to judge by the mosaics. An aqueduct limits the villa on the north and east. The servants' quarters are not yet excavated; they probably lay to the southwest, to the left of the monumental entrance (1). The whole is complicated, consistent, functional, organic, clearly the work of a master architect who will challenge comparison with the builder of the Sanctuary of Fortune at Praeneste or with Hadrian himself.

The mosaics must have been done in a hurry by huge gangs of craftsmen, probably imported from North Africa, since the technique resembles that of mosaics at Volubilis, Hippo, Carthage, and Lepcis. Mosaic-making is slow work; nowadays it takes a careful workman six days to lay a square meter of tesserae. To finish the job in the space of a few years must have required a swarm of as many as 500 artisans.

Apart from their vast extent and their subject-matter—of which more in the sequel—the mosaics are of prime importance for the contribution they make to dating the villa.

About its date there is controversy. Professor Biagio Pace (who excavated here in the '30's), relying on stylistic similarities to late (fifth century A.D.) mosaics in Ravenna and Constantinople, would date the villa in about A.D. 410, and ascribe its ownership to a rich Sicilian landed proprietor. Pace's pupil G. V. Gentili, who was in charge of the 1950 excavations, argues, following the Norwegian archaeologist H. P. L'Orange, for an earlier date. One piece of evidence not adduced by him is conclusive in his favor. The double-apsed entrance (8) to the baths contains a spirited mosaic depicting the Circus Maximus in Rome, full of life and movement, with the chariots of the four stables, the Greens, Blues, Whites, and Reds, all represented. The Green—the Emperor's favorite—wins, not without a collision. Down the center of the oval track runs the *spina,* or division-wall, surmounted by various monuments, including a single obelisk in the center (Fig. 13.3). Now it is known that Augustus set up an obelisk in the Circus Maximus, and that in A.D. 357 Constantius added another: therefore any representation of the Circus with only one obelisk must be earlier than 357. Pace's late date is therefore excluded.

Is there any possibility of still more precise dating? Gentili thinks there is. Beginning from the *a priori* proposition that a complex architecturally and artistically as grand as this must be beyond the means of any private citizen, however rich, he assumes that the villa must have been built to the order of an Emperor. Which one? To answer this question he looked among the mosaics for possible portraits, and he found them in several places. For example, in the vestibule (13) between the baths and the trapezoidal peristyle (15) there is an obvious portrait study of the mistress of the villa flanked by two children, presumably her son and daughter. The son has a squint. He is represented again, with the same squint, in the northeast apse of the *frigidarium* (9), in the room of the small hunting scene

FIG. 13.3 Piazza Armerina, Imperial Villa, Circus Maximus mosaic.
(Dorothy MacKendrick photo)

FIG. 13.4 Piazza Armerina, Imperial Villa, small hunting
scene, mosaic.   (Pace, *Mosaici*, Fig. 30)

(23), and in the vestibule of Cupid and Pan (35). (The effect of the squint is achieved by setting one eye with a square tessera, the other with a triangular one.)

Now was the time to have recourse to the study, there to take down from the shelves the works of the Byzantine chronicler John Malalas. He records that Maxentius, the son of the Emperor Maximian Herculius (A.D. 286-305), Diocletian's colleague, was cross-eyed. Armed with this firm clue, Gentili examined the mosaics again, looking for proof or disproof that the villa belonged to Maximian. He found proof. Knowing that Maximian Herculius equated himself with Hercules, as his name shows, he looked for, and found, evidence in a colossal sculptured head of Hercules from the basilica apse, and in the mosaic, of preoccupation with that hero and his exploits. Over and over again, in the borders of robes, in foliage, and self-standing (in 4) he found representations of ivy, which was Hercules' symbol: the initial of its Latin name, *hedera,* is the initial of the hero's name. Furthermore, one of the most extensive and important mosaics in the villa, that in the state dining room (46), has as its subject the labors of Hercules. Gentili's case looks conclusively proven; it was buttressed when he took up the Circus mosaic (8), to back it with concrete and replace it, and found under it a hypocaust containing coins of the late third century, presumably dropped by the workmen who laid the mosaic in the first place.

The subjects of the mosaics are in part more or less conventional mythological scenes. Odysseus hoodwinks the one-eyed Sicilian giant Polyphemus, making him drunk with a great bowl of wine (27); an obliging dolphin rescues the musician Arion from a watery grave (32), and Orpheus with his lyre charms a vast array of animals, including a goldfinch, a lizard, and a snail (39). Still more interesting are the mosaics which show Maximian's interests. He appears to have had three obsessions: hunting, the circus, and his children. The three scenes of the chase (23,26,33) have prompted L'Orange to suggest that the villa was built as a sumptuous hunting-lodge, but the great basilica shows that it was adapted also to the uses of more formal protocol; the Imperial court must sometimes have met here.

The smaller hunting scene (23) is divided into five bands (Fig. 13.4). At the top, two eager hounds, one gray, one red, are off in full cry after a fox. Next below, a young hunter identified by Gentili as Constantius Chlorus, Maximian's adopted son, accompanied by our old friend the squint-eyed Maxentius, sacrifices to Diana, the goddess of the hunt. The third band is devoted to fowling—with bird-lime—and falconry, the fourth to the fox, gone to ground and besieged in his den by the dogs. In the fifth, on the left a stag is about to be caught in a net stretched across a forest path in the unsporting Roman way; on the right is a boar-hunt with an unorthodox hunter just about to make the kill by dropping a large rock from above on the boar's head. In the center is a vivid huntsman's picnic. The hunters, wearing puttees, are sitting under a red awning. While they are waiting, one of them feeds the dog. A black boy blows on the fire, over which a succulent-looking trussed bird is roasting. Servants fetch bread from a wicker basket; another basket harbors two ample amphorae of wine.

This is an intimate *genre* scene. More impressive is the large hunting scene which crowds the whole 190-foot length of the double-apsed corridor (26). Here the aim portrayed is to catch exotic North African animals alive for the wild beast hunts in amphitheaters like the Coliseum. In the south apse is a female figure symbolizing Africa, flanked by a tiger and an amiable small elephant with a reticulated hide. The figure in the opposite apse who has a bear on one side, a panther on the other may be Rome, the animals symbolizing her dominion over palm and pine. In this case Africa is the point of departure of the captured beasts, Rome their destination. Between the two apses the hunting scenes unfold amid fantastic architecture in a rolling, wooded landscape sloping down to the sea in the center, teeming with fish. On land, animals attack each other (a leopard draws blood from a stag's belly), and hunters in rich embroidered tunics hurl javelins, in the presence of the Emperor, at snarling lions and tigers at bay, set traps baited with kid for panthers (the kid being spread-eagled in a way that looks curiously like a parody of the Crucifixion). The hunters act as bearers—their heads camouflaged with leafy twigs, like Birnam wood coming to Dunsinane—or drag a lassoed bison toward the red ship that will transport it to Italy. A horseman, having stolen a tiger cub, delays the mother's advance by dropping another cub in her path. A hippopotamus and a rhinoceros are among the game; smaller animals are hauled to the ships in crates on ox-carts; a live trussed boar is carried slung on a pole; a recalcitrant ostrich and an antelope are being pushed up a gangway (Fig. 13.5), while the gangway of another ship is groaning under the weight of an elephant with a checkerboard hide like the one flanking Africa in the apse. Most curious of all, just in front of this same apse the tables are turned: a man has taken refuge in a cage against the attack of a fabulous winged griffin, with the head of a bird of prey. The crowded, vivid, barbarous artistry of this mosaic brings us to the very threshold of the Byzantine age; in Rome's past, only the Barberini mosaic at Palestrina can match it.

In Maximian's family even the children were brought up to take part in blood sports. Room 36, a child's room, perhaps Maxentius'—his squint-eyed portrait recurs in the anteroom (35)—portrays a child's hunt, in three bands, full of characteristic Roman insensibility to animal suffering. In the upper band, a boy has hit a spotted hare full in the breast with a hunting spear, while another has lassoed a duckling. The middle band portrays hunting mishaps: a small animal nips one fallen small boy in the leg; a cock attacks another with its beak and spurs. In the bottom reg-

FIG. 13.5   Piazza Armerina, Imperial Villa, large hunting scene, mosaic (detail). (MPI)

FIG. 13.6   Piazza Armerina, Imperial Villa, Labors of Hercules, mosaic (detail).
(Pace, *Mosaici*, Pl. 7)

ister one boy clubs a peacock, a second defends himself with a shield against a buzzard, and a third has plunged his hunting spear into the heart of a goat.

The child's Circus (33), unlike the hunt, is rather fantastic than brutal. Around a *spina* with a single obelisk, as in room 8, run four miniature chariots drawn by pairs of birds in the appropriate stable colors: green wood-pigeons, blue plovers, red flamingoes, and white geese. As usual, Green wins, and is awarded the palm. Servants with amphorae sprinkle the track to lay the dust. It is all vivid, detailed, alive, more illuminating than a dozen pages in a handbook.

The masterpiece among the mosaics is clearly the labors of Hercules cycle in the *triclinium* (46). These were part of a standard repertory, available for copying from a book of cartoons (we have seen this sort of thing in Pompeii), but here the artist has stamped his own personality on the hackneyed scenes. In his hands they are at once learnedly allusive and bloodily violent. Thus the Augean stables, which Hercules cleaned by diverting a river to run through them, are simply suggested by a river and a pitchfork. Violence is often rather hinted at than insisted on, as in the slit-like eye of the dying Nemean lion, or the Picasso-like protruding eye of the terrified horse of Diomedes (Fig. 13.6). Sometimes the effect is gained by a topical touch, as when Geryon, the triple-headed giant, is given a suit of scaly armor, like the barbarians (cataphractarii) on Trajan's column. But the full baroque excess, as insistent as in the frieze from the Pergamene altar, or the Laocoön group, comes out in the scene in the east lobe where five huge giants, foreshortened with a technique which anticipates Michelangelo's on the ceiling of the Sistine Chapel, convulsively, despairingly, imploringly, yet full of impotent rage, turn their deep-sunk eyes to heaven as they strive to pull from their flesh Hercules' deadly arrows, steeped in the blood of the Centaur Nessus. In the north lobe the apotheosis of Hercules is no doubt the mosaicist's enforced tribute to his Imperial master, but in the scenes of metamorphosis in the entrance-ways to the apses—Daphne into a laurel, Cyparissus into a cypress, Ambrosia into a vine—he is following his own paradoxical bent, accepting as it were the challenge of expressing so dynamic a thing as the change from one form to another in the obdurate medium of mosaic.

The ten "Bikini girls" (38) come last, because these mosaics, which overlie another set, are obviously later than the rest. They owe their fame to the scantiness of their costumes, as brief as any to be seen on modern European beaches. Gentili thinks they are female athletes, being awarded prizes, but Pace may be nearer the truth in supposing that they are pantomime actresses, with tambourines and *maracas,* performing in a sort of aquacade, the blue *tesserae* in which they stand representing water. There is ancient evidence for this curiously decadent art-form. Martial speaks of actresses dressed—or undressed—as Nereids swimming about in the Coliseum, and the Church fathers fulminate against such spectacles. When the orchestra of the most august of theaters, that of Dionysus in Athens, was remodelled in Roman times to hold water, we must suppose, since the space is too small for mock naval battles, that the place once sacred to the choruses of Aeschylus, Sophocles, and Euripides was thereafter used for the aquatic antics of just such actresses as the Piazza Armerina mosaics portray. Tastelessness and grandeur, conspicuous waste and a daring architectural plan: this paradoxical blend, so characteristic of the villa, explains both what is meant by decline and why it took the Empire so long to fall.

The villa at Piazza Armerina belongs to an age when Christians were persecuted: the motifs in the mosaics are almost aggressively pagan. But Maximian's son-in-law Constantine became in the end a convert to Christianity, and built, beginning about A.D. 322, in honor of St. Peter, a great basilica church on the Vatican Hill, replaced in the Renaissance by the present building. In 1939, at the death of Pope Pius XI, who had asked to be buried in the crypt of St. Peter's, excavations for his tomb created the occasion for transforming the crypt into a lower church. In lowering the floor level of the crypt for this purpose, the workmen came, only eight inches down, upon the pavement of Old St. Peter's, Constantine's church. This in turn rested upon mausolea with their tops sliced off, and their interiors rammed full of earth. At the direction of Pius XII, these mausolea were scientifically excavated.

What was revealed was a pagan Roman cemetery, in some places thirty feet below the floor of the present church. The mausolea were all in use and in good repair when Constantine began his church in A.D. 322: the earliest brick stamp found in the area dates from the reign of Vespasian, A.D. 69-79. The excavations were carried out under conditions comparable in difficulty only to the recovery of the Altar of Peace: the same constant battle with seepage, the same problem of underpinning one structure in order to read the message of another. Under these formidable difficulties, the cemetery was cleared, and archaeologists found the reason why Constantine moved a million cubic feet of earth and went so far as to violate sepulchres to build Old St. Peter's on just this site. Whatever modern walls it was necessary to build were carefully marked with Pius XII brick-stamps, that future archaeologists might be in no doubt as to which masonry was modern and which ancient. The cemetery may now be visited by small groups with special permission, under the expert guidance of a polyglot archaeologist. The story he has to tell was not published until over ten years after the excavation began, in a massive two-volume *Report* which stands fifteen and three-quarters inches high, contains 171 text figures and 119 plates, and weighs fourteen pounds. Fortunately its objectivity is as impressive as its bulk. The archaeological evidence is lucidly set forth, and no conclusions are drawn which exceed it.

We know from Tacitus that Nero, in his search for scapegoats on whom to shift the blame for Rome's great fire of A.D. 64, martyred Christians in an amphitheater on the Vatican Hill, and tradition has it that in this amphitheater St. Peter, too, suffered martyrdom. It was to test the validity of this tradition that Pius XII ordered the cemetery under St. Peter's excavated. What was found was a series of twenty-one mausolea and one open area (P in the plan, Fig. 13.7), all facing southward onto a Roman street. The mausolea are plain brick on the outside, highly baroque within, enriched with mosaics, wall-paintings, and stucco-work. There are both cremation and inhumation burials, but when the mausolea were filled in inhumation was beginning to predominate. Of the mausolea only M is entirely Christian in décor; others began as pagan, later admitting Christian burials, or adapt pagan motifs to Christian symbolism. M contains the earliest known Christian mosaics, which Ward Perkins and Miss Toynbee call a microcosm of the dramatic history of Christianity's peaceful penetration of the pagan Roman Empire. They are dated by technique and motifs to the middle of the third century A.D. The subjects are Jonah and the whale, the Fisher of Men, the Good Shepherd, and, in the vault, Christ figured as the sun. The wall paintings of the cemetery are mostly pagan, the contractors' stock-in-trade, depicting in myth or in symbol the soul's victory over death. The great artistic interest of the mausolea is in the stucco-work, both in relief and in the round, superior in quality to that of the subterranean basilica at the Porta Maggiore. Some of it is of unparalleled scale and complexity, excellently preserved (Fig. 13.8), and now protected from dampness by large, constantly burning electric heaters. Of stone sculpture in the round there is very little; it was probably removed by Constantine's workmen. But there are many marble sarcophagi with pagan and Christian

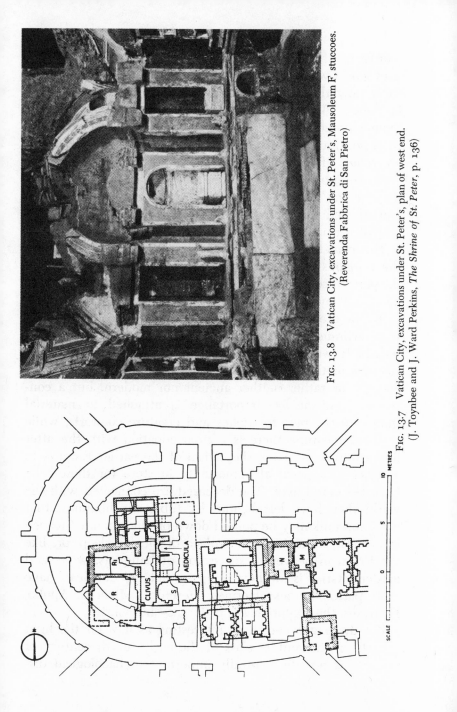

FIG. 13.8 Vatican City, excavations under St. Peter's, Mausoleum F, stuccoes.
(Reverenda Fabbrica di San Pietro)

FIG. 13.7 Vatican City, excavations under St. Peter's, plan of west end.
(J. Toynbee and J. Ward Perkins, *The Shrine of St. Peter*, p. 136)

motifs, testifying to the artistic revival enjoyed by the Roman world with the peace of the Church in A.D. 312. They show how the stonemasons carved them as blanks, filling in details like inscriptions and portrait busts to the customer's order. There is a pathetic one of a baby, who died, the inscription tells us, when he was six months old. There are reliefs of Biblical scenes: the children in the fiery furnace, Joseph and his brethren, the three Magi, and what may be the earliest Christian cross, dated about A.D. 340; (an alleged cross at Herculaneum is more probably the scar of a ripped-away wall bracket).

The cemetery tells us something about the status and the religious convictions of its owners and occupants. Of the persons recorded in its inscriptions, over half have Greek names. They are freedmen or descendants of freedmen, many in the Imperial civil service. Some are tradesmen, some artisans. Only one was of Senatorial rank: his daughter's body was wrapped in purple and veiled in gold. The richness of the tombs bespeaks an attitude that is modern enough, or rather neither ancient nor modern, but a constant. Paradoxically, importance is attached to material things, to the race for riches and creature comforts, while at the same time there is a preoccupation with the after life, a return, after the skepticism of the earlier Empire, to a belief in a personal immortality in store for those who have led moral lives. The deceased are connected with the world they have left behind by tubes for libations, that wine and milk may be poured down on their bones. Heaven is variously conceived: as a place of blessed sleep, or, like the Etruscan heaven, a succession of banquets, wine, and gardens. Grief is swallowed up in victory; the dead have their patron heroes: Hermes, Hercules, Minerva, Apollo, Dionysus, the Egyptian Isis or Horus—and Christ.

But the pagan cemetery, interesting as it is for the light it casts on the middle class of the early fourth century of our era, is not the centrally important archaeological dis-

covery under St. Peter's, nor does it supply the motive for
Constantine's location of his church just here. That motive
the excavators found in the open space they named "Campo
P." Campo P is separated from mausoleum R by a sloping
passage, called the Clivus; the drain under the passage
contains tiles with stamps dated between the years 147-161,
which fall within the reign of Antoninus Pius. A painted
brick wall, since made famous as the Red Wall, separates
the Clivus from Campo P. Into this wall are cut three super-
posed niches, two in the fabric of the wall itself, one beneath
its foundations, which were actually raised on a sort of
bridge at this point to protect the cavity. In front of the
niches traces were found of a modest architectural façade,
called the Aedicula, or little shrine.

In the cavity the excavators found human bones, which
they have never identified further than to describe them
as those of a person of advanced age and robust physique.
The Aedicula penetrated above the pavement of Old St.
Peter's and formed its architectural focus. The conclusion
is inevitable that Constantine in A.D. 322 planned his basilica
to rise just here, at great trouble and expense, because he
believed the lowest niche, under the Red Wall, to enshrine
a relic of overarching importance, nothing less than the
bones of St. Peter. There is thus no doubt whatever, on
objective evidence, that the Aedicula was reverenced in
the fourth Christian century as marking the burial place of
the founder of the Roman church.

But this is not the end of the problem. The next question
is, "How early can the burial, by objective archaeological
evidence, be demonstrated to be?" The answer to this question must be sought, if anywhere, in the context of Campo
P. This proved on excavation to be an area of poor graves,
marked, like those of the necropolis of the Port of Ostia
on Isola Sacra, simply by a surround and a pitched roof of
tiles, without any of the pomp of costly marble sarcophagus
or richly stuccoed mausoleum. It is to the class which would

be buried in such pathetic graves as these that the earliest
Roman Christians (of the age of Nero [A.D. 64]) must have
belonged. (Since the *Report* was published, Professor Magi,
whom we have already met in connection with the Cancelleria reliefs, has discovered, under the Vatican City parking
lot, another cemetery, also of poor graves, of the first century
A.D.; there is no cogent proof that they are Christian.) The
graves in Campo P (Fig. 13.9) were found to lie at various
levels: the deepest must be the earliest. The deepest is the

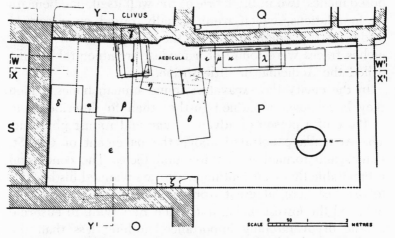

FIG. 13.9   Vatican City, excavations under St. Peter's, Campo P.
(Toynbee and Ward Perkins, *op. cit.*, p. 141)

one called by the excavators Gamma (see plan, γ, Fig. 13.9):
it lies five-and-a-half feet below the pavement of Campo P,
and it partly underlies, and is therefore older than, the
foundations of the Red Wall, which in turn is dated by the
Clivus drain about the middle of the second century A.D.
Grave Theta (θ) is higher, and therefore later, than Gamma.
It is a poor grave, protected by tiles, one of which bears a
stamp of Vespasian's reign (A.D. 69-79). It is unsafe method
to date an archaeological find by a single brick stamp which
could be second-hand, used at any date later than its firing,
even much later. But the stamp creates at least a presump-

tion that Theta may be dated as early as A.D. 79, and, if so, Gamma must be earlier still. Since both these graves appear to have been dug in such a way as to respect the area just in front of the Aedicula, it follows that the bones in the lowest niche must be earlier than either grave.

This is the process by which it is possible (but not rigorously necessary, on the evidence) to date the bones before A.D. 79, perhaps in the reign of Nero; perhaps they are the bones of a victim of the persecution of A.D. 64; perhaps they are the bones of St. Peter. They were evidently disturbed in antiquity, for this is not a proper burial, but simply a collection of bones; the head, for example, is missing. The original burial must have lain athwart the line of the later Red Wall: when the builders of the Red Wall hit upon it, they may, knowing the legend of St. Peter's martyrdom in the amphitheater somewhere near this spot, have assumed that this was his grave, and so they arched up the Red Wall's foundations to avoid disturbing it. The next step was to build the Aedicula (Fig. 13.10), an act associated in literary sources with Pope Anacletus (traditional dates, A.D. 76-88), but since not even the most pious Catholics suppose the Aedicula to be this early, an emendation of the name into Anicetus (ca. 155-165) is defensible: it is paleographically plausible, and it suits the date of the Red Wall. The traces of the Aedicula as found were asymmetrical: its north supporting column had been moved to make room for a wall that was built sometime before Constantine to buttress the Red Wall, which had developed a bad crack from top to bottom. The excavators found the north face of this buttress wall covered with a palimpsest of graffiti, only one of which—in Greek—refers to St. Peter by name, though some others may do so in a cryptic way, and all testify that this spot was one of particular sanctity, much frequented by pilgrims.

The shrine under St. Peter's is not the only spot in Rome associated with St. Peter. Another is under the Church of

San Sebastiano, two-and-a-half miles out, just off the Appian
Way. Here excavation has found *graffiti* mentioning St.
Peter and St. Paul, a room for taking ceremonial meals, and

FIG. 13.10   Vatican City, excavations under St. Peter's. Aedicula, reconstruction by G. U. S. Corbett. (Toynbee and Ward Perkins, *op. cit.*, p. 161)

Christian tombs of the third century A.D. Some scholars
believe, but without cogent archaeological evidence, that
St. Peter's body, in whole or in part, was moved to this

retired spot off the main road, from the Vatican Hill, for safety during the persecutions under the Emperor Valerian in A.D. 258. This would explain the association of the San Sebastiano site with the apostle; the assumption that the bones were returned to the Aedicula after the danger was past would explain—though it is not the only possible explanation—the disturbed state in which the excavators found them.

In any case, in the years between the building of the Aedicula and the centering of Constantine's church upon it, there was continuity of pious commemoration of the spot. This is proved by the *graffiti* on the buttress wall, and by a series of burials, Alpha, Beta, Delta, Epsilon, and Mu (α, β, δ, ε, μ) all motivated by a desire to be buried as close as possible to the Aedicula, and all, to judge by their contents—remains of cloth in Beta, for example, showed gold threads—belonging to important people. Some scholars (not including the excavators) have supposed that these are the graves of early Popes.

This was the state of affairs in Campo P when the building of Constantine's basilica began. The Aedicula was made the focus of the whole building plan: it was left projecting above the pavement of the new church, and it was covered by a canopy upheld by twisted columns. (It is an extraordinary coincidence that Bernini, when he built the canopy over the altar of the Renaissance church, chose twisted columns to uphold it, though he could not possibly have known that Constantine's canopy also involved this detail.) Constantine's architect, in the classical tradition, paid the secular Roman basilica the compliment of creative imitation.

It was not until about A.D. 600 that the altar was placed directly over the shrine, and the presbytery raised to accommodate it. By that time, the tradition was firmly established that pious pilgrims should leave a votive coin in front of the Aedicula: here in the fill the excavators found 1900 coins, Roman, papal, Italian, and from all over Europe,

ranging in date from before A.D. 161 uninterruptedly down
to the fourteenth century. Also about A.D. 600, at the same
time as the placing of the altar directly over the shrine, the
two upper niches in the Red Wall were combined into one,
the Niche of the Pallia, where the vestments of newly-
consecrated archbishops were put to be sanctified by close
contact with the bones of the first Bishop of Rome: a shaft
in the floor of the niche led down to the grave.

The shrine and the Constantinian church survived the
sacks of Rome both by the Goths in A.D. 410, and by the
Vandals in A.D. 455; the Saracens in A.D. 846 were not so
respectful. In their search for treasure they handled the
Aedicula very roughly, and it is likely that it is from this
sack, and not from the persecution of A.D. 258, that the
disturbance of the bones should be dated. In any case, after
the sack the life of the shrine went on as before, and in the
Renaissance church as in its predecessor the shrine remained the focal point, one of the most venerated spots
in Christendom.

With the shrine of St. Peter, venerable, still vital, going
back to the two roots of western civilization, pagan Rome
(itself the transmitter of Greek culture) and Christianity,
it is fitting that we should end our survey of what archaeology has to tell us about the culture to which ours owes so
much. The two complexes, the grandiose pagan villa and
the humble Christian shrine, which we have discussed in
this chapter, are interrelated. The villa is one of the last
manifestations of a culture that is played out, the shrine
marks the beginning of a new culture that will produce its
own grandiose monuments and in its turn be threatened
by decline. In a sense, with the simplicity of St. Peter's
shrine the historical cycle returns to the simplicity of primitive Rome. But it is not simply a matter of returning to
beginnings and starting over again; the new culture stands

upon the shoulders of the old. The Christian shrine has the look of a pagan tomb-monument in the Isola Sacra necropolis; Constantine's church has the look of a pagan Roman basilica. The language of the Mass is still Latin; the Pope is Pontifex Maximus. The striking thing is the continuity, and this is the most important lesson that archaeology has to teach. Again beneath St. Peter's, as at so many other ancient sites, what the archaeologist digs up is not things but people. The remains in the niche under the Red Wall are not dry bones; they are live history. The breathing of life into that history is a major and largely unsung triumph of the modern science of archaeology, patiently at work over the last eighty years. To come to know a fragment of our past is to recognize a piece of ourselves. Perhaps, as archaeology interprets history, making the mute stones speak, we may come to know our past so well that we shall not be condemned to repeat it.

BIBLIOGRAPHY

CHAPTER 1: *Prehistoric Italy*

R. J. C. Atkinson, *Field Archaeology* (London, 1946)

P. Barocelli, "Terremare, Palatino, orientazione dei *castra* e delle città romane," *Bulletino Communale* 70 (1942), 131-144

John Bradford, "The Apulia Expedition: An Interim Report," *Antiquity* 24 (1950) 84-95

————, *Ancient Landscapes* (London, 1957), 85-110

F. von Duhn and F. Messerschmidt, *Italische Gräberkunde*, 2 vols. (Heidelberg, 1924-1939)

C. F. C. Hawkes, *The Prehistoric Foundations of Europe* (London, 1940)

G. Kaschnitz-Weinberg, "Italien mit Sardinien, Sizilien, and Malta," in W. Otto and R. Herbig, *Handbuch der Archäologie*, 2 (Munich, 1954), 311-397

G. Lilliu, "1000 Years of Prehistory: Sardinia, the *Nuraghe* of Barumini and its Village—a Recent Large-scale Excavation," *Illustrated London News* 232 (1958), 388-391

H. L. Movius, Jr., "Age Determination by Radiocarbon Content," *Antiquity* 24 (1950), 99-101

T. J. Peet, *The Stone and Bronze Ages in Italy* (Oxford, 1909)

D. Randall-MacIver, *Villanovans and Early Etruscans* (Oxford, 1924)

————, *The Iron Age in Italy* (Oxford, 1927)

————, *Italy before the Romans* (Oxford, 1928)

G. Säflund, "Le terremare," *Skrifter Utgivna av Svenska Institutet i Rom* 7 (1939)

R. B. K. Stevenson, "The Neolithic Cultures of Southeast Italy," *Proceedings of the Prehistoric Society* 13 (1947), 85-100

J. Whatmough, *The Foundations of Roman Italy* (London, 1937)

R. E. M. Wheeler, *Archaeology from the Earth* (Oxford, 1954, reprinted in Pelican Books, 1956)

CHAPTER 2: *The Etruscans*

N. Alfieri, "The Etruscans of the Po and the Discovery of Spina," *Italy's Life*, No. 24 (1957), 91-104

————— and P. E. Arias, *Spina* (Florence, 1958)

P. E. Arias, "Considerazioni sulla città etrusca a Pian di Misano (Marzabotto)," *Atti e Memorie della Deputazione di Storia Patria per le Provincie dell' Emilia e di Romagna,* 4 (1953), 223-234

S. Aurigemma, *Il R. Museo di Spina in Ferrara* (Ferrara, 1936)

R. Bloch, "Volsinies étrusque: essai historique et topographique," *Mélanges d'archéologie et d'histoire de l'École française de Rome,* 59 (1947), 9-39

J. Bradford, *Ancient Landscapes,* 111-144

E. Brizio, "Relazione sugli scavi eseguiti a Marzabotto presso Bologna dal novembre 1888 a tutto maggio 1889," *Monumenti Antichi,* 1 (1891), cols. 248-426

Corpus Inscriptionum Etruscarum, II.i,3 (Tarquinia) (Leipzig, 1936)

G. Dennis, *Cities and Cemeteries of Etruria,*[3] 2 vols. (London, 1883)

M. Falkner, "Epigraphisches und archäologisches zur Stele von Lemnos," in W. Brandenstein, *Frühgeschichte und Sprachwissenschaft* (Vienna, 1948), 91-109

C. M. Lerici, "Periscopic Sighting and Photography to the Archaeologist's Aid," *Ill. London News* 232 (1958), 774-775

M. Pallottino, *Etruscologia*[3] (Milan, 1955), Engl. trans., Pelican books, 1955

—————, *Etruscan Painting* (Geneva, 1952)

L. Pareti, *La Tomba Regolini-Galassi* (Vatican City, 1947)

E. Pulgram, *The Tongues of Italy* (Cambridge, Mass., 1958)

G. Ricci *et al.,* "Caere: Scavi di R. Mengarelli," *Mon. Ant.* 42 (1955), cols. 1-1186

J. B. Ward Perkins, "The Problem of Etruscan Origins," *Harvard Studies in Classical Philology* 64 (1959) 1-26

G. E. W. Wolstenholme and C. M. O'Connor, eds., *Ciba Foundation Symposium on Medical Biology and Etruscan Origins* (London and Boston, 1959). Important contributions by H. Hencken (29-47), and J. B. Ward Perkins (89-92), among others.

CHAPTER 3: *Early Rome*

F. E. Brown, "The Regia," *Memoirs of the American Academy in Rome* 12 (1935), 67-88

L. Curtius, A. Newrath, and E. Nash, *Das antike Rom*[3] (Vienna, 1957)

A. Degrassi, *Inscriptiones Latinae liberae rei publicae*, I (Florence, 1957)

T. Frank, "Roman Buildings of the Republic: an Attempt to Date them from their Materials," *Papers and Monographs of the Am.Acad. in Rome* 3 (1924)

E. Gjerstad, "Il comizio romano dell' età reppublicana," *Skrifter* 5 (1941), 97-158

————, "Early Rome I," *ib.* 17 (1953)

————, "The Fortifications of Early Rome," *ib.* 18 (1954), 50-65

P. G. Goidanich, "L'iscrizione arcaica del Foro Romano e il suo ambiente archeologico," *Memorie dell' Accademia d'Italia*, series 7, vol. 3 (1943), 317-501

R. Lanciani, *Ancient Rome in the Light of Recent Discoveries* (Boston, 1888)

G. Lugli, *I monumenti antichi di Roma e suburbio*, 3 (Rome, 1938), 23-50

————, *Roma antica: il centro monumentale* (Rome, 1946)

Oxford Classical Dictionary (Oxford, 1949), art. "Tabulae Pontificum"

S. B. Platner and T. Ashby, *A Topographical Dictionary of Ancient Rome* (Oxford, 1929)

S. M. Puglisi, "Gli abitatori primitivi del Palatino," *Mon. Ant.* 41 (1951), cols. 1-98

L. Richardson, Jr., "Cosa and Rome: Comitium and Curia," *Archaeology* 10 (1957), 49-55

I. S. Ryberg, *An Archaeological Record of Rome from the Seventh to the Second Centuries B.C.* (London, 1940)

G. Säflund, "Le mure di Roma reppublicana," *Skrifter* 1 (1932)

M. R. Scherer, *Marvels of Ancient Rome* (New York and London, 1955)

I. G. Scott, "Early Roman Traditions in the Light of Archeology," *Mem. Am. Acad. in Rome* 7 (1929), 7-116

CHAPTER 4: *Roman Colonies in Italy*

G. Becatti, "Sviluppo urbanistico," in G. Calza, *Scavi di Ostia*, 1 (Rome, 1953)

J. Bradford, *Ancient Landscapes*, 145-216

F. E. Brown, "Cosa I: History and Topography," *Mem. Am. Acad. in Rome* 21 (1951), 7-113

F. Castagnoli, "I più antichi esempi conservati di divisioni agrarie romane," *Bulletino del Museo della Civiltà Romana* 18 (1953-1955), 1-9

————, "La centuriazione de Cosa," *Mem. Am. Acad. in Rome* 24 (1956), 147-165

————, "Le ricerche sui resti della centuriazione," *Note e discussioni erudite* a cura di Augusto Campana, 7 (Rome, 1958)

F. de Visscher and F. de Ruyt, "Les Fouilles d'Alba Fucens (Italie centrale) en 1949 et 1950," *L'Antiquité Clas-sique* 20 (1951), 47-84 and later reports in successive volumes. See also report of 1955 campaign, *Notizie degli Scavi* (1957), 163-170

G. Guiccardini Corsi Salviati, "La centuriazione romana e un' opera attuale di bonifica agraria," *Studi Etruschi* 20 (1948-1949), 291-296

P. MacKendrick, "Asphodel, White Wine, and Enriched Thunderbolts," *Greece and Rome*, new series, 1 (1954), 1-11

————, "Roman Colonization and the Frontier Hypothesis," in W. D. Wyman and C. B. Kroeber, eds., *The Frontier in Perspective* (Madison, 1957), 3-19

J. Mertens and S. J. de Laet, "Massa d'Alba (Aquila): Scavi di Alba Fucense," *Not. Scav.*, ser. 8, vol. 4 (1950), 248-288

————, "L'urbanizzazione del centro di Alba Fucense," *Memorie dell' Accademia dei Lincei*, ser. 8, vol. 5 (1954), 171-194

L. Richardson, Jr., "Excavations at Cosa in Etruria, 1948-1952," *Antiquity* 27 (1953), 102-103

Doris M. Taylor, "Cosa: Black-glaze Pottery," *Mem. Am. Acad. in Rome* 25 (1957), 68-193

J. B. Ward Perkins, "Early Roman Towns in Italy," *Town Planning Review* 26 (1955), 127-154

CHAPTER 5: *Nabobs as Builders: Sulla, Pompey, Caesar*

F. Fasolo and G. Gullini, *Il Santuario della Fortuna Primigenia a Palestrina*, 2 vols. (Rome, 1953)

G. Gullini, *Guida del Santuario della Fortuna Primigenia a Palestrina* (Rome, 1956)

J. A. Hanson, *Roman Theater-Temples* (Princeton, 1958)

H. Kähler, review of Fasolo and Gullini, *Gnomon* 30 (1958), 366-383

————, "Das Fortunaheiligtum von Palestrina Praeneste," *Annales Universitatis Saraviensis* (*Philosophie-Lettres*) 7 (1958), 189-240

Phyllis W. Lehmann, "The Setting of Hellenistic Temples," *Journal of the Society of Architectural Historians* 13.4 (1954), 15-20

G. Lugli, *Roma antica* (Rome, 1946), 177-179, 245-258 (Caesar's buildings)

————, *I monumenti antichi*, 3 (Rome, 1938), 70-83 (Pompey's theater)

Platner and Ashby, *op. cit.*, under Chapter 3

Giovanna Quattrocchi, *Il Museo Archeologico Prenestino* (Rome, 1956)

Eugénie Strong, "The Art of the Roman Republic," *Cambridge Ancient History* 9 (1932), 803-841

E. B. Van Deman, "The Sullan Forum," *Journal of Roman Studies* 12 (1922), 1-31

C. C. Van Essen, *Sulla als Bouwheer* (Groningen, 1940)

CHAPTER 6: *Augustus· Buildings as Propaganda*

B. Andreae, "Archäologische Funde und Grabungen im Bereich der Soprintendenzen von Rom 1949-1956/7," *Arch. Anzeiger* (1957) cols. 110-358

Curtius, Newrath, and Nash, *op. cit.*, under Chapter 3

A. Degrassi, "Elogia," *Inscriptiones Italiae* 13.3 (Rome, 1937)

A. Degrassi, "L'edifizio dei Fasti Capitolini," *Rendiconti della pontifica accademia di archeologia* 21 (1945-1946), 57-104

————, "Fasti," *Inscriptiones Italiae* 13.1 (Rome, 1947)

G. Lugli, *I monumenti antichi*, 3 (Rome, 1938), 194-211 (mausoleum)

————, *Monumenti minori del Foro Romano* (Rome, 1947), 77-84 (arch)

G. Moretti, *Ara Pacis Augustae*, 2 vols., (Rome, 1948)

H. Riemann, "Pacis Ara," in Pauly-Wissowa-Kroll-Mittelhaus, *Realenkyklopädie* 18 (1942), cols. 2082-2107

I. S. Ryberg, "The Procession of the Ara Pacis," *Mem. Am. Acad. in Rome* 19 (1949), 79-101

————, "Rites of the State Religion in Roman Art," *ib.* 22 (1955)

J. M. C. Toynbee, "The Ara Pacis Reconsidered and Historical Art in Roman Italy," *Proceedings of the British Academy* 39 (1953), 67-95

CHAPTER 7: *Hypocrite, Madman, Fool, and Knave*

S. Aurigemma, *La basilica sotterranea neopitagorica di Porta Maggiore in Roma* (Rome, 1954)

G. Bandinelli, "Il monumento sotterraneo di Porta Maggiore in Roma," *Mon. Ant.* 31 (1927), cols. 601-848

J. Carcopino, *La Basilique pythagoricienne de la porte majeure* (Paris, 1926)

G. Cultrera, "Nemi—la prima fase dei lavori per il recupero delle navi romane," *Not. Scav.* (1932), 206-292

G. Iacopi, *I ritrovamenti dell' antro cosidetto "di Tiberio" a Sperlonga* (Rome, 1958)

G. Ucelli, *Le navi di Nemi* (Rome, 1940)

E. B. Van Deman, "The Sacra Via of Nero," *Mem. Am. Acad. in Rome* 5 (1925), 115-126

C. C. Van Essen, "La topographie de la Domus Aurea Neronis," *Mededeelingen der Kon. Nederland. Akad. van Wetenschappen*, afd. Letterkunde, nieuwe Reeks, Deel 17 (Amsterdam, 1954), 371-398

J. B. Ward Perkins, "Nero's Golden House," *Antiquity* 30 (1956), 209-219

F. Weege, "Das goldene Haus des Nero," *Jahrbuch d. deutsch. arch. Inst.* 28 (1913), 127-244

CHAPTER 8: *The Victims of Vesuvius*

R. C. Carrington, *Pompeii* (Oxford, 1936)

E. C. Corti, *The Destruction and Resurrection of Pompeii and Herculaneum* (London, 1951, unaltered from original German of 1940)

M. Della Corte, *Case ed abitanti di Pompeii*[2] (Pompeii, 1954)

E. Diehl, *Pompeianische Wandinschriften*[2] (Bonn, 1930)

A. Maiuri, *La Villa dei Misteri*,[2] 2 vols. (Rome, 1947)

————, *Ercolano*[4] (Ministry of Public Instruction *Guides*, Rome, 1954)

————, *Ercolano: I nuovi scavi (1927-1958)* I (Rome, 1958)

————, *Pompeii*[8] (MPI *Guides*, Rome, 1956)

L. Richardson, Jr., "Pompeii: the Casa dei Dioscuri and its Painters," *Mem. Am. Acad. in Rome* 23 (1955)

V. Spinazzola, *Pompeii alla luce degli scavi nuovi di Via dell'Abbondanza (Anni 1910-1923)*, 2 vols. and vol. of plates (Rome, 1953)

A. W. Van Buren, "Pompeii," in *RE*, (1952) cols. 1999-2038

CHAPTER 9: *Flavian Rome*

P. H. von Blanckenhagen, *Flavische Architektur* (Berlin, 1940)

A. M. Colini, "Forum Pacis," *Bull. Comm.* 65 (1938), 7-40
————, *Stadium Domitiani* (Rome, 1943)

G. Cozzo, *Ingegneria Romana* (Roma, 1928)

G. Lugli, *Roma antica* (Roma, 1946), 269-276 (Forum Pacis, Forum Transitorium), 319-348 (Coliseum), 486-493, 509-516 (Palace of Domitian.)

F. Magi, *I Rilievi Flavi del Palazzo della Cancelleria* (Rome, 1945)

M. Scherer, *op. cit.* in Ch. 3, 49-62 (Palatine); 75-76 (Arch of Titus), 80-89 (Coliseum), 101-102 (Forum "of Nerva")

J. M. C. Toynbee, *The Flavian Reliefs from the Palazzo della Cancelleria in Rome* (Oxford, 1957)

CHAPTER 10: *Trajan: Port, Forum, Market, Column*

G. Becatti, *Scavi di Ostia* 2 (Rome, 1954) (Mithraea)

G. Boni, "Roma—Esplorazione del Forum Ulpium," *Not. Scav.* (1907), 361-427

J. Bradford, *Ancient Landscapes*, 248-256 (Claudius' and Trajan's harbors)

G. Calza, *Scavi di Ostia*, 1 (Rome, 1953)
———— and G. Becatti, *Ostia*⁴ (MPI *Guides*, Rome, 1957)
————, *La necropoli del Porto di Roma nell' Isola Sacra* (Rome, 1940)

J. Carcopino, *Daily Life in Ancient Rome* (New Haven, 1940), 173-184 (businessmen and manual laborers)

P. Ducati, *L'arte classica*³ (Turin, 1948), 619-628 (Trajan's Forum and Column)

K. Lehmann-Hartleben, "Die antiken Hafenanlagen des Mittelmeeres," *Klio*, Beiheft 14 (1923), 182-198 (Claudius' and Trajan's harbors)

G. Lugli, *Roma antica* (Rome, 1946), 278-307 (Trajan's Forum and Market)
———— and G. Filibeck, *Il Porto di Roma imperiale e l'agro Portuense* (Rome, 1935)

R. Meiggs, art. "Ostia," in *Oxf. Class. Dict.* (Oxford, 1949)

P. Romanelli, *La colonna traiana: relievi fotografici eseguiti in occasione dei lavori di protezione antiaerea* (Rome, 1942)

E. D. Thatcher, "The Open Rooms of the Terme del Foro at Ostia," *Mem. Am. Acad. in Rome* 24 (1956), 167-264

CHAPTER 11: *An Emperor-Architect: Hadrian*

S. Aurigemma, *Villa adriana*[3] (Tivoli, 1955)

H. Bloch, "I bolli laterizi e la storia edilizia romana," *Bull. Comm.* 65 (1937), 115-187

E. Clark, *Rome and a Villa* (New York, 1952), 141-194

H. Kähler, *Hadrian und seine Villa bei Tivoli* (Berlin, 1950)

G. Lugli, *I monumenti antichi*, 3 (Roma, 1938), 123-150 (Pantheon), 693-708 (Hadrian's mausoleum)

————, *Roma antica* (Rome, 1946), 234-240 (Temple of Venus and Rome)

D. S. Robertson, *A Handbook of Greek and Roman Architecture*[2] (Cambridge, 1954), 246-251 (Pantheon), 252-254, 316 (Piazza d'Oro)

A. W. Van Buren, "Recent Finds at Hadrian's Tiburtine Villa," *Am. Journ. of Archaeology* 59 (1955), 215-217 (Canopus)

M. Yourcenar, *Mémoires d'Hadrien* (Paris, 1951; Engl. trans., New York, 1954)

L. Ziehen, art. "Pantheion," in *RE* 18 (1949), cols. 729-741

CHAPTER 12: *Roman Engineering*

American Architect 98 (Oct. 5, 1910), 113-118 (Pennsylvania Station)

W. J. Anderson, R. P. Spiers, and T. Ashby, *The Architecture of Ancient Rome* (London, 1927), 99-113 (Baths)

T. Ashby, *Aqueducts of Ancient Rome* (Oxford, 1935)

Van Wyck Brooks, *The Dream of Arcadia* (New York, 1958), 239 ff.

R. J. Forbes, *Notes on the History of Ancient Roads and their Construction* (Amsterdam, 1934), 115-168

M. W. Frederiksen and J. B. Ward Perkins, "The Ancient Road Systems of the Central and Northern Ager Faliscus," *Papers of the British School at Rome* 12 (1957), 67-208

H. S. Jones, *Companion to Roman History* (Oxford, 1912), 40-49 (Roads)

L. Mumford, "The Disappearance of Pennsylvania Station," *New Yorker* 34 (June 7, 1958), 106-113

H. Plommer, *Ancient and Classical Architecture* (London, 1956), 338-344 (Baths)

Sir Albert Richardson, R.A., Letter to New York *Times*, Mar. 1, 1959

I. A. Richmond, *The City Wall of Imperial Rome* (Oxford, 1930)

G. H. Stevenson, "Communications and Commerce," in *The Legacy of Rome* (ed. C. Bailey, Oxford, 1923), 141-172

E. B. Van Deman, *The Building of the Roman Aqueducts* (Washington, 1934)

C. C. Van Essen, "The Via Valeria from Tivoli to Collarmele," *Papers Br. Sch. at Rome* 12 (1957), 22-38

CHAPTER 13: *Caesar and Christ*

B. M. Apollonj-Ghetti, A. Ferrua, E. Josi, E. Kirschbaum, *Esplorazioni sotto la confessione di San Pietro in Vaticano eseguite negli anni 1940-1949,* 2 vols. (Rome, 1951)

G. V. Gentili, "Piazza Armerina: grandiosa villa romana in contrada Casale," *Not. Scav.* (1951), 291-335

————, *The Imperial Villa of Piazza Armerina* (MPI Guides, Rome, 1956)

H. P. L'Orange and E. Dyggve, "Is it a Palace of Maximian Herculeus that the excavations of Piazza Armerina bring to light?," *Symbolae Osloenses* 29 (1952), 114-128

M. Guarducci, *La tomba di Pietro* (Rome, 1959; there is also an English translation)

E. Kirschbaum, *The Tombs of Peter and Paul* (New York, 1959)

B. Pace, *I mosaici di Piazza Armerina* (Rome, 1955)

J. M. C. Toynbee and J. B. Ward Perkins, *The Shrine of St. Peter and the Vatican Excavations* (London, 1956)

INDEX OF PROPER NAMES